TM

KT-231-028

References for the Rest of Us!®

BESTSELLING BOOK SERIES

Do you find that traditional reference books are overloaded with technical details and advice you'll never use? Do you postpone important life decisions because you just don't want to deal with them? Then our *For Dummies*® business and general reference book series is for you.

For Dummies business and general reference books are written for those frustrated and hard-working souls who know they aren't dumb, but find that the myriad of personal and business issues and the accompanying horror stories make them feel helpless. *For Dummies* books use a lighthearted approach, a down-to-earth style, and even cartoons and humorous icons to dispel fears and build confidence. Lighthearted but not lightweight, these books are perfect survival guides to solve your everyday personal and business problems.

> *"More than a publishing phenomenon, 'Dummies' is a sign of the times."*
>
> — The New York Times

> *"...you won't go wrong buying them."*
>
> — Walter Mossberg, Wall Street Journal, on For Dummies books

> *"A world of detailed and authoritative information is packed into them..."*
>
> — U.S. News and World Report

Already, millions of satisfied readers agree. They have made For Dummies the #1 introductory level computer book series and a best-selling business book series. They have written asking for more. So, if you're looking for the best and easiest way to learn about business and other general reference topics, look to For Dummies to give you a helping hand.

Wiley Publishing, Inc.

5/09

Coaching & Mentoring

FOR

DUMMIES®

Coaching & Mentoring

FOR

DUMMIES®

by Marty Brounstein

Wiley Publishing, Inc.

Coaching & Mentoring For Dummies®

Published by
Wiley Publishing, Inc.
111 River Street
Hoboken, NJ 07030
www.wiley.com

For general information on our other products and services or to obtain technical support, please contact our Customer Care Department within the U.S. at 877-762-2974, outside the U.S. at 317-572-3993, or fax 317-572-4002.

Wiley also publishes its books in a variety of electronic formats. Some content that appears in print may not be available in electronic books.

Library of Congress Cataloging-in-Publication Data:

Library of Congress Control Number: 00-01100

ISBN: 978-0-7645-5223-6

15 14 13 12
1B/RV/QU/QY/IN

About the Author

Marty Brounstein is the Principal of The Practical Solutions Group, a training and consulting firm based in the San Francisco Bay area that specializes in management and organizational effectiveness. Marty's consulting work includes one-on-one coaching with managers and executives, assistance to groups working to become productive teams, and guidance and direction for organizations who are establishing practices for high performance and employee retention. His training programs target management as well as employee-development issues from leadership to effective communications.

As a consultant, speaker, and trainer since 1991, Marty has served a wide variety of organizations from hi-tech to government, for-profit to nonprofit. He has bachelor's degrees in education and history and a master's degree in industrial relations. Prior to beginning his consulting career, he spent a couple of years as a human resources executive. *Coaching & Mentoring For Dummies* is his third management book; he is the co-author of *Effective Recruiting Strategies: A Marketing Approach* and the author of *Handling The Difficult Employee: Solving Performance Problems.*

To contact Marty regarding consulting, speaking, or training services, call (650) 341-8001 or e-mail him at mabruns@earthlink.net.

Dedication

To Goldie Brounstein, a very special lady in my life whom I was lucky to call "Mom." I wish you were here today so that I could hand you this book — I know you would be very proud.

Author's Acknowledgments

I want to thank the staff of Hungry Minds who provided the opportunity to write this book and gave me positive support throughout the project: Kathy Welton, Mark Butler, Karen Hansen, and Tere Drenth. Thanks, too, to friend and colleague Carl Welte for his technical support on this book.

In addition, while too many to name, the managers and executives with whom I've had a chance to work over the past ten years have served as inspiration for this book. Those who demonstrate the coaching work that I teach serve as the examples you see in this book. They know that coaching works, and I thank them for the fine job they do and also for the opportunities I've had to learn from them.

Publisher's Acknowledgments

We're proud of this book; please send us your comments through our online registration form located at www.dummies.com/register.

Some of the people who helped bring this book to market include the following:

Acquisitions, Editorial, and Media Development

Project Editor: Tere Drenth

Acquisitions Editor: Karen Hansen

Acquisitions Coordinator: Jill Alexander

General Reviewer: Carl Welte

Editorial Director: Kristin A. Cocks

Production

Project Coordinator: Emily Wichlinski

Layout and Graphics: Amy Adrian, Joe Bucki, Brian Massey, Barry Offringa, Tracy Oliver, Brent Savage, Jacque Schneider, Erin Zeltner

Proofreaders: Laura Albert, Corey Bowen, Susan Sims, Charles Spencer

Indexer: Sherry Massey

Special Help

Andrea Boucher, Mark Butler, Amanda M. Foxworth, Michelle Hacker, Melba Hopper

---

Publishing and Editorial for Consumer Dummies

Diane Graves Steele, Vice President and Publisher, Consumer Dummies

Joyce Pepple, Acquisitions Director, Consumer Dummies

Kristin A. Cocks, Product Development Director, Consumer Dummies

Michael Spring, Vice President and Publisher, Travel

Brice Gosnell, Publishing Director, Travel

Suzanne Jannetta, Editorial Director, Travel

Publishing for Technology Dummies

Richard Swadley, Vice President and Executive Group Publisher

Andy Cummings, Vice President and Publisher

Composition Services

Gerry Fahey, Vice President of Production Services

Debbie Stailey, Director of Composition Services

Contents at a Glance

Cartoons at a Glance

By Rich Tennant

The 5th Wave By Rich Tennant

"I was giving them a rousing motivational speech from my college football days, at the end of which everyone jumped up and butted heads."

page 9

The 5th Wave By Rich Tennant

"It's the crew, Captain Columbus. As we appear to be approaching the horizon line at full sail, they'd like to hear your 'Round World Motivational Lecture' one more time."

page 161

The 5th Wave By Rich Tennant

"I think it's time we cut the mentoring umbilical cord, Stacey."

page 113

The 5th Wave By Rich Tennant

"I think Dick Foster should get the promotion. He's got the vision, the drive, and let's face it, that big white hat doesn't hurt either."

page 217

The 5th Wave By Rich Tennant

"Your supervisor tells me you're the guy I talk to for fast tracking a project."

page 291

The 5th Wave By Rich Tennant

"I sort of have my own way of delivering a non-threatening performance review..."

page 65

Fax: 978-546-7747
E-mail: richtennant@the5thwave.com
World Wide Web: www.the5thwave.com

Table of Contents

Introduction

Walk into any bookstore today and you'll see a large section of books under the topic of "management," with titles that come in a wide variety of sizes and shapes, from leadership to time management. What you won't see, however, are a lot of books that deal with coaching and mentoring employees. The ones you may see usually are by sports figures trying to pass on their nuggets of wisdom to the business world — yet many of these sports coaches or players don't have any experience working in the business world.

But go back to the office and what do you hear?

- Your boss or some other senior manager telling you how you need to coach your employees so they know how to effectively perform their jobs
- Employees talking about how they wish they had managers who were mentors

What is everyone talking about and how do you learn to coach and mentor? You've probably seen many business books highlighting trends that turn out to be fads that come and go. Learning to coach as a manager, however, is here to stay. The demands to get top performance out of the staff you manage — the essence of what coaching focuses on — won't go away in your lifetime.

Welcome to *Coaching & Mentoring For Dummies.* You're about to read a management book that gives you the guidance as a manager to understand what coaching is — and how to do it well. It is a book that you can refer to time and time again for tips and ideas on how to get the best out of employees' performances. And the approach of the book is fun and practical: You get an easy-to-read resource that provides you with how-to instruction.

About This Book

This book is written for managers of all levels. Some managers, often called supervisors, have responsibility for a few staff members in one functional group such as sales, accounting, and operations. Those called middle managers have responsibility for a few such groups or greater numbers in the same group. Executives, often with department head, director, or vice president titles, have responsibility for many groups in one overall department or for multiple functions and a few departments. Regardless of where you find yourself in these structures and what level of authority you carry, what you and other managers share in common is the responsibility for the performance of others.

Most managers know, regardless of their levels of experience, that the people-performance issues are the greatest challenges of the jobs. The secret to success in the job is to be able to multiply your effectiveness through others. You can't do everything yourself as a manager. When your employees are performing effectively, you as a manager are doing your job. Coaching is the pathway for multiplying your effectiveness through others, for getting the best out of people's performance. Managers who have discovered how to do this are in great demand in today's business world.

This book provides the foundation for understanding what business coaching is all about and helps you gain or improve the coaching skills that drive employee performance and commitment. These skills, which serve as the main topics of the book, involve the following:

✔ Getting employees to deliver the results you need

✔ Guiding employees to think and do for themselves

✔ Motivating employees to take on responsibility and perform effectively

✔ Growing employee capabilities that lead to career development and success

If you're a manager who's in need of achieving these results, this book is for you. Whether you work in the public or private sector, chances are, you operate in an ever-changing, fast-paced environment. You probably face many challenges and pressures in doing your job as a manager, such as the following:

✔ Do more with fewer resources.

✔ Implement organizational and business changes.

✔ Find ways to increase efficiency and productivity.

✔ Meet greater customer expectations.

✔ Deliver results and retain good employees.

With these types of demands, developing your staff to be effective performers and to function self-sufficiently is the key to your success. Yet too many managers still operate in a task-focused or a must-maintain-control fashion. They manage in a way that hasn't kept pace with the demands and changes that are upon them. They haven't discovered how to multiply their effectiveness through others. They haven't read *Coaching & Mentoring For Dummies!*

Conventions Used in This Book

Coaching, as defined in this book, has two aspects to it:

- ✔ It's an approach to how someone functions in the role of being a manager. In the approach of managing as a coach, the manager operates as the leader, developer, and guide of the team and its individuals.
- ✔ It's a set of management skills aimed at getting the most productivity out of employee performance. These skills or tools require hard work and often, a change in old habits, but they work.

Together, these two aspects of coaching give managers the best weapons to deliver results and positively influence employee commitment.

In the business world, the terms "coaching" and "mentoring" are often used synonymously. In this book, that's not always the case. When you hear employees talk about wanting a manager who is a mentor, they are in essence talking about wanting a manager who carries on as a coach. They want a manager who cares about their development and who challenges them to grow and perform to their best — in brief, what managing as a coach means.

- ✔ Coaching is the sum of all the skills — the coaching skills of giving performance feedback, delegating, motivating employee performance, and so on.
- ✔ Mentoring is one set in the overall skills of coaching. It is a significant part of coaching and the set that focuses on guiding employees to do for themselves. Mentoring promotes self-development and self-sufficiency and is covered in detail in Part III of this book.

In addition, when discussing the skills of coaching throughout this book, I use the term "tools" to mean "skills." Tools are handy ideas and practices that work and can be put into action. The skills of coaching explained in this book are such tools.

The book also talks about certain behaviors that are important for making coaching work: behaviors such as being assertive, leading by example, and listening. The book doesn't suggest that a certain management style or personality style is what you need to be effective at coaching. You have to be able to work with people and build relationships with them to make coaching work, but no set style or personality exists as being the one for coaching success. Thank goodness! Coaching allows for diversity of styles.

Coaching does, however, advocate that you be flexible because you manage a variety of individuals with different needs and skill levels. Rigid, one-style-fits-all in how you manage staff doesn't work well when coaching.

Foolish Assumptions

The book takes the assumption that you, as a reader, have a basic understanding of what the job of being manager entails. You have the responsibilities for business functions and for the performance of people, not just yourself. It assumes that managing and evaluating staff performance is a major part of your job, or you are someone who aspires to take on such responsibilities in your career one day. For a good reference to find out more about the functions of a management role, read *Managing For Dummies* by Bob Nelson and Peter Economy (IDG Books Worldwide, Inc.).

In addition, in this book, I steer clear of academic debates on the differences between management and leadership. Management positions are conventionally viewed as leadership roles. The book takes the assumption that effective leadership is part of being an effective manager. In simple terms, leadership is influencing others to achieve desired outcomes, and this is a critical part of what is needed to make coaching work.

How This Book Is Organized

This book flows from the conceptual to the practical. It first introduces the concept of coaching and the idea of building employee commitment — and how coaching is the best way to influence high levels of commitment.

The rest of the book gives the practical application of coaching, in which the skills of coaching are taught with examples of how to include them in your management practices. (The theme of how coaching influences employee commitment is carried through the rest of the book, however: Each coaching skill and how it impacts commitment is examined.)

The following sections provide a summary of what you'll find in each section of the book.

Part I: Building Employee Commitment through Coaching

This part lays the conceptual foundation for the book. First, it defines what coaching means and why it's important in today's business environment. This part then introduces a management model to guide efforts for building high levels of employee commitment as well as the behaviors that managers need to coach and influence commitment.

This part also explores the issue of diversity, which became a critical management issue starting in the last few decades of the 20th century. It makes the connection between coaching and managing diversity.

Finally, before moving ahead into specific coaching tools, this part shows you how to manage your time and stay connected with your staff. Coaching takes place through two-way conversation and collaborative efforts, so that you have to take the time to work with people to coach them effectively.

Part II: Performance Coaching for Results

In this part, I explore three different coaching tools, all of which help you to focus employees and manage their performance to deliver quality results. This part begins with the skill of giving performance feedback through constructive feedback rather than through praise and criticism. From there, you practice setting goals and developing performance plans. Finally, you find out how to give periodic performance reviews that help you manage these plans, instead of waiting for an annual performance review to evaluate progress.

Part III: The Fine Art of Mentoring and Tutoring

This part explains what mentoring and tutoring are all about and defines the behaviors that comprise this significant coaching tool. It also helps you reflect on common management behaviors that have the opposite effect of what they want to achieve with employee performance — behaviors that stifle employee thinking and hinder employee responsibility.

This part also helps you hone one of the most sophisticated and powerful mentoring skills: tutoring with questions. Here, you understand how the power of questionning, far more than getting answers, helps you find ways for employees to perform self-sufficiently. The part closes by exploring the core of what mentoring involves: taking an interest in employees and guiding their development for top performance, referred to here as "taking employees under your wing."

Part IV: Motivating and Empowering Your Staff

Empowerment, which has turned into a buzzword of sorts, is about giving people autonomy to do their jobs along with the support to do them well. Empowerment also holds employees accountable to deliver the proper results. To empower employees, you need to understand what makes them tick and what motivates them, which is covered in the first chapter in this part. This part goes on to provide practical strategies and skills that help you motivate employee performance to increase quality and assure commitment.

In this part, you also find out how to delegate in a way that empowers employees and produces good results at the same time. A five-step coaching tool is provided that helps ensure success.

Part V: Grooming and Growing Your Employees

Part V puts a heavy emphasis on coaching to help stimulate professional development and career growth for employees. It explains the message of career self-reliance and helps employees put this into practice for their own career resiliency and development.

The part also gives you tools to train employees when you need to give formal instruction and to best use others as resources to maximize training efforts. I also give you a tool that helps you focus employees on a path of development that often can bring career growth, and I touch on how to coach for improvement when performance isn't at the level it needs to be.

Part VI: The Part of Tens

This fun part gives you summary tidbits and information that wrap up the book and help you understand the value of coaching. This information, given in pieces of ten, helps dispel the myths of coaching, lists skills to develop to support your foundation for effective coaching, and helps you review how coaching can positively impact employee commitment.

Icons Used in This Book

Throughout this book, you may notice small graphics in the margins, called *icons,* which are meant to grab your attention and support what you're reading. Here are the ones you will see in this book.

This icon symbolizes practical tips, ideas, and strategies to make your coaching efforts work.

The example icon signals a real or made-up story that illustrates a point being discussed or highlights a manager's experience with a coaching effort.

Pearls of wisdom are those "aha!" nuggets of information that are meant to stimulate thought and provide you with insight worth hanging onto.

This icon is a reminder of good ideas or points of information to use when you put coaching into practice.

This icon serves as a warning of what not to do in your behavior or management practices because they detract from your coaching effectively.

Where to Go from Here

The book is written so that each chapter stands on its own, so if you like to skip around when you read, you can do that with this book and not feel out of place. Occasionally, references are made to other chapters that you can turn back to if you need refreshing on a topic. You may, however, want to start with Chapters 1 and 2 because they give the conceptual foundation that the rest of the book builds upon.

Certainly, if you prefer the traditional flow of reading from start to finish, you'll find that this book flows very nicely for you. Either way, enjoy!

Part I

Building Employee Commitment through Coaching

The 5th Wave   By Rich Tennant

"I was giving them a rousing motivational speech from my college football days, at the end of which everyone jumped up and butted heads."

In this part . . .

As you begin to coach, you need to understand what coaching means and recognize that the critical aim of coaching is to impact employees. This part gets you started.

Also in this part, you discover how coaching supports your efforts to manage diversity and how you can maximize your time when coaching your staff.

Chapter 1

Get Off the Bench and Be the Coach!

. . . .

In This Chapter

▶ Defining what coaching means in the business world

▶ Contrasting two common types of managers: coaches versus doers

▶ Making the change to managing as a coach

▶ Taking a look at the tools of coaching

. . . .

You're a manager, possibly a first-level supervisor, middle manager, or executive. Whether you came upon the role recently or have many years of experience, you know that the job of being a manager is not getting any easier. You carry a great deal of responsibility, and with the pace of change these days, more may be coming your way before you know it. Whoa!

At the same time, you're expected to lead your group(s) and make them productive. And while you're at it, you have to keep your employees motivated and committed — you can't afford turnover problems. (Of course, if you're not feeling just a tad overwhelmed at times, you're not alive!)

If trying to do it all yourself isn't working as well as you would like (it never does), and because magic wands don't exist (none has been found so far), the solution, which your employees want you to figure out, is that you have to manage as a coach. Yes, a coach. You've probably heard others suggest this idea but may have wondered what coaching is, how you do it, and whether it will really help you as a manager. You've come to the right place — where the secrets for coaching success await you.

This chapter lays the conceptual foundation for the book. It introduces what coaching in the business world is all about and delves into its benefits, particularly how coaching can help you be a winning manager in the 21st century.

Getting the Lowdown on Business Coaching

You probably relate the term "coaching" to the sports world, but you don't have to be a sports coach or fan to be a manager who coaches effectively in the business world.

The definition of coaching, in a business context, has the two following aspects:

- ✓ Coaching is an approach to management — how one carries out the role of being a manager.
- ✓ Coaching is a set of skills for managing employee performance to deliver results.

Being a coach means that you see and approach the role of manager as a leader: one who challenges and develops your employees' skills and abilities to achieve the best performance results. In other words, if you manage as a coach, your staff members learn, grow, and work hard, too. As you seek to get the best out of their performance, you also have to work very hard.

As a coach, you develop and possess various skills and efforts that are aimed at guiding employees to achieve high productivity and positive results. The more you manage as a coach, the easier you'll find coaching as a manager because you'll be putting those skills into practice. A preview of some of these critical coaching skills or tools is coming up in the next section.

Sneaking a quick look at the tools of coaching

Understanding and putting coaching tools into practice is a critical step in becoming a coach. Here's a quick look at various coaching tools, all of which are covered throughout this book:

- ✓ Setting goals and performance plans
- ✓ Giving performance feedback
- ✓ Conducting periodic performance reviews
- ✓ Guiding development through mentoring and tutoring
- ✓ Tutoring with questions
- ✓ Taking employees under your wing

✔ Motivating employee performance

✔ Delegating to empower and increase productivity

✔ Training for skill development

✔ Stimulating and supporting career development

✔ Intervening to build improvement in performance

The focus of these eleven coaching skills is on performance, which is the emphasis of coaching — getting the best out of people's performance. Notice that "being nice" isn't used to describe how you perform these coaching tools. Coaching isn't about being nice any more than it's about being mean.

Coaching applies to any personality type, and while it does involve building working relationships, the nature of those relationships vary by individual. Some employees need pushing and firmness; others need little direction and a light touch. Sometimes you need to give direction and other times, support. That is, the use of the coaching skills or tools are tailored to fit individual skill levels and needs.

You carry out these coaching skills through conversation and collaboration. These skills involve working with an employee in order for that person to go back to his or her job and perform successfully. Spending quality time (rather than quantity time) with others is the crux of how you execute these coaching skills.

Fine, but do I really need to be a coach?

Raise your hand if any one of the following challenges and pressures affect you in your job as a manager:

✔ Do more with fewer resources.

✔ Get employees to adapt to change.

✔ Find ways to increase efficiency and productivity.

✔ Create an environment to retain employees.

✔ Meet greater customer expectations.

✔ Deliver results.

Is your arm tired yet? In today's increasingly fast-paced, ever-changing, and highly competitive environments, demands such as these are affecting many organizations — especially their managers. Demands and pressures cut across all types of businesses — private and public sectors, for-profit and not-for-profit enterprises — and across all levels of management, from the top executive to a newly promoted first-level supervisor.

Sorry, no sports analogies

Two, four, six, hike! Keep your eye on the ball. Bend those wrists after your jump shot. While many analogies are made between coaching in the sports world and coaching in the business world, managing employees as a coach is far different from coaching a football, baseball, or basketball team.

✔ As a manager, you probably get paid more than your employees, which is often not the case in professional sports.

✔ Sports are all about winning, while business is more than that. Clear-cut winners and losers are less evident in the business world. Adapting, improving, surviving, and keeping customers satisfied are major focuses of many managers.

✔ If you manage in an autocratic and verbally harsh way to motivate your employees the way that many sports coaches do (some quite successfully) with their players, you will only succeed at being viewed as a tyrannical and difficult boss. Remember, professional athletes get paid to play; employees get paid to work. The environments aren't the same.

✔ Sports coaches don't play. They may be ex-players, but their jobs are to stay on the bench. Many managers in the business world are working managers. They frequently help perform the technical functions that their work groups do, and some even work the front lines right alongside their staff members. Business coaches have to get off the bench.

So if you're a big sports fan or someone who has experience playing or coaching in sports, will that help you be more effective at coaching employees? Not really — although this knowledge may come in handy when you bet in the office football pool.

Yet what has not always kept pace with all these changes and expectations is the way that managers manage. Far too many managers still operate in a task-focused or a must-maintain-control fashion. If I just do more hands-on myself and tell everybody to do more, and everyone will get along just fine, right? Or I can toss in a few buzzwords or phrases to help: "All right everyone, you've been empowered. Now work smarter, not harder." The problem is, managing this way just doesn't work.

Because today's challenges aren't going away anytime soon, managing as a coach is a necessity not only for your success, but also for your survival. Coaching is about helping others become more effective, developing employees to perform to their best ability and to function as self-sufficiently as possible, and challenging employees to take on responsibility instead of waiting to be told what to do. It also means supporting and involving your employees in the process.

Coaching influences employee adaptability, productivity, and retention. It helps you make better use of your time. But many new and different efforts are needed. The road to success starts by making the shift from managing as a doer to managing as a coach. Read on!

Managing as a Coach versus as a Doer

Coaching is an approach to management: how you function in the position of a manager. While different leadership or management styles exist, how managers approach their roles tends to be one of two ways — as a coach or as a doer. The following are descriptions of how the two approaches generally function:

- ✔ **Coach approach:** Managers work to achieve the best operational performance results by developing and maximizing the talents and abilities of employees to their fullest.

  Those who manage as a coach still perform tasks; in fact, many work alongside their staffs doing some of the same duties. Yet those who approach management as a coach recognize they also need to lead and develop others to top performance, because that is how the tasks best get done. Such managers live by the principle of *and;* that is, they approach their jobs as a balance of managing both task issues *and* people issues. They see the two as connected. They see managing people as part of managing the work the people do.

- ✔ **Doer approach:** In this approach, managers tend to focus more on task issues of the job (and also the technical issues of their work), as well as on the group's performance. Their attention tends to go first to the things they themselves have to do and to the areas of greatest comfort — task and technical issues. Doers, as a result, tend to function as senior individual contributors.

  While the style of doers varies from controlling to very hands-off to a combination of the two, the doer approach to management tends to live by the principle of *or.* They have task issues to handle *or* people issues to handle. These issues are often viewed as separate sides of the manager's role rather than interrelated ones. So doers tend to put much less emphasis on how people are performing, which is usually less comfortable to deal with, than on getting things done.

A common feature of both management approaches is that managers have their own tasks to perform. Few ever focus solely on managing others. The key difference in the two approaches, however, is on where a manager focuses his or her attention.

Table 1-1 gives you a quick preview of the tendencies that coach and doer managers exhibit when handling six of the most common management functions. To help you see this difference in greater detail, the following sections illustrate how managers using the two approaches would handle various functions. (As you check out the general tendencies of each approach, keep in mind that general tendencies mean just that; things don't work exactly the same way all the time.)

Table 1-1	Coaches versus Doers: Approaches to Management Functions	
Management Function	*Coach*	*Doer*
Planning	Invests time in doing it.	Has little time for planning ahead.
	Often involves others in shaping plans.	Tends to operate on a day-to-day or short-term basis.
	Is future-focused.	Often crisis-driven and fire fighting.
Goal setting	Works with others to develop goals and plans to achieve them.	If operates with goals, tends to give staff their goals — little employee involvement.
	Ensures that goals are written and expectations are clear, and then manages by them.	Often tends to be activity- and task-oriented as opposed to results- and goal-driven.
Giving performance feedback	Does so on an ongoing basis. Feedback is tied to what employees are doing.	Seldom, unless something goes wrong, or gives occasional, vague praise.
	Provides both positive and negative feedback so staff knows where they stand.	May do so at annual review time.
Dealing with performance issues	Addresses issues in a timely way with solutions-oriented approach.	Many avoid dealing with these issues. Is outside of comfort zone.
	Works with employees to map out plans for improvement.	May seek punitive measures as the first action to deal with problems.
Delegating	Does so as much as possible to maximize resources and increase productivity.	Finds letting go of responsibility to others hard to do and thus delegates little beyond simple tasks.
	Provides necessary support, lets people handle the job, and holds them accountable.	If willing to delegate, dumps assignments — gives little guidance and support.

Management Function	Coach	Doer
Mentoring and developing staff	Takes an active interest and involvement in employee learning and growth.	Tends not to put much attention in this area.
	Supports training and encourages opportunities to expand employee capabilities.	Takes a learn-on-your-own approach to employee development.

Planning

Planning is a critical management function that entails looking to the future and setting a course of action to get there.

- ✔ **Coach approach to planning:** The manager as coach takes time to plan — after all, you don't get ahead unless you plan ahead. The coach realizes this and doesn't just focus on what is happening now, but constantly looks to the future and often involves others in shaping plans to reach future goals. This future-focus is often part of the conversation that a coaching manager has with his or her staff.

- ✔ **Doer approach to planning:** The doer manager tends not to spend much time planning — too much to deal with now to worry about that later-on stuff. Doers tend to have a day-to-day focus, reacting to the problems at hand and incurring frequent interruptions. In other words, their days are often full of other people interrupting them with one problem after another. Crisis management and fire fighting are words many doers spew and live by. They are often quite busy.

The coach manager can sometimes fall into this reactive mode. When a coaching manager, however, senses that people are getting caught too much into fire fighting, he or she gives attention to working on fire prevention.

Goal setting

Goal setting is defining what needs to be accomplished in performance to achieve desired results.

- ✔ **Coach approach to goal setting:** The coach manager often involves group members in shaping the group's goals, and most definitely works with individual team members so that they know what their individual goals are. When you work for someone who manages as a coach, you know what your priorities are and what's expected of you. In fact, goals and plans are usually written so that no one has to rely on memory.

✔ **Doer approach to goal setting:** If goals exist, the doer approach tends to give people their goals. Less time is spent discussing and working together to shape goals and plans.

In many cases, no set or articulated goals exist. Doer managers tend to be more task-oriented than goal-focused. They know what needs to get done now and maybe in the near future. But goals are the bigger-picture stuff — a series of tasks that together accomplish an end result. Goals are about achieving significant results. The major improvements to be made and the targets to be hit aren't often on the doer's radar screen, or if goals exist, they're rarely part of conversations between managers and employees. As a result, the doer manager's staff tends to be absorbed with activities and being busy (or at least looking that way) instead of being focused on important results to achieve.

Giving performance feedback

Performance feedback is letting others know what you've observed in their efforts and performance. It is acknowledging what people have done and how they've performed.

✔ **Coach approach to giving performance feedback:** The coaching manager provides ongoing feedback to his or her staff members, who know where they stand in terms of their performance. When something is done well, performance feedback is given; when something needs to done better, performance feedback is given.

The coach works to give the feedback, both positive and negative, with specifics and timeliness — as near as possible to the time the performance occurred. The coach provides feedback about both the individuals' work and behaviors. Whatever issues of performance are involved, when something is worth acknowledging, the coach avoids the *couch potato syndrome* — sitting back and saying nothing. These managers get off the couch and verbalize their observations.

✔ **Doer approach to giving performance feedback:** The doer manager tends to give feedback less frequently and with less specifics. Employees tend to hear from them only when something goes wrong or during their annual review time. Otherwise, no news usually means good news, or so employees hope. Little recognition takes place, and areas for improvement are often glossed over.

Employees working for a doer often aren't sure where they stand in their performance, or some may think their performance is better than it really is. In the latter case, no news means distorted views.

Dealing with performance issues

Sometimes, employees aren't performing to the level you need. Such situations are one of the biggest challenges for managers.

> ✓ **Coach approach to dealing with performance issues:** When someone is not performing as well as needed, the coach approach is to work *with* the person first. The emphasis is on coaching to improve, working together to clarify expectations, developing plans of action that target improvement, and providing support to help make improvement happen.
>
> The coach doesn't wait for performance issues to turn into big problems, either. He or she responds with early intervention using a positive, solutions-oriented, firm touch.

> ✓ **Doer approach to dealing with performance issues:** The doer manager quite often follows the *management-by-osmosis* path in dealing with performance problems — avoiding them and hoping for the best. The idea is that employees will read your mind and figure out that better performance is needed.
>
> You don't have to be an experienced manager to figure out what happens when performance issues aren't dealt with — they get worse. But for many doers, dealing with a performance issue is as far from the comfort zone as you can go, so they practice big-time avoidance.
>
> For some doers, often after avoiding the problem for awhile, the mode of operation is to get tough, if not down-right punitive: threatening the employee with his job, putting the poor performer on written warning, or better yet, getting him or her out of there for good. These punitive-type efforts, especially when done as the first, main effort, tend to cause shock, bitterness, and anger from employees. This is akin to having your doctor tell you to hit your head against the wall to relieve your headache. Not too solutions-oriented, is it?
>
> In other words, throw a group of doer managers a technical problem and what do they do? They go into problem-solving mode. Throw them a personnel-related problem, and they either run from it or kill it.

Delegating

Delegating is entrusting others with assignments and responsibilities. The coach and doer contrast greatly in how they handle this function.

> ✓ **Coach approach to delegating:** The coach delegates as much as possible for one simple reason — you can't do everything yourself. The coach looks to maximize the resources at hand and increase productivity.

The coach delegates meaningful responsibilities and projects, not just busy-work tasks, and provides the necessary support, resources, and accountability that employees need to do their jobs well. Allowing failure slows everyone down. The coach gives attention not only to day-to-day happenings, but also to important matters that are often ignored or left alone. Planning and going after important issues, not just urgent issues, is where the coach manager asserts leadership.

✔ **Doer approach to delegating:** Take a guess at the doer approach to delegating. For many a doer manager, delegating meaningful responsibilities and assignments to staff is not a frequent practice. How come? For many, delegating beyond assigning simple tasks feels like a loss of control. In addition, the doer lives by the old adage that if you want to get a job done right, you do it yourself.

Because styles vary, some doer-types think that they do delegate. However, their form of delegating is more often dumping. "Here, you do it (because I don't want to), and don't screw the job up or bother me with it." Support or resources to help — what are those things? Not surprisingly, such assignments often end up making one person look bad — the dumpee.

Mentoring and developing staff

Mentoring and developing involves making the effort and showing interest in helping your staff grow in their skills and capabilities. It involves teaching, encouraging, and challenging them to do their best.

✔ **Coach approach to mentoring and developing staff:** Such managers thrive on working with their employees and helping them develop their skills and capabilities. They ask questions more than they give answers, they give their staff challenging opportunities and work, and frequently they exchange feedback to spur learning and growth. They regularly take an interest in employees' careers and job situations and encourage training and other learning experiences.

From the coach perspective, the more capable your employees, the more productive and self-sufficient they are. Developing strong people resources is a source of pride, not a source of insecurity.

✔ **Doer approach to mentoring and developing staff:** Quite often, the doer is too busy to spend time mentoring and stimulating employee development — the comfort to do this is lacking. If employees are particularly observant, they can still learn from the doer because many doers are knowledgeable and skilled in their work. But employees tend not to learn *with* the doer. (And if employees watch carefully, sometimes they may learn what not to do.) Beyond good, old-fashioned on-the-job training (OJT) in which you learn on your own, any organized or focused efforts on employee development are infrequent occurrences.

I'm a Doer, You're a Doer — So Many Managers Are Doers

Many doer managers are hard workers and high achievers, and are sometimes even technically brilliant. But in terms of effectiveness in a management role and the ability to develop others to deliver high levels of performance, doers tend to fall short in comparison to managers who are coaches.

Yet in my experience as an employee, a manager, and as a consultant working for a number of years with managers at all levels in a wide variety of organizations, I find that the vast majority of managers tend to function more as doers than as coaches. In fact, when I discuss this point with most managers, from first-level supervisors to top executives, they agree with me and are often insightful at answering the question, "How come?"

So, why do more managers function as doers? Take a look at the following:

✔ **Who gets promoted?** How do people usually get started in management roles? They are promoted from the ranks of the individual worker-bees. And the ones who earn the promotions are generally good doers — that is, those who are technically competent. Few people who are technically incompetent are made managers. (Although sometimes you probably wonder how a few managers got their jobs. Did they have revealing pictures on the company president?)

The high-performing salesperson is promoted to sales manager. The top engineer becomes the engineering manager, the hard working accountant is promoted to accounting supervisor, and so on. The logical career path for good performers is to move into management. But the preparation for the role and the demonstration of leadership abilities required for the role are seldom seen. And after they're promoted from the ranks, organized training and mentoring efforts on how to become an effective manager generally don't occur on a regular basis, beyond the one-day shot at an external or internal seminar.

Many doers continue to earn promotions and work their way to higher levels of management because they are high achievers and show technical competence, if not brilliance. If they have strong personalities, they have an added advantage. A track record of coaching and developing others and functioning as a real leader (rather than as a senior individual contributor) aren't usually major prerequisites for advancement.

✔ **Who are your role models?** Because most managers are doers, having been promoted because of their worker-bee mentality, most managerial role models are doers. And although you may admire their technical expertise, you may have less admiration for their leadership and coaching skills. Because little training or mentoring is done to guide them in different ways of managing, a lot of monkey-see, monkey-do behavior goes on.

In addition, the recognition and rewards that managers get often has little to do with their abilities to coach and develop others. Certainly, they are rewarded when they are effective coaches, but more often, the recognition and rewards come because managers show that they are strong performers and high achievers in their areas of expertise (sales, finance, engineering, operations, and so on). A vice-president or department head, for example, often has years of management experience. But experience tells only how long someone performed, not how well they performed.

✔ **What do managers work to develop?** The final reason for an abundance of doer managers relates to the background and the expertise of most managers: A vast majority of managers have their educational degrees in a field related to their career work — engineering, business, marketing, public administration, finance, and so on, and not in management. While some managers may have degrees unrelated to their current managerial functions or no college degrees at all, you seldom find that they have a degree or related training in management with an emphasis on coaching.

So, what they lack in education related to their current position, they make up for in what they have learned through experience in their jobs, right? More often than not, managers tend to focus their own educational development (through seminars, conferences, reading material, and so on) on their technical fields of expertise. Ongoing concentrated learning efforts in leadership and coaching aren't the norm for too many people in management roles. Do a comparison for yourself. How many hours have you devoted to management development versus technical development during the past year or two?

Many managers and executives overlook the fact that management is a discipline itself — a field of study. Mastery is never achieved. Being effective requires continuous learning, because managing people and helping them achieve their best performance is no small feat. It's a never-ending challenge for . . . well, truth, justice, and good results. (Bet you thought I was going to say the American way.) No, you don't have to be a superman or superwoman to know how to coach. You just have to be open to learning and willing to work hard at it.

If you see yourself as one of the millions who tend to manage more like a doer than a coach, should you be worried? Not really, unless worrying is what motivates you to make changes in the way you manage.

But if the doer shoe fits, here are a few points to keep in mind.

✔ Doers aren't bad people — they just need to focus on coaching.

✔ You're part of a very big club.

✔ Coaches are doers, too. They carry out tasks, but also focus on leading, developing, and maximizing the resources they have to get the best performance results.

✔ Technical competence is important for coaching effectively. You certainly have to understand the functions that people work at in order to help develop them to better performances in these functions.

The key, then, is to work at making the shift from doer to coach. You begin the shift by grasping the concept of approaching your management role as a coach. This concept involves understanding that your people and task-management responsibilities go hand-in-hand; they're not separate entities. This is the view of *and* (balancing task issues *and* people issues) versus the tunnel vision of *or* (handling task issues *or* people issues).

I can illustrate this point with a story of an engineering manager. He was given two main responsibilities: Take a production group that now reports to him out of a restructuring situation and build them into a productive team *and* lend his technical expertise to a cross-functional engineering project.

The engineering manager had been in management a few years, but the job at hand was a new experience for him. To help him work effectively with this new group, the manager's manager made training and consulting resources available, but it was up to the engineering manager to make use of the resources. What did he do?

After some initial efforts to start meetings with the production group and after facilitating a few hours of team training for them, the manager became engrossed with the responsibilities of the engineering project. Within a short time, 90 percent of his time went to the project, the rest to the group he was supposed to manage.

What happened to the group? Not hard to guess: They floundered. Chaos reigned and morale suffered. The training and cross-training that was available hardly occurred, and plans for building the team were never set.

What approach did the engineering manager take? That of classic doer. The engineering manager got caught in the tunnel vision of *or*. He approached his job with an all or nothing mindset, giving his attention to either one major responsibility or the other.

He quickly gravitated to the area of greatest comfort, his technical side. Little coaching and leadership took place. The engineering manager was not able to balance his responsibilities and see that both tasks — his new group to manage and his project to complete — were equally important. In his previous position, he had managed a few engineers who worked fairly independently, so his doer tendencies had never gotten in the way. With his new group, however, coaching skills were in great demand but he responded as a doer.

The view of *and* (balancing task issues *and* people issues), is critical for making the shift from doer to coach. You, as a manager, have many priorities, some related to the work activities within the group or groups you manage and others related to matters that take your time and attention outside your group. These priorities may range from working on your own projects to spending time with your boss to interacting with customers. The view of *and* says you have to see all of your priorities and coach your employees so that they will function as productively and self-sufficiently as possible.

Chapter 2

Laying a Foundation that Builds Commitment

Take any group of managers and ask them if they want employees with high levels of commitment. Except for the rare person (who probably then needs to be committed — sorry, no pun intended), the answer will come up a resounding "yes!"

Employees with high levels of commitment are the ones most dedicated to the job and the organization. They're the ones who show drive and initiative, who work hard, and who aren't satisfied until they deliver top results. They're also the ones most likely to stick around and not leave the company. Simply stated, employees with high levels of commitment make a manager's job much easier and much more effective.

Achieving this commitment is no small feat. This chapter shows you how.

Tuning In to Personal versus Positional Influence

Influence, as defined here, means to have an effect on other people and on outcomes. From a negative perspective, influence can mean the use of manipulation and coercion. But from a positive stance, it can mean using your influence to gain an added value or a good effect. And when managers exercise leadership, they influence — positively or negatively.

Although managers are seen as leaders in organizations, not all managers assert much leadership. Many managers are somewhat *laissez-faire* in their style of leadership; that is, they are hands-off and passive. Such managers tend not to have too much influence over their employees. On the contrary, managers who do exhibit influence tend to do so in one of two ways, by use of positional influence or personal influence.

In the next two sections, I take a look at how these two styles of influence usually work. In addition, Table 2-1 gives an overview of how managers tend to assert their leadership influence. One type of influence, that of personal influence, is far more effective for coaching than the other.

Table 2-1	Management Influence
Management by Positional Influence	*Management by Personal Influence*
Exercise authority	Exercise personal qualities
Look to maintain the chain of command	Look to build working relationships
Seek control	Seek employee ownership and involvement
Likely result: compliance	Likely result: commitment

Managing by positional influence

Management roles are positions of authority in organizations. Managers who wield *positional influence* view their titles as important and expect employees to respect their authority. For managers who use positional influence, having authority — and pushing it as needed — is how results are best achieved. Managers who exert their positional influence also seek the following:

✔ **Maintain the chain of command:** Private and public organizations historically have been patterned around hierarchy — the many levels of positions from the non-management ranks through the management ranks. In military terms, the hierarchy represents a chain of command to be followed and never circumvented. Positional-influence managers generally follow this thinking. For them, the flow of communication and decision making needs to adhere to this chain of command. The hierarchy of management is to be abided by and respected, starting with the authority of their own position.

✔ **Gain control:** Management literature of the 1960s and 1970s touted four main functions of a manager: To plan, lead, organize, and control. Managers who exert positional influence tend to really like that control part. Things are working right when everything is under their control and running the way they want it. In the groups they manage, they grant the approval for most decisions and give the solutions for most problems. The extreme types here are what employees call *control freaks.*

Control isn't necessarily a negative factor. Managers certainly need to monitor progress, know that everything is working and under control, and work with their employees to make modifications as needed. Most employees want this kind of organization or control. They tend not to respond well to chaos, but they tend not to respond well to stifling or controlling managers either.

✔ **Promote compliance:** The result of this management influence is often employee compliance — people do what they're told and work does get done, and sometimes, quality performance does occur.

Managing by personal influence

Now take a look at what happens on the other side of the coin. Managers who exhibit *personal influence* strive to earn respect from others rather than expecting it automatically because of their titles. They do so by demonstrating traits and behaviors such as honesty, respect for others, and all that leadership-by-example stuff. By exerting personal influence, they seek the following:

✔ **Build working relationships:** Personal-influence managers attempt to establish positive working relationships with their employees instead of worrying about who has what authority in the organization. They do so by getting to know their employees professionally and personally so that the qualities that make both the manager and their employees good people and good workers can come out. Ongoing two-way communication is the norm in these relationships.

The emphasis here is on building working relationships as opposed to personal relationships. These managers know that understanding both the professional and personal facets of an individual is helpful in working with that person. These bosses are the ones who can be friendly with their staff members without trying to become friends with their employees. A friendly boss is far different than a boss who is trying to be your friend.

✔ **Seek employee ownership and involvement:** Managers who exert personal influence encourage employees to take ownership in their jobs — that is, they delegate responsibility, provide support and guidance as needed, and expect results to be delivered. Employee involvement and initiative are invited. Control for these managers doesn't come from telling employees how to do their jobs; it comes by having people follow through on the responsibilities they're given.

✔ **Develop commitment:** The likely result of management by personal influence is commitment. Managers who demonstrate positive personal qualities, build constructive working relationships, and drive employee autonomy with accountability increase the likelihood of getting commitment in return. Management of this kind creates situations in which employees respect their managers. Employees like working for someone who knows and cares for who they are and, at the same time, provides challenges and opportunities to grow. The roots of employee commitment come from this kind of environment.

Seeking Commitment versus Compliance in Today's Workforce

Positional influence and personal influence have radically different effects on employees and their performance. Commitment tends to yield greater productivity and employee retention than compliance does — especially in today's work world in which job security, and therefore, loyalty to the company, has been eroded.

At the same time, from the 1970s until now, the U.S. workforce itself has been changing greatly. Beyond the changes in the demographic makeup of the workforce, changes like the following have been happening:

✔ Education levels have been rising.

✔ Technical skills and knowledge of computer use have been on the increase.

✔ Desire for challenge and meaning in one's work is on the upswing.

If the job situation isn't quite right, today's highly skilled workers are likely to look and go elsewhere — even out of state — for employment. Today, the norm for the workforce is to have multiple jobs in their lifetimes, if not multiple careers. The employers' concerns about so-called unstable *job-hoppers* (individuals who have held many jobs, with short life spans at those jobs) are shifting more to concerns about applicants who have spent many years at one job — for surely these applicants lack creativity and flexibility!

Are these employees prepared to follow orders and revere authority? In subtle to more overt ways, employee responses come back with a resounding, "Don't tell me what to do!" The more managers attempt to push compliance and their positional influence, the more employees push back with various forms of resistance.

When compliance encouraged, you find employees doing the minimum, taking little initiative, blaming you — the manager — for everything that goes wrong, and sitting back, taking little responsibility on their own. These employees still do what they're told, but their efforts are likely to be minimal and fall short of achieving the quality results you need and want.

Maintaining your personal influence under pressure

While many managers want to build positive working relationships with their employees, the nature of the relationship often changes when pressure and stressful situations come into the picture. At those times, their mode of operation shifts to the compliance side.

For example, imagine that yesterday I was willing to be friendly and discuss ideas with you, but now stress has arrived, so today, do what I say! Or yesterday I was willing to show interest in your work and career, but stress has arrived, so now I am too busy to be bothered with you.

Managers who skip back and forth in their mode of operation limit their credibility for having much personal influence. If you always give orders and push authority, at least your manner is clear and consistent and therefore, easier to deal with. If you shift back and forth, in which case your employees are always trying to figure out whether you're going to be open to listening and engaging in two-way discussions, you'll quickly lose credibility.

Your best bet is to find ways to always build positive realtionships with your employees, in spite of stressful situations.

Finding ways to build commitment offers the best hope for ensuring employee retention and productivity. When commitment occurs, you see employees with drive, creativity, positive morale, and a willingness to make the extra effort and take responsibility. Ongoing research done on employee retention points out more and more that the major factor that keeps employees with an organization is the quality of the relationship they have with their managers. Pay alone is not enough. If people are working for a manager who cares about them and their careers and who provides them with challenges in their work, their reasons for staying far outweigh their reasons for moving elsewhere to work.

Personal influence, not positional influence, builds connections between employees and managers and commits employees to your company.

Managing as a Tone Setter

Effective coaching is based on building positive working relationships and exercising personal influence with your employees. These efforts are what stimulate the development of mutual trust. One of the critical aspects of the leadership side of management is *tone setting,* in which managers understand that their own behavior often sets the tone for the behavior and overall performance for the group(s) they manage.

In other words, how your employees work and conduct themselves on the job is a reflection of how you, their manager, work and conduct yourself. And the higher you go up the organizational ladder, the greater the number of people you influence and affect.

Show me a manager who, rather than face a problem, looks to find blame when problems occur, and I'll show you a group of defensive employees who often walk on eggshells. On the flip side, show me a manager who, rather than place blame, always avoids dealing with problems, and I'll show you a group of frustrated employees working in chaos. And another example: Show me a manager who openly complains about management whenever he gets frustrated about something in his job, and I'll show you a group that frequently whines and complains, especially about its manager.

These examples illustrate how the tone-setter role can come back to haunt you as a manager. You need to stay aware that your own faults and weaknesses may be magnified within the staff you manage. Of course, even if you lead by positive example, there's no guarantee that you will get positive behavior and performance in return, but doing so certainly increases the likelihood. Therefore, for managers to exert influence and coach effectively, maintaining awareness of their tone-setter roles is important.

Over the years, I've asked a number of management and non-management groups to identify the leadership-by-example behaviors that managers need to exhibit to set the right tone for their groups. These groups have most often identified the following sixteen behaviors, which I refer to as the *Sweet 16:*

- ✔ Listens to understand; isn't judgmental.
- ✔ Follows through and meets commitments.
- ✔ Takes an interest in employees as people.
- ✔ Works productively and meets deadlines.
- ✔ Is flexible and open-minded.
- ✔ Treats others with respect.
- ✔ Stays calm under pressure.
- ✔ Addresses issues timely and constructively.
- ✔ Shares information and stays in touch.
- ✔ Collaborates with others.
- ✔ Is solutions-oriented and doesn't blame.
- ✔ Recognizes good performance of others.
- ✔ Displays honesty and integrity.
- ✔ Shows interest and enthusiasm for the work of individuals and the group.

✔ Shows up on time for meetings and other important events.

✔ Takes a positive focus in interactions.

When you make these behaviors regular practices, they earn you respect in return. Most important, they build your personal influence as a manager, which puts you on the road to ensuring the commitment of your employees. It's easier to ask your employees for high levels of performance and professional conduct when you demonstrate these efforts yourself.

So how are you doing as a manager at making these behaviors consistent practices? Evaluate yourself. On a scale of 1 to 5 — with 1 being seldom and 5 being frequent — with what frequency do you exhibit each of the Sweet 16 behaviors in your management practices? After this self-evaluation, if you're open to the feedback, ask your employees to rate how frequently they see you exhibiting each of these leadership-by-example behaviors. As a gauge of how you are doing (and don't shoot any of your employees if they give you a low frequency rating), consider an 80 percent level a competency level (80 percent is a total score of 64 out of 80.) Anything above 80 percent is outstanding. Be honest with yourself! What is most important here is not your overall score, which is just a gauge, but the level of your awareness of whether and how frequently you demonstrate behaviors that build your personal influence as a manager.

The toughest person to manage in your group is none other than yourself. When you recognize this fact, you can work on you, and then you can apply the coaching practices that stimulate high levels of performance and employee commitment.

The Collaborative and Assertive Nature of Coaching

Coaching is carried out in an effort of collaboration. What's collaboration? Grab a dictionary, and you see something to the effect that collaboration is the act of working together. *Collaboration* is cooperating and willingly assisting others in some kind of effort.

Now moving to the other end of the manager's pendulum, what's not collaboration? Here are some examples of what managers often do that is *not* collaboration:

✔ Are frequently uninvolved in the work that employees are doing.

✔ Tell people how to do their jobs.

✔ Correct all the mistakes employees make and solve all the problems employees encounter — *for* them.

These examples of not collaborating fit well with the doer approach to management, covered in Chapter 1, which is in many ways the opposite of the coaching approach. Collaboration, on the other hand, is about working with someone else to set plans, solve problems, gain skills, and focus performance in the right direction.

The collaborative nature of coaching recognizes that managers and employees don't have the same level of responsibilities, and it doesn't seek consensus on all decisions. Managers practicing assertiveness and collaboration don't focus on making employees happy or on sitting with employees to help them get all their work done — *hand-holding,* as the expression goes. These approaches focus on communication, on taking action and responsibility, and on performance. Instead of coercion or acquiescence in stressful and challenging situations, assertive and collaborative coaches engage in dialogue with their employees. Even though these managers are decisive about getting an action done, they are willing to listen and are open to discussion. They are positive, firm, consultative, and understanding in the face of pressure.

Engage in two-way conversations

The collaborative nature of coaching requires two-way conversations. Two-way conversations occur when two people are willing to listen to each other's points of view and express their own points of view. Two-way conversations are discussions, not debates, dialogues, or lectures. They also convey that the employee and what she has to say are important and deserve to be heard with respect. You don't have to agree with each other, but you must be willing to understand one another and maintain dignity in your working relationship.

Assert yourself

For the two-way conversation and the collaborative nature of coaching to work, managers must be assertive in their manner and actions. In your role as manager, *assertiveness* is your ability to communicate and take action in a positive, sincere, and confident manner that maintains respect for others. Assertiveness translates into such actions as communicating directly, using language constructively, addressing problems with a focus on solutions, following through, taking initiative, and leading the way to bring issues to closure.

Coaching assertively involves flexibility tailored to the individual employee and the situation at hand. Sometimes this flexibility means being encouraging; other times it means being firm. Sometimes this means being persistent; other times it means being patient. Sometimes this means pushing a person to take action; other times it means backing off and seeing what the individual will do. Coaching assertively encourages input and ideas but doesn't compromise high standards of performance. It encourages dialogue but not endless discussion with no closure.

Internalizing collaboration

While many managers understand on an intellectual level that coaching is an assertive, collaborative effort that takes place through two-way conversation, they don't act upon it until this understanding reaches an emotional level. Only then are these concepts internalized and truly understood and practiced. The shift begins at times like the following:

✔ When a disagreement is recognized as an opportunity for listening and entering dialogue rather than as a time for arguing or just backing away.

✔ When a manager reacts to an employee's resistance by seeking to find out why the resistance occurred in the first place and

how the issue can be settled, instead of using the resistance as an excuse to yell and order or to appease and do nothing at all.

✔ When problems in an employees' work are seen as opportunities to ask questions and challenge employees to come up with solutions — versus telling them how to fix their problems or by letting problems linger.

When these kinds of shifts take place, you're starting to coach. Your focus shifts as well to be performance-based rather than personal-based, to working together rather than working against, to figuring out what works best to get a job done rather than seeing everything as either right or wrong.

Hold the pickles, onions, and aggressiveness!

Being assertive isn't the same as being aggressive. While both approaches are action-oriented, they are quite different in their manner and behavior. An assertive manager allows dialogue; an aggressive one permits little listening and holds one-way conversations. An assertive manager addresses problems in a solutions-oriented manner; an aggressive one addresses problems in a shoot-first-and-then-blame manner. An assertive manager is direct; an aggressive one is blunt. Being assertive means being willing to take charge; being aggressive means being hard-charging — my way or the highway. In simple terms, assertiveness invites collaboration; aggressiveness seeks compliance.

So, let me repeat: The collaborative nature of coaching requires assertive managers, not aggressive ones.

Don't be passive

Passive and nonassertive approaches don't work when trying to achieve collaboration, either. Being meek, hesitant, indirect, and *laissez-faire* in manner and actions renders coaching useless. The give-and-take and constructive dialogue of coaching doesn't occur when managers are passive in their approach with employees.

Testing your collaboration skills

To help clarify the value of the assertive nature of coaching, check out the following responses made by managers who approach their roles in different ways.

Here's the scenario: One of your employees expresses an idea for the direction in which she would like to see a project go, and you, the manager, don't agree with her idea.

✔ **Aggressive response:** "That idea will never work. I disagree with it totally. I don't know what you were thinking, and who asked for your ideas anyway!"

Here, you create a one-way conversation — end of discussion.

✔ **Passive response:** "Well that idea has possibilities. Maybe we could consider it. If you

want to work on it, uh . . . maybe you don't have to. But I do appreciate that you have ideas. But if you want to explore it more, we could."

Here you create confusion and leave the issue hanging because of an indirect and hesitant response.

✔ **Assertive response:** "I have some concerns about whether that idea will help the project. Here they are (constructively expressed). Please address my concerns or clarify any misunderstandings."

Here you invite a two-way conversation, collaborative problem solving, and an opportunity for closure on how to proceed with the project.

The Five Pillars for Building Commitment

In this section, I review the *five pillars for building commitment,* a model for your efforts as a coach to build commitment and achieve high levels of performance. The pillars serve as your guideposts. If you impact them, you impact employee performance and increase commitment levels.

✔ **Focus:** When focus is strong, employees know what they need to accomplish in their jobs, they know what is expected of them, and they are aware of the values of the group or organization. They know where the group is going and what its priorities are. While the group's plans may change, chaos and mystery are not frequent visitors.

✔ **Involvement:** When this pillar is strong, employees feel that they have some say-so over the matters that affect their day-to-day work situations. They have input into the planning, problem solving, and decision making that affect their level of responsibility. They feel included. The old, but true adage that "people support most what they help create" highlights what the pillar of involvement emphasizes.

✔ **Development:** When this pillar is strong, opportunities for learning and growth are encouraged and supported. These opportunities are both formal and informal in nature, ranging from such activities as a training course to a mentoring discussion between an employee and a senior manager. Helping people continuously strengthen their knowledge, skills, and experience are common practices.

✔ **Gratitude:** When this pillar is strong, efforts for and accomplishments of good performance are noticed and acknowledged. As with the other pillars, how gratitude is provided varies from formal to the informal practices, but efforts to recognize what employees do well occur regularly.

✔ **Accountability:** When this pillar is strong, employees are given responsibility along with the authority to carry it out, which creates in them the desire to produce results with high standards. Lax performance is not tolerated, while measuring progress and reporting results are normal practices. People produce quality results not just because it is expected of them, but, more importantly, because they enjoy experiencing a sense of achievement.

Coaching is your best set of tools for positively influencing employee commitment. All of the coaching skills previewed in Chapter 1 impact one or more of these five pillars for building employee commitment. They, of course, only do so when done as regular practices. Just a little effort now and then doesn't do the trick.

Looking at an example

The following is a commonplace scenario of good intentions. As you read the story, you may want to analyze the manager's (Jack's) efforts by considering the following questions, each of which I address later in this section:

✔ What are Jack's efforts to coach Tim, his employee?

✔ What are Jack's efforts to encourage commitment from Tim?

✔ (Ah, now the tricky one.) Regarding Jack's decision on making the corrections for the project that Tim is assigned to handle, how would you as a manager deal with this situation?

Tim was quite eager when he started his new job. Early in the job, Tim's manager, Jack, met with Tim and assigned him to handle an important project as his primary area of responsibility. Jack gave Tim a general description of what the project entailed and three directions — to do what it takes to get the job done, to come to him with questions, and to complete the project within three months.

As the weeks passed, Jack was pleased with Tim's progress. He noticed that Tim was meeting with the right people, was often working efficiently, and seemed self-sufficient. Jack held a brief review meeting with Tim a few weeks after the project started, and Tim appeared to be on the right track. Also, every now and then, Jack informally asked Tim how things were going and received an enthusiastic response of "really good."

Tim liked the freedom Jack gave him. Other than an occasional reminder to stay on schedule with the project, Tim appreciated the fact that Jack was not a harsh or demanding boss. On the other hand, Tim found that Jack was often tied up in meetings and burdened with his own projects, so Tim learned to get answers to questions elsewhere.

In a little less than three months, slightly ahead of the deadline that Jack had set, Tim informed Jack that the project was complete. When they met to go over the project, Jack's excitement about Tim's work soon turned to disappointment. Jack didn't like some of the decisions Tim had made, decisions that resulted in the project going in a somewhat different direction than Jack had envisioned.

Jack also didn't agree with some of the methods that Tim used to do his work. Jack wound up telling Tim that the project needed quite a bit of correction and that because of the tight deadline he (Jack) would handle it and let Tim work on another, smaller assignment. Tim became deflated and frustrated.

Analyzing the manager's coaching efforts

Jack had good intentions at the beginning. He gave Tim a meaningful assignment, allowed him autonomy to run with the project, and gave clear directions about when the work needed to be completed. Early on, Jack met with Tim and did a brief progress review.

After that, however, any real coaching was nonexistent. The results expected were never spelled out nor were parameters set for Tim to work within. As for feedback of any substance and progress reviews along the way, well . . . *nada*.

So after the first few weeks, the two had little regular communication — and don't forget, Tim was a new employee. Jack didn't really take an interest in what was happening for Tim and the project until the deadline. Jack illustrates the classic doer (covered in Chapter 1) who stays busy with his own affairs until something critical comes up.

Analyzing the manager's efforts to affect his employee's level of commitment

Jack gave Tim meaningful responsibility and initially a sense of autonomy in his work. So you could say that Jack made an initial effort to involve Tim. Jack also gave Tim a sense of focus at the beginning by letting Tim know the deadline within which he needed to complete the project.

These two early efforts did scratch the surface of two pillars for achieving employee commitment: involvement and focus. But Jack's lack of ongoing involvement and guidance fell short of building a working relationship and influencing high standards of performance in Tim's case. Jack failed to lay a foundation on which to build commitment. Jack then further undermined Tim's potential for commitment with the decision to leave him out of the correction phase of the project.

Ascertaining how to handle corrections for this project

This is a tough one. You have a tight deadline and a project that needs fixing. The quickest course is fix it yourself, as do many doer managers. While this decision may seem to be an easy solution (and many people, myself included, have taken just this course when faced with similar circumstances), it actually has serious shortcomings and may have more difficulties than meets the eye at first glance.

✔ When Tim is left out of the effort to correct the project, he can't learn from the experience. And, in a short period of time, trying to match Tim's knowledge of the project is no easy task, even if you have the technical expertise. Also, if you had the time, why didn't you do the project in the first place yourself?

✔ In determining what went wrong with the project, Jack is focusing on the methods Tim used. From this perspective, you can say that Jack is placing methods over results — which is common with doer managers, who often worry more about how a job should be done than about the desired outcomes. In this case, it's possible that many of the results Tim produced are acceptable. But not involving Tim in evaluating the results and not focusing on results wastes time and a valuable resource.

✔ Even if Tim is invited to just sit alongside and watch Jack make corrections, Tim will learn more from the experience than if he has no involvement in the effort at all. In most tough business decisions, two key factors must be considered: the business at hand and the impact on the people involved or affected by the decision. Jack's focus was on the first factor only, the business at hand (how to fix the project). As a result, Tim's potential for future commitment was shot down! The trust and working relationship between Tim and Jack was greatly damaged.

Consideration must be given to both factors — making the fixes himself or involving Tim in the revision process — when making critical business decisions, not just one or the other. No doubt, it's essential that Jack get hands-on with fixing the project, but doing so with Tim's help is the most performance-effective course to take for this problem and any future problems.

Coaching focuses on performance but recognizes that people are connected to the work they do. To lay the foundation for building employee commitment requires focusing on developing working relationships and on developing the performance of the individual doing the job. With coaching, they are mutually inclusive efforts, and they put you on the road to seeing the five pillars of commitment become reality.

Chapter 3

Coaching and Managing Diversity

· ·

In This Chapter

▶ Clarifying what "managing diversity" means

▶ Avoiding the assumptions that lead to problems

▶ Focusing on the issues of performance to manage — and behaviors not to tolerate

▶ Managing people as individuals

· ·

*I*n the latter half of the 1980s and into the early 1990s, the issue of diversity became big news in many American business organizations in both the private and the public sectors. Diversity initiatives were launched in organizations, various forms of sensitivity workshops ensued, the media jumped on the bandwagon, and diversity consultants came popping out of the woodwork.

Today, publicity and attention surrounding the issue of diversity has greatly dissipated. But what came out of all the earlier attention is that managers still need to know how to manage diversity. And when you sift through all the talk about what it means and what it takes to manage diversity, at the core is coaching.

In this chapter, I explore the issue of diversity, help you shed any assumptions you may have about your employees, and discuss ways to focus on two key issues: managing performance and discouraging certain behaviors.

Finding Out What Diversity Is All About

Since the 1970s, the United States has been experiencing an influx of immigrants from around the world. Having lots of folks migrate to U.S. soil isn't a new phenomenon — however, unlike earlier times when most immigrants came from Europe, more recently, new residents have come from all over the world, with the greatest number coming from Asia and Latin America. At the same time, more and more women and minorities have been entering the workforce and seeking equal opportunities. This means that the demographic makeup of the U.S. and its workforce is in flux.

Who we are as people

Beyond factors such as race, ethnicity, gender, and age, what factors influence who a person is as an individual? Here are a few examples:

- Aptitude and skills
- Biases and prejudices
- Career or occupation
- Diet and health
- Education
- Family upbringing
- Financial status
- Friends and relationships
- Geography
- Hobbies and interests
- Language(s)
- Leadership experience
- Marital status
- Media exposure (press, television, movies)
- Military experience
- Parental status
- Pets
- Physical abilities and disabilities
- Physical stature and appearance
- Political views
- Religion
- Role models and mentors
- Sexual orientation
- Siblings
- Spending habits
- Substance use or abuse
- Traumatic experiences
- Travel
- Work experience
- Work styles

As you can see, nothing gets left out! While these factors vary in importance and experience from person to person, they indicate that everyone is a complicated, fascinating, and unique soul.

As a result of these demographic changes, some business leaders, consultants, and employees see diversity (sometimes called *cultural diversity*) as a matter of race, ethnicity, age, and gender. (See the "Who we are as people" sidebar for broader examples of diversity.) And even among those in the business world who understand that the concerns of diversity are broader than race, ethnicity, age, and gender, they *still* tend to focus mainly on race, ethnicity, age, and gender.

Not surprisingly, then, you can find an abounding difference of opinions about what diversity means and approaches for dealing with it. Programs and training efforts offered by groups on diversity have had a mixture of results. Some efforts have created awareness and employee dialogue within a business context. Other efforts have reinforced and even taught new stereotypes, created more discomfort and tension, and made little connection to a business context.

Whether you like the issue of diversity, understand what it means, or view it as important, when the dust and confusion settle, managers still need to lead and manage their employees and the diversity that comes with them.

Defining diversity

The best way to start is by answering the question, "What does diversity mean?" Simply defined, *diversity* means difference or variety. Put two people in a room together and you have diversity, for as you know, no two people are exactly alike. Yet at the same time, even though the two people have their differences, they also have similarities. So as you begin to put a definition to the issue of diversity, you can say that it is about the differences and similarities among people.

But to define diversity in the workplace, you must tie the initiative to a business context, so I further clarify my definition: Diversity is about how you manage people who work in your business.

And people bring a variety of differences and similarities that make them who they are as employees. Similarities? Sure! Think, for example, of some similar expectations that employees bring to their work environment.

- ✔ They want to be treated with respect.
- ✔ They want to feel included or as if they're part of a team.
- ✔ They want the kinds of opportunity and support that will enable them to be successful in their jobs.

Putting these pieces together, I further define diversity as follows: Managing employees — all kinds of them — and creating a work environment where they are treated with respect and inclusion and are given support and opportunity to be successful as individuals, as well as the opportunity to help the business be successful.

What is the best approach for helping people of all sizes, shapes, colors, and persuasions feel respected, included, and supported? Ahem, the envelope, please. And the winner is . . . managing as a coach, not as a doer (see chapter 1).

Putting differences aside

If you're like me — and probably most folks — when you meet another person, right away you start to identify something about that person based on a few physical characteristics — race, ethnicity, gender, and age, for example. Although you and I certainly can't "guess" correctly about someone's personal background based just on these characteristics, impressions may form in your mind anyway. If you develop a negative connotation about differences and see that someone is of a different race, ethnicity, gender, or age than you, the biases you bring as a human being are going to get in the way and limit your ability to interact positively with the other person.

The key for coaching people is not that you *feel* an instant negative connotation about something or someone who is different from you. That's part of being human. The key is what you *do* about that feeling and whether you get hung up over the fact that some kind of difference exists.

Try this exercise: Think back to times when you entered a situation, and, for whatever reason, you felt different than the other people involved. Write down the feelings that you had about being different in those situations. Having done this exercise with many people through the years, I've found that the vast majority respond with comments such as these: strange, isolated, apprehensive, inhibited, awkward, and uncomfortable. What do these feelings have in common? They all have negative connotations. In fact, say the word "different" or "differences" and, more often than not, people have a negative reaction to it.

But if you take a negative connotation about differences or try to pretend people don't have them, and you will be rendered ineffective (if not hazardous to your employees' health!) as a manager. Ding, ding, ding — disqualified due to ineffective coaching.

Therefore, getting not-hung-up starts with an awareness of diversity and looking beyond impressions and what you see on the outside to getting to know who a particular employee is as an individual. This is akin to the metaphor that people are like special gifts. It's not until you get past the wrapping paper that you discover how special the gift is. Coaching, and therefore managing diversity, works when you respect and manage people as individuals. The two efforts go hand in hand.

When you apply respect and listen in a nonjudgmental way in order to understand, you actually find that learning about people's differences is fascinating — and, by the way, that's also the best way to discover everyone's commonalities, which you also then get to enjoy.

Assumptions: The Ingredient to Leave Out

What's an assumption? An *assumption* is something that is accepted as true and as fact without being proved or demonstrated. While assumptions may sometimes be useful because they help people make educated guesses when needed, generally, they lead to big problems. You've probably heard the old line about what happens when you assume something: You make a derriere out of you and me, or something like that. Actually, you make a donkey out of just yourself. When you act on an assumption before checking out the truth, even with something as simple as finishing someone else's sentence before the message is complete, you increase the potential for misunderstandings and destructive conflicts.

In fact, four assumptions that people commonly make are guaranteed to cause friction and hinder productivity if you act upon them as you manage your staff. In the list and sections that follow, I explore these four assumptions in depth so that you can steer clear of them.

- ✔ **Stereotyping:** Assuming that persons of a group different than yours are all relatively the same in their thinking and behavior.

- ✔ **Setting low expectations:** Assuming you cannot expect much from anyone of a different group because they are not very capable or willing to work hard.

- ✔ **Believing that differences are negative:** Assuming that those of a different group have nothing in common or are too difficult to ever understand.

- ✔ **Equating sameness with equality:** Assuming that managing everyone the same way is the same as managing people equally and consistently.

Coaching focuses on people's capabilities and performances, which is key to managing diversity. But before you can focus on capabilities and performances, you have to push your assumptions aside.

Assumption one: Stereotyping

Stereotyping ignores and dismisses individual differences that influence who a person is and prescribes a set of behaviors to everyone in a particular group based on personal background, physical attributes, or occupation.

- ✔ **Personal background:** Personal background can include race, ethnicity, gender, religion, sexual orientation, age, or physical abilities and disabilities. When you stereotype, you imagine that all the people of a similar personal background are relatively the same in their thoughts and behaviors.

  No one person represents thousands or millions of people just because of a shared physical attribute. While some may argue that there is always someone or a few someones who fit a stereotype, that can lead to thinking that all people of a particular group fit a certain mold based on certain physical attributes, not on their capabilities.

> ✔ **Occupation:** Another example of stereotyping is categorizing how people think and act based on their occupation — for example, "All engineers are this way, and all sales people are that way." Again, while similarities exist, so do plenty of differences about the people who do these and every other kind of job.

Assumption two: Setting low expectations

The assumption of low expectations builds off of stereotyping. An example of low expectations is that you can't expect much from anyone in a group from a certain personal background because they are neither very capable nor willing to work hard.

People often act out this assumption with comments such as, "We hired one person like that once before, and he (or she) didn't work out." One individual is used to represent countless others, so no one of this group is given the opportunity to succeed or fail on his or her merits.

Assumption three: Believing that differences are negative

Building off of stereotyping and setting low expectations, this assumption deems that those of a different group have nothing in common with you or that they are too difficult to ever understand, let alone appreciate or respect.

This assumption implies that differences, especially those that you can see, are negative — they are strange, wrong, or harmful. This assumption can result either in individuals verbally attacking the one seen as different or in individuals timidly backing away from the "other," leaving him or her feeling isolated or excluded.

Assumption four: Equating sameness with equality

This assumption takes for granted that managing everyone the same way is equivalent to managing people with equality and consistency. However, managing all the staff the same way isn't the same as managing them equally. The problem with this assumption is that it ignores individual needs and differences. Sure, everyone needs to abide by the same laws, but this assumption isn't at all flexible.

One style does not fit all

The following is a story that serves as a lesson about assumptions. It helps illustrate the dangers of managing everyone the same way and assuming that approach is the best way to deal with your staff.

Marcia got her first promotion into management a year ago. The management style of her boss, John, was to tell people what to expect and then let them get the job done — a sort of sink-or-swim-on-your-own style. Marcia inherited a challenging situation: She was expected to lead her group in developing and implementing some system and process changes designed to increase efficiency.

Marcia's group wasn't an easy one to manage. Many members had been in the company for awhile and were quite comfortable with the status quo, so she faced resistance to the changes she needed to make happen. In addition, Marcia came from the ranks of her peers, and some in the group resented the fact that Marcia was promoted over them.

John managed three other supervisors in addition to Marcia. These three individuals — Mike, Willie, and Hector — were experienced supervisors who ran efficient and stable operations that required little change. Outside of the occasional check-in with each supervisor to gauge progress and a monthly staff meeting, John let his supervisors run on their own with little guidance.

However, this style did not help Marcia deal with her ever-mounting management challenges. The more she came to John to seek support, mentoring, and resources, the more John reacted with disinterest and annoyance. The more John heard the resistance that came out of Marcia's group, the more he told Marcia that she needed to learn how to handle her problems better — and hold the line on costs, too.

By the year's end, while painful, Marcia had made a good deal of progress implementing the changes needed in her group. Despite this, in his annual performance review of Marcia, John described her shortcomings a manager as he perceived them, and he recommended that she be reassigned to a less demanding role — a non-management position — for which John wouldn't have to hold her hand.

Focusing on John's management efforts, what is going on in this situation? Possibly, the lack of support and coaching have much to do with three assumptions: stereotyping, setting low expectations, and believing that all differences are negative.

Marcia doesn't fit John's view of what a manager should be, is someone he has low expectations of, and has an obvious gender difference, which is something he's not comfortable dealing with at all. Now, whether these assumptions are coming into play for John and Marcia can be debated all day. Yet what often happens to employees in challenging situations like Marcia's when support is lacking is the feeling that maybe "who I am is the reason that you don't provide me with what I need to be successful."

A fourth assumption also may come into play — managing everyone the same way. John seeks to manage Marcia as he does his three veteran supervisors. His *laissez-faire* style works fine for them because they need little guidance or support. Marcia, as a new supervisor, one facing resistance and resentment, needs much more guidance and support.

That's what coaching and managing diversity are all about: tailoring efforts to help individual employees succeed in their jobs. Sometimes, that means working more closely with some staff than with others. John was reluctant to provide much coaching for Marcia, and his one-size-fits-all style was not effective in managing employees' different needs.

Managing people equally and consistently means that you afford everyone respect, hold everyone to a high standard of performance, and give everyone the guidance and support they need to perform successfully. So, you treat everyone equally in terms of your management *efforts,* but not necessarily the same in terms of how you *apply* those efforts.

For example, a new employee will need closer guidance than a skilled veteran. Some employees need more frequent feedback on how they are performing than others do.

Employees have different needs to achieve job success and are at different levels of skill and experience. If you try to manage them all the same way — using a one-size-fits-all management style — the chance that you may induce employee failure is greater than the chance that you may stimulate success.

Focusing on Performance and Behaviors — Not on Assumptions

Coaching employees operates with only two safe assumptions — that people mean well, and they want to and try to do a good job. Only their actions determine otherwise, not any outdated assumptions. This is why coaching works well when managing diversity.

To coach and manage diversity effectively, you need to concentrate on two areas: First, focus on performance; second, don't tolerate behaviors that hinder performance.

Emphasizing performance

Focusing on performance deals with what you're paying employees to do: their jobs. It means putting forth efforts to make employees feel respected and part of the team and to give them the guidance and support they need to develop and maximize their talents and skills.

The coaching approach focuses on helping employees be successful. The idea is that employees can fail only from their lack of competence or productivity. As frivolous as some lawsuits have been, to my knowledge, not one has been as a result of a fired employee who said, "I was discriminated against because I was a poor performer. My manager made good faith efforts to help me improve, but I just couldn't cut it. So that's why I'm suing." (Of course, fire an employee in a harsh and arbitrary manner with no coaching efforts made, and hello lawsuit.)

To help employees be their best, you need to be aware of the issues involved in managing performance. Job performance can be broken down into three main areas: attendance, work and tasks, and job-related behavior.

Attendance

Attendance has two aspects:

- ✔ **Availability:** It's pretty simple: Productivity comes from people performing their jobs, and they can't perform when they're absent. While people are absent because of illness and other legitimate reasons, the matter becomes a performance problem when an employee develops a pattern of absenteeism or is absent frequently enough that his or her work doesn't get done. (*Note:* Serious bouts of illness or disabling situations are *not* in the category of chronic absenteeism.)

- ✔ **Punctuality:** When people repeatedly don't show up on time — at the beginning of the work shift or after breaks — the problem of tardiness exists. In many kinds of jobs, especially salaried or exempt positions where overtime laws aren't applicable, tardiness isn't an issue. In such jobs, people often work long hours to get the job done, so holding them to an exact schedule is irrelevant, even undesirable. On the other hand, with some jobs, such as one that's a time-sensitive operation or one in which customer service needs exist, coming to work at 8:01 a.m. rather than 8:00 a.m. is too late.

As a manager, you have to apply common sense, not rules for the sake of rules, when determining how critical attendance — especially punctuality — is as a job-performance issue. Base your judgment on the needs of the job and the customers it serves. When someone works in a role that isn't time-sensitive and often puts in more than 40 hours a week, you can be flexible about punctuality. If you make a big deal when the person arrives at work a few minutes past your starting time, you will have an impact on performance: You will demotivate that person, and you may see his or her work limited to 40 hours a week. You may wind up with compliance rather than commitment, which is the opposite of what coaching seeks (see Chapter 2).

The work and tasks people do

Work-related issues are critical in every job performance situation. These issues deal with the technical side of employees' jobs: that is, products they make and services they perform. The issues involve output, quality, completeness of the work, and timeliness of getting the work done.

- ✔ **Output:** The amounts or volume of work that people need to produce. Output may include sales quotas, production targets, or numbers of service calls taken.

- ✔ **Quality:** How well the job is done? Is the work produced with few errors, little waste, and in good working order? These aspects of quality are critical in the work and tasks people do.

- ✔ **Completeness:** How thoroughly the work is done? Is everything complete and in order? Half-finished products are items that no one wants to receive.

- ✔ **Timeliness:** The work is getting done when it needs to get done. Meeting deadlines is another important performance issue.

Job-related behaviors

This critical issue of performance relates to employees' conduct and relations with others — behaviors needed to do a job well. Of course, these behaviors vary from job to job, but they often involve things such as teamwork, customer service, upholding operational or safety standards, courtesy and respect, and managing others.

When managing diversity and, of course, coaching, you want to put an emphasis on giving attention to the issues of performance that yield high productivity and build positive work environments. Stay away from attempting to manage issues that aren't performance-related. For example, when managers mistakenly deal with the following three issues, they may find that their efforts create problems and fail to enhance productivity.

- ✔ **Attitude:** Attitude isn't an issue of performance that you can manage. When I share this fact with managers, many want to jump out of their chairs and protest — until I ask them to define the word *attitude.* (They often have a hard time answering that question.) Attitude is how someone thinks or feels about something. It's not the same as behavior. Behavior is tied up in someone's actions; you can observe and manage behaviors.

  You know, of course, that attitude often influences people's behavior. However, you can't *see* attitude, even though you have your perceptions or opinions about it. You can't see what's inside someone else's head, and trying to judge a person's attitude, especially when you view it as bad, is minefield territory. So you need to deal with the *concrete* (the behavior you see) and not the *abstract* (the attitude you perceive behind it).

  For example, imagine that Sue is one of your employees, and she has a bad attitude toward people who have two heads. However, you have coached her to be courteous, helpful, and responsive to all types of customers — all behaviors that influence performance. Today, a two-headed customer walks into your store, and Sue must deal with this customer. Although Sue has a negative attitude about this customer, she provides courteous, helpful, and responsive service, and the customer walks away satisfied. Although Sue has a bad attitude about two-headed people — she's even told you about her attitude — she exhibits the proper behaviors. Her performance is good. (Now, two-faced people are not the same as two-headed ones; they're much worse. Oh, oh, is my bad attitude starting to show?)

✔ **Personal background:** An employee's personal background — his or her race, ethnicity, religion, age, gender, sexual orientation, and so on — doesn't determine his or her ability to perform. Skills and behaviors do that. When you base your employment-related judgments and decisions on who a person is rather than on the person's performance, you jump into the discrimination zone.

All civil rights laws exist for a reason — to protect the who-we-are-as-individuals side of us. *Discrimination* in the legal sense is acting in a prejudicial way that hurts or denies someone an opportunity because of his or her personal background. Although managers know these points of law, many still suffer from foot-in-mouth disease. As a result, they help keep lawyers busy responding to employees who are filing — and sometimes winning — discrimination lawsuits.

✔ **Style:** Style is the methods or ways (a personal touch) that individuals use when getting their jobs done, and nearly everyone has a different work style. Although certain policies and procedures must be followed in many jobs, a person often has a good deal of latitude in how he or she follows them. How neat someone's desk is or whether the employee does a task like you would seldom has any bearing on how well an employee performs.

Unless the style harms others, it's not a performance issue. When managers attempt to make such things an issue or insist that employees do tasks in a set way, employees often wind up feeling stifled and taking less initiative. Certainly, this leaves no room for creativity. When managers focus on methods of doing a job (after someone is trained to do it) rather than on the results expected, they create compliance, not commitment (see Chapter 2 for further details).

You don't need to be a cultural anthropologist to manage diversity. What a relief! You just need to manage people as individuals and focus on their performance. And when you focus your efforts so that your employees feel respected and included and that they have the guidance and support they need to perform successfully, you are not only managing diversity effectively but you're also coaching in high gear. Coaching and managing diversity do go hand-in-hand.

Stamping out insensitive behavior

The second factor in managing diversity relates to behaviors — not tolerating any behaviors that hinder performance: behaviors that are disruptive or insensitive and can offend, intimidate, or anger others. Such behaviors have a counterproductive effect — they hinder quality performance and damage morale.

Here are some examples of such behaviors for you to watch for and address immediately:

- **Off-color humor:** Jokes and other attempts at humor that are sexual in nature or make fun of a particular race, ethnicity, religion, sexual orientation, or disability.

- **Ridicule or insult:** Comments or attempts at humor that personally degrade or attack someone else. Even when done in a subtle fashion, such attempts at humor usually hurt and anger those on the receiving end.

- **Profanity and vulgarity:** I'll stay away from giving specific examples in this area — you probably heard many of them in grade school anyway! A word here or there is usually not a big deal, but many people take great offence at the continuous use of profane, vulgar, or lewd language.

- **Stereotypical remarks:** Broad generalizations of a subtle but degrading nature about groups of people. Comments that start out as, "Those kind of people are all like this," or "I'm not prejudiced, but . . . ," are usually stereotypical remarks that cross the line of respect.

- **Subtle-to-overt sabotage:** Withholding information, not giving help that people need to do their jobs, or causing damage to work items or property.

- **Threats:** Intimidation about someone's job situation or threats aimed at someone's physical safety.

- **Slurs:** Derogatory name-calling that's most commonly aimed at race, ethnicity, gender, religion, and sexual orientation.

- **Mimicking:** Ridicule that usually involves repeatedly imitating another person's accent, especially when English is a second language.

- **Exclusion:** Ostracizing someone from the work group to isolate the person — a destructive behavior that hinders performance.

The list can go on, but these behaviors have instant negative impact on individuals and the work environment when tolerated by managers. And it's even worse if the manager is exhibiting these behaviors.

As a coach, you must recognize that unprofessional and disrespectful conduct have no place in any work environment. These kinds of behaviors aren't what you're paying employees to do. (Hi, I'm applying for the position of offensive jerk. I have extensive qualifications. How much do you pay?) People have the right to feel safe at work.

When an employee commits these transgressions, take the appropriate action to rectify the situation. Often, the first action may be to try to rehabilitate the transgressor; that is, coach to improve and refocus the person on the right behaviors and performance to do (see Chapter 16). Then you set and follow through on consequences if the person still has difficulty performing in a positive and professional manner, as in "Sorry, we don't hire offensive nincompoops — we're trying to keep payroll costs down."

Chapter 4

Finding the Time to Stay Connected

Coaching is a collaborative effort that takes place through two-way conversation. This means talking "live" with your employees and spending time with them — and this is what scares many managers, especially doers as they shift to being coaches. (Flip to Chapters 1 and 2 for more background information.)

Many doer managers fear that making the effort to really coach will take too much time. Devoting time and attention to employees is required to make coaching work. Yet, as the doer ponders, who has any more time to give? That's the beginning of the misconception about how coaching works.

Coaches recognize the importance of staying connected and involved with employees. Staying connected is what builds the working relationship and the personal influence that affect employee performance. This chapter shows you how to build commitments and boost performance by staying connected with your staff.

Coaches versus Doers: Views on Using Time

Managers, whether they use a coach or a doer approach, can easily say that they never have enough time. Few managers at any level in any of today's organizations have *enough* time — a manager's job is seldom a 40-hour-per-week role. So while the doer and the coach may feel pinched for time, their view and use of time tend to be quite different. The two following sections explore those differences.

Time and the doer

Doer managers often find themselves in *crisis mode.* Because they seldom delegate key decisions or responsibilities or develop others to the point that they can help tackle day-to-day problems, doers get stuck in a fire-fighting mode of dealing with one problem after another. Employees can walk into their offices with a problem (which I refer to as "the monkey") and walk out of the offices relieved that the monkey is off their backs. Where did it go? To the manager, of course, who takes on all problems and tries to solve them by him- or herself.

Because doer managers often are in crisis mode, their focus tends to be short-term. They look at what's happening today — or maybe next week. Don't ask them where their groups will be in a year or even in six months. Don't ask them what issues they need to start working on in order to meet the future demands of their business. They have too many fires to fight today to worry or even think about the future. Who has time to do that anyway?

Because managers' styles vary, doer managers may find themselves at one extreme or the other: Either they are constantly interrupted or they find themselves in activities that isolate them from their staff members.

✔ **Interruption-driven manager:** The days of an interruption-driven manager are often filled with people popping into their offices with urgent issues or just for social chatter. And when no one is dropping in, the phone is ringing. They sometimes try to do both at the same time: Talk on the phone and talk to the person standing in front of them. They often sound rushed and are late for meetings; nonetheless, their time is seldom organized or structured in any way. They may spend as much as 60 minutes with just one employee during a week. Unfortunately, that time is just one minute of attention given 60 times over. Efficiency is not their strong suit.

✔ **Isolated manager:** The isolated types aren't very accessible. Meetings may keep them away from their offices. They have e-mail to catch up on — almost as though writing and responding to e-mail messages are their main responsibilities. Are they ever visible? On occasion. Have a serious problem and they may show up to tell everybody what to do. Then they leave and become consumed in their management activities. The isolated types are sort of like a bird swooping in and dropping its bomb: They create havoc in their hit-and-run involvement with their employees. They have neither the time for consistent attention nor an interest in what is going on.

Time and the coach

Coaching managers view their time like money; it's an investment to use wisely. They view spending time with people and issues as the way to get a return on their investment. So, like money, time is not to be wasted. For example, if spending time with an employee — perhaps to help him or her get a better handle on doing an assignment — will yield more self-sufficiency for that employee, a coaching manager invests the time now and receives a payoff later.

If, on the other hand, your employees frequently interrupt you with questions, constantly giving them answers is not the best use of your time. So a coach manager will teach employees how to find their own answers so that they can become more self-sufficient.

The theme here is helping people do a better job themselves — that is, self-sufficiency. (Just don't tell your employees what you're up to!) Coaching is about getting the best performance out of people so that they can do for themselves. Because coaches see that people have an effect on the tasks to be done, they know that investing time in people in order to increase their abilities to perform well is an investment well worth making. Your reward for doing so is increased productivity. And you actually save time: Instead of going from one interruption to another, your time and attention can be spent on the critical issues, which is what managers are really being paid to do.

Because coaching managers realize that they don't have a quantity of time to give to their employees, they know that the time they spend must be *quality* time. Quite simply, they make the time count, making it productive time rather than inefficient time.

✔ Instead of being interrupted 60 times by one employee in the course of a week, a coach spends one hour with the employee preparing him or her to handle the challenges of the daily job. That's quality time.

✔ Instead of watching employees become frustrated and stuck over a problem, and instead of falling into the trap of telling them how to solve every problem they encounter (so that they cannot think for themselves) a coach spends time helping them map out a plan to solve problems. That's quality time.

✔ Instead of chasing after an employee three times a day to see whether she or he is getting tasks done (the dreaded *micromanagers,* as employees call them), a coach takes a half-hour with that employee once a week to do a status review on the project. Now that's quality time!

While the doer manager is just on the go, a coach manager says, "Make my time count." To make your time count, you have to structure and organize your time by asking the following questions:

✔ What activities will you be involved with and when?

✔ How will you organize the time you spend in those activities?

✔ What will you gain from giving them time?

A coaching manager's approach is to make these questions part of the planning process so that his or her time is spent within a particular structure and with a particular purpose.

Many managers find that their time and attention gets pulled in several directions and away from the groups that they manage — and the higher you go in an organization, the more this happens. To guard against this, they carefully scheduling their time. For example, say that you're going to be involved in some high-level meetings most of the next three days and you have a staff member who needs some focused attention. Schedule a one-on-one meeting, say for 30 minutes, with that staff member before you get involved in the other activities. In this way, you can maximize her time and yours. Without structuring your time, you would probably play hit-and-run with her over the three days, leaving her frustrated and feeling that she is low on your priority list.

Keep in mind that although some matters may not be urgent, they may be important. Coaching recognizes this fact and the need to sometimes make time for the important matters.

Two Techniques — MBWA and MBPA — for Building Connections

Staying connected requires that you understand who your employees are and what is going on with each person's performance. Staying connected, therefore, improves the relationships that stimulate high levels of performance and build commitment. Many of the effective strategies for building relationships, staying connected with your employees, and maximizing your time are informal. These strategies fit well with coaching because coaching is informal by nature.

Management by walking around

One such strategy, *MBWA,* which stands for *management by walking around,* is about managers being visible and getting to know their staff members as people, not just as employees. This strategy involves showing an interest in each staff member as a person and being able to converse at times on non-business issues. You carry out MBWA strategy by leaving your office periodically and going to your employees' offices or work areas just to engage in friendly conversation.

E-mail, voice mail, and coaching

Electronic communications provide a good vehicle for passing on information, updates, documents, and even correspondence. Often without taking up a great deal of time, you are able keep in touch electronically.

But keeping in touch via e-mail or voice mail is not the same as staying connected and involved with your employees. If you don't see them or talk with them in person, you aren't connected with them. People build relationships through "live" interactions with other people, not through interactions via computers and telephone-messaging systems.

When you need to discuss issues, set plans, or work out problems, e-mail and voice mail just don't work. Try sending feedback via e-mail or voice mail to employees about some aspect of their performance that you want them to improve upon, and just watch the hard feelings bubble over. You'll get better results by sorting out these matters, which often are sensitive, in live conversations.

That's because with two-way communication, you have an on-the-spot opportunity to explain your point or the chance to listen to the other person's point of view. E-mail and voice mail really amount to monologue. Coaching, on the other hand, works as a give-and-take dialogue.

To make MBWA work, here are a few helpful tips (paraphrased from Leonard Sayles' book, *Leadership: What Effective Managers do . . . and How They Do It*):

- ✔ Be frequent
- ✔ Evenly distribute your time among employees
- ✔ Strike a good balance between short and long contacts
- ✔ Stay flexible in length of speaking and silence

You must practice this strategy regularly. The purpose of MBWA is to build rapport and trust. If you stop by to have a friendly conversation with your staff members only once every few months and are otherwise seldom visible or sociable, your staff may wonder what you're doing hanging around and may think that something is wrong. They'll want you to go away!

No set number exists as to how frequently you need to walk around, just to talk news, interests, family, and so on. When you manage one group, an MBWA strategy may require only a few minutes every day or so. Because senior level managers must extend the strategy to many groups (and this doesn't include direct reports), they may use it with less frequency, but their reach is greater.

Nonetheless, an MBWA strategy, in its truest essence, is about being visible and talking about something other than business. You have the rest of the day to talk business. Of course, if your employees want to talk about a work issue when you come by for a brief, friendly chat — there's nothing wrong with letting them do that — but let them initiate that conversation.

As a manager using an MBWA strategy, one benefit you receive is your employees' perception that you're approachable. Many managers say that they have an open-door policy, meaning that their employees are free to come and talk with them at any time and about any concern. "My door is always open to you." However, an open-door policy works only when you, the manager, are seen outside of your office. Generally, the less visible you are, the less approachable you are — and the less approachable you are, the less likely that employees feel comfortable or believe that your door is really open for them to come in and talk. That is what an MBWA strategy does for you. It advertises that you are someone who can take a little time to go and see your employees, show interest in them, and get to know who they are as people.

This practice encourages the informal flow of communication from employees to their managers. This kind of communication makes it more likely that your employees will come to you when they have issues; it also increases the probability that they will be less defensive when you call them into your office because you have a concern to discuss with them.

In addition, an MBWA strategy helps you understand much about what is going on in the department, just by watching and listening. And as you find out more about your employees as people, including an understanding of the what makes them tick, you have a better idea of how to work with them to motivate and stimulate their performance.

Management by phoning around

MBPA, in contrast, is *management by phoning around.* It's the same as MBWA, except that you do it by . . . yes, the phone. (You probably had that one all figured out.) You can use this strategy when you manage employees who are not physically where you are, such as salespeople, field service professionals, or telecommuters. An MBPA strategy generally requires a scheduled approach, for the simple reason that you need to make sure the person you're calling is available when you call. As a result, managers often maximize everyone's time by combining the call with a business discussion. Nonetheless, the same principle applies to MBWA and MBPA strategies: Both managers and employees can find time to share in relaxing conversation and rapport-building, even when they don't see each other very often.

Being friendly versus being a friend

Although you may be able to see that building connections helps you, as a manager, develop relationships that make coaching work, perhaps you think that this MBWA and MBPA stuff is getting just a tad too personal with your employees. Is it friendships that you're after?

Good question. The relationships that you're building are effective working relationships — relationships in which manager and employee know and trust each other. To pretend that your employees don't have personal lives hinders the rapport and trust needed to work together effectively. After all, you are spending a lot of time with each other at the same workplace.

There's a big difference between being a manager who can be friendly and who cares about employees and being a manager who is trying to be everyone's caring friend. MBWA and MBPA strategies are about being the former and staying away from the latter. Difficulties often result when managers and their employees develop close personal relationships. Managers who become too close to their employees often have a hard time being objective and making tough decisions — or not becoming frustrated and baffled when their friends, also known as employees, seem to be taking advantage of their good nature.

You don't have to be someone's friend to build rapport. You don't have to be friends to take an interest in what is important in someone else's life. But you do need to know who your employees are and have some concern about them in order to be a manager that they can work with. MBWA and MBPA strategies are simple and effective communication tactics that help you stay connected with your staff and build the foundation for a strong coaching relationship.

Let's Do Lunch

Another effective strategy to stay connected with your employees is lunch — the meal that you and they most commonly consume while at work. Because the majority of people eat something for lunch, why not periodically have lunch together?

Lunch often helps people feel more relaxed because it's a break from the fast pace of the work day. So to maximize its communication and coaching benefits, have lunch together away from the office.

For the same reasons, the strategy of lunch is best done one-on-one. Group gatherings and celebrations over lunch are great on occasion. They do not, however, help you build connections with *individuals* — the essence of the two-way relationship that's essential to coaching.

What do you do at lunch with your staff member? Well, you eat. More importantly, though, the lunch get-together is a great time for social conversation (kind of *MBEA,* management by eating around), for business discussion, or a combination of the two. When your time is limited, lunch is a good vehicle for spending quality time with your staff members.

At the luncheon meeting, you can catch up on what is happening with your employees outside their work life, as well as within their work life. Lunch may give you both a chance to work on a project together, or it may give you an opportunity to be a mentor by advising an employee on how to handle a challenging situation. Sometimes the most amazing things about having lunch out of the office together are how well business matters are worked out or how people open up and talk candidly about sensitive issues. Lunch provides a neutral setting in a relaxed atmosphere, which works well with the informal two-way nature of coaching.

In trying to stay connected, you don't have to employ the strategy of lunch all the time. That isn't practical. Lunch is a good intermittent strategy; that is, while you and your employee don't go out to lunch every day or every week, saying "Let's do lunch today" isn't an unusual or odd occurrence, either.

By the way, lunch is not the place where you share all the saved-up bad news with your employee. If you do, just think what your employees would say — "Oh, oh! Joe got called by the boss to go to lunch. What did he screw up this time?" And remember, lunch is a strategy that you carry out periodically with each of your staff members, not with just one or two of them most of the time. If you have lunch frequently with the same person, then you may get the "Oh, oh" gossip in reverse — and usually with a focus on your being a manager who plays favorites.

Many managers don't take advantage of the opportunity that lunch brings for staying connected with their employees and other key people. While you may like to take a break away from everyone else or you may be stuck at your desk eating and working most of the time (uh oh, sounds like a doer — see Chapter 1), periodic lunch meetings are a great use of your time and greatly enhance a working, coaching relationship.

One-on-One Meetings

One of the most effective strategies for structuring your time and staying connected with your employees is the one-on-one meeting. This is a set meeting in which you and your employee come together to work on issues and maintain a good flow of communication. Coaching managers live off one-on-one meetings with their employees — real coaching and connections occur at these meetings.

For many doers, meetings with their individual staff members take place in hallways or on a hit-and-run basis. "Bill, come in to my office right away!" A few "What about this, what about that, or do this or do that" statements often characterize such unplanned and unfocused meetings.

Or these so-called meetings may be a series of interrupt-driven events initiated by your employees, like the ones I describe in the "Time and the doer" section earlier in this chapter, in which employees come running into your office asking for solutions to their work problems. If you keep telling them what to do (so that they don't think to do for themselves), what happens? They keep interrupting you and you keep telling them what to do, and the vicious cycle continues. As a result, you have no handle on your time. (And here's another common scenario: You are the manager at an off-site special meeting or seminar; your beeper goes off throughout the day because your employees have this terrible dependency on you for every answer and decision. Sound familiar?)

The one-on-one meeting is valuable for a coach manager. For some such managers, these meetings occur on an as-needed basis. If your employees are close at hand, when you or one of them has a need, you just set a time and get together shortly thereafter. For other managers whose time and availability are limited, having regularly scheduled one-on-one meetings works best. In either case, the time is structured rather than haphazard, and the one-on-one meeting is a regular practice rather than an unusual occurrence.

One-on-one meetings as a regular practice occur anywhere from once a week to once every few weeks, usually from 30 minutes to one hour, and longer for special situations. They don't preclude an informal touching-base or "Hi-how-are-you?" communications. Instead, one-on-one meetings provide a forum for focusing attention on issues and for in-depth communication, along with a great return on your investment of time.

Organizing a one-on-one meeting

While not every one-on-one meeting with your employees is a coaching session (you may just be getting to know your employees), every coaching session takes place in a one-on-one meeting. *Coaching sessions* are the times that you work together with a staff member to prepare that person to go out and perform: giving feedback, delegating an assignment, setting goals, developing plans, mentoring to solve a problem, and so on. To maximize the time and productivity of both parties, the meeting works best when it's organized. Because coaching is informal in nature, you may think that being organized is contrary in nature. However, that's not the case. Why? Because chaos and a lack of focus decreases employees' desires to meet with you and decreases their abilities to effectively work with you.

Having an organized flow for the meeting allows you an opportunity to be flexible as well. Sometimes, employees raise unexpected issues or you realize you need to devote more time to a matter than you first realized. You'll have a much easier time changing course or adjusting in a conversation when everyone is following a track than when there's no track at all.

So with that understanding, here is a list of questions to address as you plan and organize effective coaching meetings:

- ✔ **What is the objective for this meeting?** What are you trying to accomplish in this meeting with your staff member? You need to know this goal before going in, and you need to communicate the goal in advance so that your employee can be focused on that goal.

- ✔ **What positive outcome are you seeking?** This question is tied to the first question. It serves as a reminder, especially with tough issues, that you need to aim toward a positive result. Sometimes, you can get caught in the emotions of an issue, and as a result, lose sight of the positive goal you're seeking. For example, if you're dealing with a problem, the positive outcome you're seeking with the employee is a solution. Or if you're dealing with a situation in which confusion exists, the positive outcome is a plan that provides clear direction. (Much better than seeking confessions or pushing guilt trips!) Going into the session, you don't need to know what the exact solution or plan will be; you just need to know the positive outcome that you're aiming for.

✔ **What do you need to be prepared to do at the meeting?** You may need to give feedback about the employee's performance; you may have stimulating questions to ask, information to provide, or something to teach; or you may need to give direction or spell out expectations. Sometimes, you may need to prepare by reminding yourself to listen and be patient. Whatever the case, come ready.

✔ **What do you want your employee to come prepared to do?** Unless you want to waste your employee's time and give the individual a dose of frustration, let the staff person know how to come prepared for this meeting. Can the employee report on information, provide project status, share ideas, review plans, and so on? If you come ready and the employee comes ready, the coaching session will actually be a very productive meeting!

✔ **What particular plan or agenda for this session will encourage employee participation?** When you figure out what you're trying to accomplish at this coaching session, what steps do you have to take to get there? Think these steps through so that you increase the likelihood of accomplishing something useful. As part of this effort, remember that coaching takes place through two-way conversation. If you dominate the conversation, you'll probably be able to get your employees to nod and smile (that's when you're in real trouble), but you won't get them thinking and learning how to do things for themselves. See the "Looking at some examples" section for a few sample meeting plans.

✔ **How can this meeting help the employee perform better or more self-sufficiently for the future?** This question is related to the previous one and is a reminder of what you want to do in a coaching session. Your overall goal in every coaching session is to ensure that your employee's performance benefits from the time you invest in the session.

✔ **What follow-up should be set?** If action items come out of the meeting or if an employee is going to work on implementing an idea you discussed, should a progress review be set? In most cases, the conclusion of the coaching meeting has the employee going forward to put something into action. As the meeting closes, set a follow-up time to check progress. Doing so allows you to stay connected, builds in accountability for the employee, and shows that you care about what happens. And setting the follow-up time at the close of your meeting helps prevent you from forgetting or chasing after the employee to see whether the action item is being handled. No one likes managers to become disinterested or act like nags.

Ultimately, you want your employees to drive these one-on-one meetings. You want them to bring to the meeting the issues and ideas to discuss. In essence, the meeting is a two-way street. The employee's role is to take responsibility; yours is to provide support and add value that helps the employee perform well.

Looking at some examples

Using the questions in the previous section as a guide, use the three following sample one-on-one meeting plans as you prepare for your upcoming meetings.

Sample #1

✔ **Objective:** Have the employee correct some mistakes in performance that you noticed occurring yesterday.

✔ **Positive outcome:** Focus on solutions. The point of the meeting is not to dwell on mistakes, it's to fix them.

✔ **Plan or flow of the meeting:**

- Provide feedback about your observations of the mistakes made.

- Encourage two-way discussion. Let the employee comment on your feedback. Then solicit the person's ideas for correction and contribute ideas as needed.

- Close by recapping the solution worked out during the session (have the employee recap, as well), and set a follow-up meeting to review progress.

✔ **Come prepared:** Be ready to give the feedback and ask the questions so that the employee develops ideas for correction.

Sample #2

✔ **Objective:** To review progress on hitting a project milestone and set next steps for keeping the project on track.

✔ **Positive outcome:** A chance to recognize accomplishments, set future direction, and maintain accountability.

✔ **Plan or flow of the meeting:**

- Employee reports on deliverables produced to meet the project milestone. Your feedback is added as needed, especially to recognize good work.

- If problems are identified, engage in joint problem-solving to address them.

- With employee, set the deliverables for the next milestone to be hit in the project.

- Close by setting another status-review meeting around the next milestone.

✔ **Come prepared:** Both parties should have a list of the deliverables for which the employee is to report progress. If the employee has any issues or problems, she or he is to come prepared to explain them and recommend ideas for solutions.

Sample #3

✔ **Objective:** To evaluate how a customer meeting (a call and presentation) was handled by the employee. To be done as a debriefing after the customer meeting.

✔ **Positive outcome:** A chance to recognize what was done well and to determine what can be improved upon for future efforts.

✔ **Plan or flow of the meeting:**

- Employee evaluates his own efforts on what was done well in the presentation and customer meeting — and on what didn't go as well.

- You provide your specific feedback on these two points.

- On the areas for which improvement is needed, ask for the employee's ideas of what can be done for the next time and provide suggestions as needed.

- Close the meeting by reinforcing the efforts that were done well and by setting action items for improvements with the employee.

✔ **Come prepared:** Let the employee know that you want to conduct a debriefing after the customer meeting and that you want him or her to be ready to self-evaluate how the call went. Then let him or her handle the call while you stay in a support role.

Does the checklist and the plan for the coaching meeting need to be written out? If it helps you stay focused, then, yes. If it's not necessary, don't worry about it. Keep in mind that coaching is informal by nature.

The more you use these examples as your guide for coaching meetings, the more you will know what notes to prepare and what you don't need to write down. You will go into meetings with a positive mental road map that maximizes your time and your employees' time — and that keeps you well connected with how your employees are performing.

Part II

Performance Coaching for Results

The 5th Wave   By Rich Tennant

"I sort of have my own way of delivering a non-threatening performance review..."

In this part . . .

Coaching is about impacting employee performance. In this part, you discover three sets of coaching tools that help you drive performance to achieve the results you need: giving feedback so that employees know how they are performing, developing plans with your staff to let them know what they need to accomplish, and assessing their progress along the way.

Chapter 5

Giving Constructive Feedback, Not Praise and Criticism

. . . .

In This Chapter

▶ Contrasting constructive feedback with praise and criticism

▶ Giving performance feedback effectively

▶ Introducing a tool for tracking your feedback efforts

▶ Facilitating the discussion after the feedback and handling challenges

▶ Influencing employee commitment through constructive feedback

. . . .

*O*ne of the most powerful coaching skills is the ability to give effective *performance feedback* — information given to an employee about how he or she performs. This feedback lets the employee know whether the job was done well or whether he or she needs to improve upon the work.

This coaching skill is connected to many other coaching skills. For example, part of effective delegating is giving the delegatees feedback along the way to let them know how they are performing their assignment. Part of training and instructing employees is giving them feedback while they are learning new tasks and skills.

Quite often, non-coaching managers talk with their employees about work issues, but never directly tell them how they are performing in regard to those issues. Performance feedback, on the other hand, is direct and timely. That is, on an ongoing basis, you let employees know how effectively they are carrying out a specific effort or achieving a specific outcome — right at the time they occur. (Pretty novel concept, being straight and honest with people — tough to do, though!) This chapter helps you build your performance-feedback skills.

Using Constructive Feedback versus Praise and Criticism

Performance feedback can be given two ways: through constructive feedback or through praise and criticism. Don't fall into the trap of giving praise and criticism on employee performance.

✔ *Constructive feedback* is information-specific, issue-focused, and based on observations. It comes in two varieties:

  • *Positive feedback* is news or input to an employee about an effort well done.

  • *Negative feedback* is news to an employee about an effort that needs improvement. Negative feedback doesn't mean a terrible performance, rather a performance in which the outcomes delivered should be better. So negative is not a negative word in this case.

✔ *Praise* and *criticism,* on the other hand, are both personal judgments about a performance effort or outcome, with praise being a favorable judgment and criticism, an unfavorable judgment. Information given is general and vague, focused on the person, and based on opinions or feelings.

The following examples help show the difference between constructive feedback (either positive or negative) and praise/criticism:

✔ **Praise:** You did a great job on that project. Good work.

✔ **Positive feedback:** The contributions you made on this project were a big help. I noticed that the work you produced was thorough and accurate. In addition, whenever I needed help in coordinating the team and managing the project schedule, you stepped in and covered for me or gave me assistance, which kept the team and the project on schedule. When team members had questions, you were available to help get them answers. Thanks so much for your contributions in helping make this project a success.

✔ **Criticism:** You were not much help on this project. You were really ineffective. I hope this is not the best you can do.

✔ **Negative feedback:** Here are the concerns I have regarding your assistance on this project. As I explained at the beginning of the project, your services were needed to help coordinate the project management in terms of keeping people focused on their assignments and on the schedule. I did not see much effort of coordination occurring. For example, many of the team members came to me with questions about assignments and schedule issues, often after they could not get answers from you. Most of the time, I noticed that you were working on your part of the project, but the interactions with the others about the overall project and its progress were not evident. When I asked you to cover for me at three of the meetings, each of the meetings ended after a brief time with no minutes or action items produced. Delays have occurred in the project, and we'll now require everyone's attention to get back on track.

The two types of constructive feedback come across as far more objective, specific, and nonjudgmental than praise and criticism. Because constructive feedback is based on observations in specific terms about issues of performance, it is not a right or wrong. Constructive feedback encourages a discussion after the person gets the feedback. As a result, you and your employee can learn more about the situation and, if needed, set a positive course of action.

Praise and criticism don't encourage this dialogue. While nothing is wrong with praise — employees like to know if they did a good job — it can often be seen as hollow or lacking in substance. (To read an example of this point, check out the "Mr. Good Job" sidebar.)

Sometimes managers attempt to soften criticism by first saying, "Now don't take this personally." After that's been said, the employee will likely become defensive. Like praise, in which specifics aren't stated, criticism often leads to a battle between a manager and an employee about whose opinion is right or wrong. Because no observations are provided to give a factual basis to the input — the input is focused on personal judgments — the receiver has a difficult time understanding exactly what he needs to improve upon, and the result can be defensiveness.

For effective coaching, therefore, give your employees constructive feedback about their performance, rather than praise and criticism. In fact, if you are seeing the differences clearly, you can see that "constructive criticism" doesn't exist. How can you, as a manager, give employees, in vague terms, pointed at employees personally, based on your opinions or emotions, anything constructive about improving their performances? Good luck trying.

Mr. Good Job

To be encouraging, Mr. Good Job periodically makes his rounds among his staff to compliment them about their performance. The praise flies: "Good job, Tom." "Way to go, Sue." "You're doing a bang-up job, Mario." On one of these occasions, one of his employees asks him, "So what is good about my performance?" Momentarily silent, Mr. Good Job replies,

"You're just a good worker. Keep it up, " and then hurries back to his office.

While Mr. Good Job may win awards for overkill, input about performance, witnout specifics, tells an employee little and can leave the individual wondering if you even notice what has been done.

Giving Constructive Feedback: A Step-by-Step Guide

The guidelines for giving constructive feedback are relatively the same, whether you're giving positive or negative feedback. These methods fall into four categories: content, manner, timing, and frequency, each covered in the following sections.

Content

Content is *what you say* in the constructive feedback.

1. **Identify the issue of performance involved.**

   In your first sentence, identify the topic or issue that the feedback will be about. For example, "I want to discuss with you your progress on the ABC project." ABC project is the issue of the feedback.

2. **Provide the specifics of what occurred.**

   Give the examples or other evidence to provide the picture of what took place in the employee's effort of performance. (Without the specifics, you only have praise or criticism.) Start each key point with an "I" message, such as, "I have noticed," "I have observed," "I have seen," or when the need exists to pass on feedback from others, "I have had reported to me." "I" messages help you be issue-focused and get into the specifics.

Manner

Manner is *how you say* the constructive feedback. As you may know, how you say something often carries more weight than what you have to say — manner is an important element when giving feedback.

- ✔ **Be direct when delivering your message.** Get to the point and avoid, to use a great expression, beating around the bush. For many managers, bush-beating tends to be more of an issue when giving negative feedback than when giving positive feedback. Both should be given in a straight-forward manner.

- ✔ **Avoid "need to" phrases, which send implied messages that something that didn't go well.** For example, "Jane, you need to get your reports turned in on time, and you need to spell check them." This message is not really performance feedback. It implies that Jane did not do something well with her reports, but it doesn't report exactly to Jane what happened. Providing clarity on what occurred is the aim of feedback.

✔ **Be sincere and avoid giving mixed messages.** Sincerity says that you mean what you say with care and respect. Mixed messages are referred to as "yes, but" messages. For example, "John, you have worked hard on this project, but. . . ." What follows is something the person is not doing well and is the real point of the message. The attempt to be nice first — sugar-coating the message — is negated, and the real sincerity of the message is diluted. (See the "Constructive feedback scenario" sidebar for an example of how to give positive and negative feedback without mixing the two.) The word "but," along with its cousins "however" and "although," when said in the middle of a thought, create contradictions or mixed messages. In essence, putting "but" in the middle tells the other person, "Don't believe a thing I said before."

Constructive feedback scenario

Suppose Sheri is one of your top technically-trained staff members. In fact, in her latest project, her technical skills have been put to good use. So far, the work she has produced has been thorough and accurate, and she has been helpful and responsive to other team members when they've encountered problems. At the same time, Sheri's work has been late . . . again. Now she's two weeks past the second milestone. Because she is a key player in the project, her slowness has resulted in a delay for the overall project. You want to make sure the project stays on schedule and meets its final deadline. Now you need to give feedback to Sheri.

What do you say? You want to hit the key guidelines: The issue of performance needs to be clearly identified; you need to be specific, direct, and sincere, with no mixed messages; and you want to give observations, not interpretations.

This scenario is challenging. Does it warrant both positive and negative feedback? To guide your judgment of whether to use both types of constructive feedback (both positive and negative feedback) in the same conversation, do so only when they are relevant to the issue at hand.

If you attempt to give positive feedback along with negative feedback when the positive isn't really relevant, you're sugarcoating your message and undermining your sincerity. However, when both are relevant, don't blend their points — that creates confusion and may send a mixed message. Let the points you want to make in each type of feedback stand on their own; don't connect them in the same thought. In your opening sentence, introduce that you have two sets of feedback to give.

Here's an example of giving both kinds of feedback when they're both relevant:

> "Sheri, I want to give you feedback on your progress so far with Project X. You've performed some aspects of the project very well and I also have one area of concern I want to work out with you.
>
> In the deliverables you have produced for each milestone, I have noticed they have been thorough and completely accurate. The research done outlines the issues we needed addressed with this project. I have also noticed that you have been responsive to fellow team members' questions and challenges and taken time to help them get problems solved. Thanks for the great teamwork.

(continued)

(continued)

The issue of concern deals with meeting deadlines. Work for the second milestone was turned in two weeks past due, as occurred with the first milestone. These delays have contributed to delays with our project schedule, and that is my major concern, especially with the need to deliver this project on time."

As you see in this example, both positive and negative feedback were given because both were relevant to the issue at hand — the progress shown with Project X. Both types of feedback were given with their own specifics, so no praise or criticism, and each point stood on its own. The manager didn't use transition words, such as "however" or "but," that blend points together and create mixed messages. If you only want to comment on the missing deadlines issue rather than assessing progress with the entire project, you go with just the negative feedback. Remember, though, that if you continuously only comment on what the person doesn't do well and overlook what is done well, you may demotivate the employee and lose the value of your feedback.

Here is another example of where both positive and negative feedback fit together.

"Tom, I had a chance to read over your assessment report and want to give you some feedback about it. Most of it was good, and I saw one area that could use some work.

First, the report detailed very well your findings from the interviews with the team members. It clearly identified what their concerns are and what they see as the efforts the team is doing well. I wanted to get a good sense of what is working and what isn't working, and this assessment outlined those issues. Well done.

The area I saw that needs some work was the last part of your report on recommendations. It contained more of a list of ideas with little explanation or reasons for them. As you will see by the questions I wrote in this section for you to review, I didn't get a clear grasp as to what all the recommendations mean and which ones would be most helpful."

✔ **In positive feedback situations, express appreciation.** Appreciation can be expressed in many ways: "Great job," "Thanks for all your help on this project," or "I really appreciate the good work you did here." Appreciation alone is praise. Yet when you add it to the *specifics* of constructive feedback, your message carries an extra oomph of sincerity.

Take a look at this example: "Sue, we had a backlog this past week and without being asked, I noticed you pitched in and helped John get everything caught up. Your handling of all the processing work while John did the callbacks made for an efficient effort and showed good teamwork. Everything you did was accurate, as well. Thanks so much for helping out. Such initiative is a real value to the team."

In this example, the last two sentences express appreciation after the content of the feedback was given. It also gets at the purpose of positive feedback — to reinforce good performance. Behavior that is rewarded is repeated, so reward the right behaviors.

✔ **In negative feedback situations, express concern.** A tone of concern communicates a sense of importance and care and provides the appropriate level of sincerity to the message. Tones such as anger, frustration, disappointment, and the ever-popular sarcasm tend to color the language of the message and turn attempts at negative feedback into criticism. The content of the message gets lost in the noise and harshness.

The purpose of negative feedback is to create awareness that can lead to correction or improvement in performance. If you can't give negative feedback in a helpful manner, in the language and tone of concern, you defeat its purpose.

✔ **Give the feedback person-to-person, not through messengers of technology.** The nature of constructive feedback is verbal and informal. That can be done only by talking live to the employee, either face-to-face — or by phone when you physically can't be together. E-mail and voice mail don't work for constructive feedback (see Chapter 4), because they don't allow live, two-way conversation to follow. Nor does the sincerity of the message come across as well, whether it's positive or negative feedback. Talk one-on-one with people when giving feedback — most of them don't bite.

✔ **State observations, not interpretations.** Observations are what you see occur; interpretations are your analysis or opinion of what you see occur. Tell what you've noticed, not what you think of it, and report the behavior you notice at a concrete level, instead of as a characterization of the behavior. Observations have a far more factual and nonjudgmental aspect than do interpretations.

To see what I mean, compare these interactions: "You have been moody and uncooperative today" (interpretation and criticism). "Today I noticed that you often had your head down on your desk, and you either didn't answer the phone to take customer calls until reminded to do so or you answered on the fourth ring, which has me concerned" (observation).

The same reasoning applies to positive feedback. Instead of saying to an employee, "You were wonderful with that customer today," (interpretation and praise), report the observations of the behavior you saw, "I noticed you answered the customer's questions accurately and in lay terms. In fact, the customer remarked how helpful you were in explaining how our products work. Well done."

Timing

Timing answers this question: When do you give an employee feedback for a performance effort worth acknowledging?

The answer is ASAP (as soon as possible). Feedback is meant to be given in real-time, as close as possible to when the performance incident occurs so that the events are fresh in everyone's minds. When feedback is given well after the fact, the value of the constructive feedback is lessened.

When giving negative feedback, you may want to apply the a different time-line: ASAR (as soon as reasonable/ready — that is, when *you're* ready). Sometimes when an incident happens, you aren't feeling too good about it, and you need time to cool off and get your thoughts in order before you give negative feedback (so that your manner displays a tone of concern). Doing that may mean giving the feedback tomorrow rather than right now, but tomorrow is still timely, and your feedback will come across as far more constructive.

Frequency

Frequency answers the question, "How often should your employees receive constructive feedback on their performance?"

This last guideline is the most important one of all. It is the one that makes all the other guidelines work. So how often should constructive feedback be given? The answer is, on an ongoing basis that reflects each employee's actual performance.

Constructive feedback shouldn't be contrived. You use it to acknowledge real performance, and you do so as a regular practice. But be careful not to take the positive for granted. As you look at the performance of your employees, how many produce more efforts and outcomes that warrant negative feedback than positive? Like most managers, more than likely you see more outcomes of positive performance occurring. Yet, often, employees hear about performance only when something goes wrong. If the positive performance is taken for granted, constructive feedback doesn't work because it isn't reflecting most people's actual performance. So regularly giving positive feedback is the secret for coaching success with constructive feedback.

I can't give you a set ratio of positive to negative feedback, nor can I give you a set frequency for giving feedback. These things vary by individual and by what is happening in that person's performance. Generally speaking, the newer the employee, the more frequent the feedback. Overall, the idea here is quite simple: Try to catch and respond to employees doing the job *right* just as much as you catch and respond to them doing something that isn't quite right — and don't acknowledge how they are performing only once or twice a year.

Significant-events list

A significant-events list (shown Figure 5-1) serves as a tool for recording the constructive feedback you give to your employees. It helps you track what's happening in people's performance rather than relying on your memory. And relying on your memory is the most unreliable practice you can have.

The significant-events list consists of your notes on the performance feedback that you give. Remember to do the following when filling out the significant-events list:

✔ **When you record the feedback you give, write summary notes.** Two to three lines per incident of performance should do in most cases. Recording feedback should be quick and easy.

✔ **Everything that you record on the list has been verbally stated to the employee.** Don't write notes about employee performance that you haven't already communicated to that person — only write what you say. You have no hidden agendas or surprises for employees. (Although those could be contained in a future book, *How to Demotivate Employee Performance.*)

A significant-events list yields some substantial benefits. When you go to write a performance review, typically asked for on an annual basis, your task is an easy one. You merely summarize the feedback you've been giving to the employee all year long. Also, maintaining this tool helps you see trends in employee performance and then set strategies as needed for further coaching efforts. Most importantly (drum roll please), the significant-events list helps you manage the toughest person you have in your group — yourself. With this tool, you can see whether you're giving constructive feedback that reflects each employee's actual performance. This information keeps you honest and helps you avoid the mistake of taking the positive for granted.

The Discussion after Giving Feedback

Constructive feedback (either positive or negative) is a direct report to an employee about how he or she performed a specific task or other incident related to performance. While the feedback starts out as a one-way conversation — so that you can clearly identify what occurred — the feedback needs to promote a dialogue from that point on.

Significant-Events List

Employee: _____

Date	Event

Figure 5-1:
Significant-
events list.

Often, when giving positive feedback, little discussion is needed; you may even end up talking about other matters with an employee. However, the rule of big toe (or rule of thumb for you non-soccer fans) when giving negative feedback is that discussion between you and an employee after the feedback is a must. A discussion allows the employee to digest what was heard and then work with you on how to make the situation better as you both go forward.

After you break the mindset that negative feedback is an uncomfortable thing to do — or that it's just about telling bad news — you'll probably find that it gives you a great coaching opportunity to promote learning and enhance your employees' performance.

In fact, answer this question: If you didn't do something well in your performance, would you want to be told about it? Few people would answer "no" to this question for a simple reason: Most people want to be informed about how they're doing — they just don't want to be hit over the head with the news. Be constructive, not harsh, and then let the discussion begin.

Keeping a positive outcome in mind

When you give negative feedback, enter the discussion phase with a positive outcome in mind, and state it clearly to the employee. Doing so influences the dynamic of the conversation and gives it a positive direction. For example, after giving feedback, you may say," I want to explore with you what you can do to stay on schedule and make your total efforts with the project a success." This is a positive outcome, with a focus on solutions, and it invites the employee to participate in a two-way conversation. This is much better than what many managers may say or imply — such as, "I want to know why you can't meet our milestones, and you better not let this project have any more delays. Stay on top of your assignments and spend less time talking with your team members." That's not a good tactic: pushing blame and giving orders. This interaction isn't much of an invitation to a productive post-feedback discussion with the employee.

After stating your intended positive outcome in a post-feedback discussion, do more asking than telling and more listening than speaking.

1. **Initiate employee involvement with a question.**

   For example, ask " What are some factors affecting your ability to meet the milestones?"

2. **Listen to get an understanding from the employee's perspective as to what has been happening.**

3. **Move the discussion toward the positive outcome you are seeking.**

   For example, ask "What ideas can you offer to ensure that you stay on schedule for the remainder of the project?" Let the employee help shape the efforts to produce the positive outcome: Often, this means creating a solution.

   Offer your input as needed, but conduct the discussion as an exchange of ideas, not as a dictation of your ideas to the employee.

Two-way discussions, as described here, push employees to think and take responsibility. (Scary thoughts, eh?) And as you know, when people help create their own solutions, they are more committed to making them happen. Building self-sufficiency and commitment is what coaching is all about.

After the positive outcome is worked out, bring the conversation to a close. If the matter is important for monitoring progress, set a follow-up date with the employee to do just that.

Dealing with defensive reactions

A handful of employees are sensitive and react defensively whenever you attempt to give them negative feedback. Certainly, defensive people make discussions difficult.

Here are some ways that you can prevent defensiveness, minimize its effect on your meeting, and help you work through a defensive situation, should it arise.

- ✔ **Give negative feedback, not criticism.** Make sure that you follow the guidelines for giving constructive feedback; namely that you are issue-focused, specific, direct, and that you base your feedback on observations. If you fall into the giving-criticism trap, you are often inviting defensiveness, regardless of your intentions. Critical comments with a personal focus based on characterizations, not substance, usually come across as extremely judgmental. If you come across as judgmental with a sensitive employee, let the fireworks begin.

- ✔ **Give sincere and straightforward negative feedback.** Time for a little physics. For every action, there is a reaction. (Lesson over — that's the extent of my physics knowledge.) In interactions between two people, while you don't control another person, you can influence how that individual receives your message by the way you deliver it.

  - • Deliver the message with anger or harshness in your tone, and you are likely to get anger and harshness in return.

  - • Deliver the message in a hesitant and apprehensive manner, and you're likely to face someone becoming quite anxious, wondering what is so terrible that you can't tell it straight.

When giving negative feedback, communicate the appropriate sense of concern in both your language and your tone so that your message comes across with care and importance. You are out to help, not hurt, with your feedback.

✔ **Give employees feedback on how they receive feedback.** If you give performance feedback constructively, you have the opportunity to coach your employees on how to receive feedback constructively. Let them know that you are going to give feedback as a regular practice and set the expectation that you want them to receive it well and learn from it. Make sure that you, too, are open to the feedback that you get from them.

As you give constructive feedback, positively reinforce when your employees receive it well. Give negative feedback when they don't receive it well. Remember, state your observations, not your interpretations.

- **An interpretation:** "You react defensively when I attempt to give you feedback on your performance."

- **An observation:** "Sometimes when I attempt to give you feedback about mistakes or areas for improvement in your performance, I notice that your voice gets louder. I'm interrupted before I can finish my message, your face often becomes flushed, and you frown. These behaviors make it difficult for me to give the feedback that I need to give."

Often, it's a good idea not to give feedback on how employees receive feedback in the heat of the moment, but later, as an issue by itself. Then, if the employee reacts defensively and demonstrates the very behavior you're describing, you can report it right on the spot. "Hold on. That's the behavior I am talking about, and that's what I'd like you to change." It is kind of like being caught on *Candid Camera*. People can better understand the behavior you want improved upon when you capture them doing the actions live and, in essence, can show it to them.

✔ **Aim for positive outcomes.** When giving negative feedback, discussion between you and an employee is a must. Give the feedback at the start of the conversation, and then allow a two-way discussion to automatically follow. No hit and run such as, "Here's what you are not doing well, specific-specific, blah, blah. Now go on and get out of here." If your style is to state the feedback and attempt to end the conversation at that point, regardless of how specific you are, your abruptness can be like a kick in the teeth (or other body parts, if you like) and invites a defensive person to become quite reactive. Force a message down a employees throat and he or she won't swallow without a fight.

When you finish giving the negative feedback, state the positive outcome you're seeking and initiate a discussion with a question that invites the employee's participation. Listen patiently and responsively; if you debate, you get defensiveness in return. Stay focused on the positive outcome you're seeking. The whole dynamic of the interaction changes as a result. When you dwell on problems, you get blame going both ways. When you dwell on solutions, you get collaboration and often creativity. (This tip is even safe to try at home.)

✔ **Announce the behavior you want to see.** This serves to set an expectation and prepare the employee for the behavior you want exhibited. You state the behavior you want to see before giving the constructive feedback, as a kind of introduction to the conversation. Make sure that you state in positive terms what you want to see rather than the behavior that you don't want to see. Instead of saying to the employee, "When I give you this feedback, I don't want you to react defensively" (guess how the employee will react to that?), you can say in positive terms, "I want to give you feedback about an issue, and I want you to listen patiently and openly the whole time, and then work with me to come to a positive solution."

A manager recently told me that she followed this tip with one of her employees who often became defensive when receiving negative feedback. Although the employed squeezed the arms of his chair very tightly, he stayed in control during the whole conversation. He heard the feedback all the way through and engaged in discussion to help figure out a solution to correct the problem at hand.

Stating this behavior expectation up front allows you to refocus the employee, should defensive behavior rear its ugly head. For example, as the employee starts to get defensive, "Hold on, remember, please stay patient and open the whole time in this conversation."

✔ **Give ongoing constructive feedback that reflects actual performance.** This tip is the biggest and best one for minimizing, if not preventing, employee defensiveness when hearing negative feedback: Acknowledge all aspects of an employee's performance, not just the problems or mistakes. If you give feedback to your employees only when something goes wrong, you encourage their quick-to-react-and-get-defensive behaviors.

Try to achieve balance in your efforts of giving constructive feedback, and do so on a regular basis so that your employees are used to hearing from you about how they are performing — what they have done well and what they need to do better. They know where they stand and that their positive efforts are not taken for granted. So when you say, "Hey Jane, please come in my office for a few minutes," you don't get a "what-did-I-do-this-time?" reaction.

Impacting the Pillars of Commitment with a Regular Dose of Feedback

Coaching can have a great influence on stimulating employee commitment. The five pillars that are the foundation for building commitment (see Chapter 2 for further details) are impacted by the coaching tool of constructive feedback. In this section, I take a look at how regular constructive feedback — both positive and negative — affects these pillars.

✔ **Development:** As employees grow in their knowledge and skill, the appropriate level of positive and negative feedback helps reinforce their development and build the confidence that goes along with the growing competence. Kind of like sunshine and water for a growing plant.

✔ **Gratitude:** Positive feedback is one of the most cost-effective ways to recognize employees and let them know that you care about their good performances.

✔ **Accountability:** Both forms of constructive feedback drive the pillar of accountability. They reinforce that high standards are expected and that what is done in performance is cared about and noticed.

✔ **Focus:** The pillar of focus is also affected by ongoing constructive feedback. Positive feedback reinforces that employees are going in the right direction in their performance — attention is put on the right priorities and things that are being done well. Negative feedback helps the employee who is getting off track to refocus and head in the right direction, especially through the discussion that follows the feedback.

✔ **Involvement:** This pillar of commitment is affected less directly when the feedback is initially given. But when two-way discussions take place after the feedback, employees have a good deal of say-so about how they will perform as they move forward.

Often these five pillars of commitment come together simultaneously when constructive feedback is given. This one coaching skill — constructive feedback — which is far better than just praise or criticism, helps to ensure beneficial results in performance and influences employee commitment. So let the constructive feedback start flying!

Chapter 6

Setting Performance Plans the SMART Way

In This Chapter
▶ Defining the key elements of results-focused performance plans
▶ Discovering how to set measurable and results-oriented goals and standards
▶ Identifying important issues for goals that capture total performance
▶ Coaching collaboratively with employees to develop performance plans
▶ Examining how performance plans help stimulate employee commitment

Managing by plan is one of the fundamentals for effective coaching; it is actually the million dollar secret that drives results. (I think the figure used to be $64,000 — taken from the $64,000 question in the old TV game show — but this secret is greater in value and takes inflation into account.) Simply, a *plan* sets a course of action. It provides direction and, most importantly, focus — one of the five pillars for building commitment (covered extensively in Chapter 2 and reviewed at the end of this chapter).

Development plans, improvement plans, project plans, motivation plans, and delegating plans are some of the fundamental tools for coaching success — and they're all subsets of *performance plans,* which provide guidance and direction for an employee's overall performance. Sometimes called *work plans,* they spell out what you're paying the employee to accomplish. When well defined, they tell employees, "Here is what you have to contribute to earn your keep." When done right, the employee has helped shape the performance plan and can thus take ownership of it.

Managing without plans, as is commonly done by managers using the doer approach (see Chapter 1 for more on doer managers), keeps employees busy but not necessarily productive. People have no trouble filling an eight-hour workday with various activities. Who isn't busy? With performance plans, however, a shift takes place. How busy you are carries much less importance than what you are accomplishing in your performance. A shift from focusing on activities to focusing on results is a great benefit for you and your employees.

Mixing the Key Ingredients in Performance Plans

To work with your employees in setting their performance plans, you need to know what goes in the plans. This section outlines the key ingredients in putting together results-focused performance plans.

The worksheet shown in Figure 6-1 gives you a guide for coaching your employees in the development of their performance plans. The ingredients for cooking the plans are a dose of goals or standards (similar spices), a few cups of action plans, and a strong pinch of measurement. The following bullets define each ingredient:

✔ **Goal:** Sometimes referred to as an *objective*, a goal is a performance effort that you want to accomplish or a target that you want to reach. A goal answers these questions: What result are you seeking that will help your business or organization? What important undertaking do you want to accomplish?

✔ **Standard:** A standard is similar to a goal in that it, too, focuses on achieving results. It is a behavior expectation, a level of performance to achieve, or positive results to maintain. Standards are often defined in performance areas such as quality, management effectiveness, teamwork, and service.

Goals and standards are meant to be challenging yet attainable; something the employee can accomplish but has to work to accomplish. If the bar (not the drinking establishment — the results expected) is too low, you aren't getting the progress and results you need from your group. If the bar is too high or you're asking employees to take on goals that they don't have real control over, you're inviting frustration — and for many employees, a good dose of demotivation. Thus, you can see the advantages of a collaborative goal-setting process.

✔ **Action plans:** These focus on how the goals and standards are to be achieved. Action plans are the milestones, key steps, or main efforts your employees will take to accomplish the goal or standard. Generally, three to six action plans are enough for each goal or standard.

✔ **Measurement:** The last ingredient that goes into the pot . . . or rather, the plan. This element defines your means for measuring the results being sought. Measurement spells out the tangible ways or sources of evidence, both quantitative and qualitative, by which the goals and standards are to be evaluated.

Performance Planning Worksheet

Covers period from _____ to _____

Goal/standard: _____
_____
_____

Action plans: _____
_____
_____
_____
_____

Measurement: _____

Goal/standard: _____
_____

Action plans: _____
_____
_____
_____

Measurement: _____
_____

Figure 6-1:
Use this
worksheet
to set per-
formance
plans.

While goals and standards are the key ingredient in the performance plan, without action plans, the goals are less likely to occur. The action plans provide a roadmap; they are the how-to's for achieving your goals. Without this roadmap, you have no direction. It would be like saying, "I know what I want to accomplish, but I don't know how to go about making that happen." (Good luck on your lost journey.) Defining your means of measurement upfront makes it easy for you to clearly evaluate your progress: You know the results (and evidence of them) that you're looking for in the evaluation. With performance plans, you never have to rely on a gut feeling to determine whether your goal is met.

Writing SMART Performance Plans

You can drive employee performance on the path of promising results when you find out how to develop goals and standards the SMART way: SMART is the acronym that provides guidelines on how to write goals and standards.

Here are the SMART guidelines:

- ✔ **S = Specific and clear:** In most cases, a goal or standard should be written in one sentence. The message needs to be clear and specific — to anyone who reads it, not just to you and your employees. The language shouldn't be vague or confusing.

- ✔ **M = Measurable:** When a statement of the goal or standard is read, the reader can tell that the results sought can be measured. Goals don't just have to be quantifiable to be measured; some goals or standards can be measured through qualitative means (see the "Measuring them thar goals and standards" sidebar for more information on this topic).

- ✔ **A = Action-oriented:** Action verbs lead and drive the goal or standard statement. Here are some examples with the right pizzazz for goals: develop, achieve, implement, create, produce, and maintain. While "learn" is an action verb, it doesn't usually work for goals and standards because it doesn't produce results. To learn skills or knowledge may often be part of an action plan that helps you reach a goal, but learning doesn't in itself achieve an end result. (See the following bullet for more explanation of focusing on results.)

- ✔ **R = Results-focused:** This answers the so-what factor — what are you hoping to gain, what is the reason you want to do this, what are you looking to accomplish? After you and your employees comprehend the results focus, the aha kicks in (Aha! Now I get it). And writing goals and standards becomes easy to do.

Quite often, when people attempt to develop their goals, they tend to be activity- or task-focused, rather than results-focused. For example, an employee in manufacturing writes this statement as his goal: "Develop and implement a quality process to help manufacturing." But his statement refers to an activity, not a goal. He doesn't state what result is being sought. Here, on the other hand, is a results-focused goal: "Develop and implement a quality improvement process that reduces the defects in the manufacturing process from the current 25 percent level to a 10 percent level within 12 months, by the end of the year 2001."

As another example, here is a task-focused standard for a receptionist's job. "Answer every call by the third ring." In this example, no result is defined (other than good wrist action). This one is a task (which is limited in scope and short in duration), not a goal or standard. Conversely, here is a standard: "In your telephone interactions, maintain on a consistent basis a level of service that internal and external customers report as helpful, responsive, and courteous — starting January 1, 2000, and ongoing." Of course, answering the phone by the third ring may indeed be one of the action plans for achieving this standard.

✔ **T = Time frame:** T indicates when the goal or standard needs to be accomplished — a target date. Target dates are the best guesses for completion, but they give a time frame to aim for, which is much better than the common, "I'll get it done sometime next year." The time frame can also be ongoing, which is often the case with standards because the level of performance needed to produce results must be maintained on an ongoing basis.

Measuring them thar goals and standards

Paul Simon, the famous musician and entertainer, recorded a song about 50 ways to leave your lover. It was quite a catchy tune. However, when measuring goals and standards, fewer ways of getting the job done are needed. In fact, seven will do the trick, Rick. So hop on the bus, Gus. You don't need to be coy, Roy. Just listen to me . . . about how to measure goals and standards: The following methods of measurement can help.

✔ **Quantifiable means:** *Quantifiable* means measurement by numbers: sales figures reached, widgets or other item amounts produced, costs reduced, and time saved are some of the common targets for goals. These numbers are usually key indicators that businesses as a whole count and track, so goals in these areas are often easy to measure. And thanks to computers, the statistical reports showing the results are often at your fingertips.

✔ **Feedback and survey:** Constructive feedback on performance is another measure of how someone is performing. This feedback, to measure a performance goal or standard, can come from you and from other sources, such as internal and external customers. A survey is a more formal means for gathering customer feedback and a great way to measure customer satisfaction with the service you are working to deliver.

(continued)

(continued)

✔ **Audit, test, inspection:** In the areas of finance and accounting, an audit is a common strategy used to measure how you are doing with your task or goal. You can apply a test many ways. For example, tests are used in the high-tech world to find out whether a product does what it was designed to do. The military uses inspections to measure results, but in business terms, an inspection can be an arranged progress check or an audit in areas such as safety, quality, or service. Some companies use a *tester* — a person (whom the employee doesn't know) who appears as a "customer." The tester "experiences" the service and then reports what happened.

✔ **Documentation:** Reports, plans, correspondence, notes, and other documents are often records of results that occurred. Thus, they are useful as a means for measuring the results of goals and standards.

✔ **Timelines:** Did the rocket launch when it was supposed to launch? Did the product get shipped to market when it was supposed to be shipped? Evaluating whether a goal was met on time can be one of the most important results to measure — and it's often quite easy to measure.

✔ **Work products or samples:** This means of measuring goals and standards is especially useful if you are from Missouri, the "show me" state. For example, you ask an employee to show the tangibles of his or her work toward meeting a goal, and he or she shows you. ("Is the widget fully assembled and operational? Let me see it." "Is the telecommuting policy developed? Let me see it.")

✔ **Observation, when combined with feedback or documentation:** Watching a salesperson sell to a customer and watching a service attendant interact with a customer are but a couple of examples in which observation helps you measure whether the performance results you're seeking are happening. Then just share what you observe. In the clinical and scientific worlds, observations are often critical for evaluating the results of an experiment. What did the rat do when the cheese got moldy?

You can measure most goals and standards by more than one of these means. For each goal and standard, you want to define in specific terms how the results will be measured by all the means applicable. By doing this with the employee when the performance plans are set, monitoring progress and evaluating the results are easy. The employee can track his or her own results, and you know the sources (evidence) to look at in order to see whether the goals are attaining the desired results. This approach is a simple and objective one, not a contest of opinions.

Sampling some SMART performance plans

Here are a few performance plans that give you examples of goals and standards, along with their appropriate action plans and measurements. To set a context, imagine that these performance plans take place over a six-month period, starting at the beginning of a given calendar year. Also keep in mind that they are set *with* your staff members, not *for* them.

Sample #1

✔ **Goal:** Create and implement process improvements that reduce the current cycle time for month-end-closing activities with the general ledger from four days to three (25 percent) by July 1, 2001.

✔ **Action plans:**

1. By March 15, 2001, document current processes for handling month-end-closing activities and the average time for each process.

2. By April 30, 2001, gather input from other staff in the department and draft a plan for a streamlined process.

3. After reviewing the streamlined plan with management, perform a test run of the process improvements for May's month-end closing.

4. Evaluate the test results and make necessary modifications to handle June's month-end closing.

✔ **Measurements:**

- Primarily, the cycle time for month-end close, starting June, 2001

- Secondarily, the documented process improvement plan

Sample #2

✔ **Goal:** By July 1, 2001, develop a marketing kit that provides the field sales force with tools that they find useful in increasing their effectiveness in selling our company's product.

✔ **Action plans:**

1. By Feb. 15, 2001, survey the sales force to assess their needs for marketing literature, product samples, and other items that will help their sales efforts.

2. Working with marketing communication vendors and engineering, by April 1, 2001, draft literature and create product samples and other necessary items for a prototype marketing kit.

3. By May 1, 2001, conduct focus groups of internal managers and field sales representatives and select customers to test the value and usefulness of the marketing kit.

4. By June 1, 2001, complete necessary modifications of marketing kit based on feedback gathered from the focus groups.

5. Conduct training sessions with the sales force to familiarize them with how to use the marketing kit in their presentations to customers, completed by July 1, 2001.

✔ **Measurements:**

- Timelines — is the kit ready to use and has the sales force been trained on its use by the target date of the goal?

- Feedback gathered on the usefulness of the marketing kit in their sales efforts from the sales force. Take this measure on a monthly basis for the first quarter after implementation.

- Similar kind of feedback gathered from a select group of customers after the kit is in use.

Sample #3

✔ **Standard:** On a consistent basis, demonstrate cooperation, assistance, and support of your XYZ team members that shows reliable contributions and helps the team meet its four output goals for the first half of 2001.

✔ **Action plans:**

- On all assignments, complete your parts within the set deadlines without rework being needed.

- Pitch in and offer assistance to others on the team and respond in a timely way to their requests, as well.

- Maintain a positive, helpful, and respectful manner in interactions with team members.

- Address concerns that may arise directly with the source and constructively work out solutions in the process.

✔ **Measurements:**

- The assignments you do — their quality and timeliness — and how they contribute to the team's ability to meet its four output goals

- The observations and feedback made by your manager on your work and on the teamwork behaviors outlined in the action plans

- The feedback informally received and formally gathered from team members on your work and on the teamwork behaviors outlined in the action plans

Sample #4

✔ **Standard:** Consistently produce bug-free code on your final product deliverables for each project you work on by the project deadlines for the first half of 2001.

✔ **Action plans:**

- Set realistic deadlines for code delivery, factoring in time to do testing; follow through and adhere to schedules.

- Develop and run tests for the code you write before passing on the deliverables as complete.

- Work with appropriate team members and your manager to resolve difficult bug problems that may arise.

✔ **Measurements:**

- Delivery deadlines being met.

- Number of errors or bugs in final deliverables on each project.

- Consistency of code running with applicable hardware. Does the software application do what it is supposed to do?

Encompassing total performance

SMART performance plans are meant to encompass the person's total performance. How employees spend their time — the tasks and activities they are doing — is tied to the results or outcomes they need to produce. You don't want your employees spending time in areas that don't produce the results needed. If they're spending time in something that you think is important, make sure a goal or standard is set to capture that area of performance.

Therefore, goals aren't something extra in an employee's performance. They are the focus of the employee's performance. Everything each individual works on and all the key job-related behaviors needed are aimed at producing meaningful results. They are part of the total performance plan.

When you manage by plan in this way, you help your employees make the shift from an activity focus to a results focus. They can see their jobs on the broad-perspective level; that is, how what they are seeking to accomplish helps the business be successful. (It's as though you are saying, "Sorry, you are no longer being paid to shuffle paper and mindlessly fill out forms. Now you have to accomplish goals that serve customers well and run processes efficiently." Oh no! Kind of like pouring water on the wicked witch in *The Wizard of Oz*.)

You join in this shift when you manage as a coach with performance plans because *how* your employees spend their time becomes much less important than the *results* they are producing; *how* they do their jobs becomes less important than the *outcomes* they are achieving. For example, with a sales rep, when you make the shift, your focus swings from things like whether the employee is spending time with personal phone calls to whether the desired number of customer orders are being brought in. (What about the old rules to enforce? Oh no! They are dying. More water on the wicked witch.)

To encompass an employee's total performance when setting performance plans, set goals and standards with them in areas such as the following:

✔ Output targets

✔ Quality indicators

✔ Service expectations for customer satisfaction

✔ Major projects

✔ Important solutions or changes needed

✔ Key duties to maintain for results

✔ Areas for performance improvement

✔ Key job-related behaviors for reinforcement and for maintaining results

✔ Attendance targets

✔ Professional development

When you define the important issues that the employee needs to work on to produce meaningful results, you have a SMART goal or standard set that incorporates each issue. Thus, the person's overall performance plan encompasses his or her full job. No set number exists as to how many goals or standards an employee should have. Generally speaking, most employee performance plans consist of five to eight goals or standards — not more than ten. Beyond double figures, you either have more than the person can chew or you have set a task list and are not focusing on important results.

To gain practice in tying goals and standards to measurable results, start with your own job as a manager. What are the important areas you need to tackle to produce meaningful results? Set a goal or standard around each one. Make sure you set a standard targeting management effectiveness — a key part of every manager's performance plan.

Mutually Setting Performance Plans

Throughout this chapter, you may notice that when terms such as "performance plans" or "goals" are mentioned in a sentence with the word "employees," the word "with" is often used to connect them. Getting the most success out of SMART performance plans means that you set plans *with* your employees, as opposed to *for* them. It's a mutual process — something that you do together.

Goals and plans are funny things. If you give them to your employees, "Here are your goals to get done," employees may nod and smile at you, but then they walk away holding your goals, not theirs. If something goes wrong, they can blame the manager who gave them unrealistic goals. Conversely, when

employees are part of the process to shape the goals and standards that they need to accomplish, they tend to see them as their own. The difference is compliance versus commitment (see Chapter 2 for more on building commitment). Therefore, you want the process to be mutual and collaborative.

Your role as a manager in this two-way process is to provide the employees with direction. Tell them where the business and the group are going, what the high-level targets or objectives are, and what key issues to tackle. The role of the employees is to set challenging yet attainable goals and standards that align with this direction and to outline the key steps or roadmaps (the action plans) on how to achieve the goals or standards.

You certainly contribute input and ideas to this discussion, not as to the way things are to be done but as part of a two-way, give-and-take dialogue to help shape the performance plans, which the employees will own and for which they will be accountable. Letting employees step up and take responsibility are a key to coaching success and building commitment.

Because many employees initially may not be familiar with how to set results-based performance plans, here is a good process to follow to mutually set plans:

1. **Prepare your employees for the meeting to set their performance plans.**

   Provide direction on the priorities and targets for the coming period. To help your staff understand this direction, give them a copy of your own performance plans. Doing this also helps them understand the key ingredients that go into a performance plan.

   Ask them to come ready with a list of ideas for their own goals and standards that align with this direction. Here are a few questions that stimulate thinking:

   a. What should you accomplish to help the group achieve what it needs to accomplish?

   b. What changes or improvements need to be made to help us work more efficiently?

   c. What key behaviors or responsibilities need to be reinforced or maintained to achieve high levels of performance?

   d. In what areas of performance do you want to seek development?

2. **Facilitate the planning meeting.**

   At the one-on-one planning meeting, incorporating the employee's ideas, draft each performance plan one at a time. Maintain a two-way conversation and have the employee do the writing as together you shape the plans. Go in this order for each plan:

a. Write the goal/standard statement following the SMART guidelines (see the "Writing SMART Performance Plans" section earlier in this chapter).

b. Outline the action plans.

c. Define the ways progress will be measured. What are the sources of evidence that will track progress?

In particular, have the employee take the lead in developing the action plans portion. He or she is the one who needs to meet the goals and standards and the one who often knows best how to get the job done. Telling people how to do their jobs invites compliance, not commitment.

If differences in points of view come up while setting the goals or standards, discuss them thoroughly and hear each other out. If you have concerns about what an employee wants to do, express them constructively and have the employee address them — and visa versa if the employee has concerns about your ideas. Then collaboratively propose ideas that settle the differences.

Remember the high-level needs or priorities that need to be met? Use them as the focus for the solutions you work out. Hold firm if an employee wants to have a goal contrary to the direction needed. On the other hand, if an employee is ambitious and aligned with the direction, more often than not, you can let the person run with it and learn from experience. The individual may surprise you and accomplish the target precisely because she was the one who set it. Regarding action plans, unless the employee is proposing a method to blow up the place, you usually defer to the individual's judgment because she or he is the one who does the job.

3. **Finalize the plans.**

Have the employee recap what has been written and agreed upon and then type up the plans and provide you with a copy. Have the employee keep his or her performance plans visible while going forward.

After your staff members have a good handle on how to write results-based performance plans, you can use the planning meeting to review and finalize their drafts instead of creating the draft together. Initially, they may need close guidance, but giving that kind of early guidance saves time in the long run. (If you ask your staff to draft plans when they have no idea how to write a plan, they are lost, and you spend a lot of time sending drafts back and forth.)

Keep performance plans current and within a reasonable time period. Performance plans should receive a final evaluation within one year and then be reset. Because of today's fast-paced and ever-changing business environments, six-month plans are even more reasonable. Resetting every half-year can work quite well as long as dialogue is maintained along the way to incorporate change. (You find more on how to do that in Chapter 7.) Staying current, flexible, and results-focused with your employees — now there's a smart manager.

Helping Build the Pillars of Commitment with a Good Dose of SMART Performance Plans

Take a look at how setting performance plans, when done as a regular coaching practice — collaboratively and SMARTly — affect the pillars of commitment (see Chapter 2 for more on the pillars of commitment). Which ones are impacted and how so?

✔ **Focus:** Performance plans greatly influence focus, helping employees determine what their priorities are and what needs to be accomplished.

Be sure that your goals and standards follow the SMART guidelines, keeping them results-focused (see the "Writing SMART Performance Plans" section earlier in this chapter).

✔ **Involvement:** The mutual effort of setting performance plans impacts the employees' involvement. Because the plans are set with the employees, they have direct input in shaping their own goals and standards. In setting the action plans, employees take the lead in defining the steps to take to accomplish the goals and standards — which achieves a high degree of involvement.

The key to using the process of setting performance plans as an effective coaching tool is to set them collaboratively.

✔ **Accountability:** Keeping the performance plans visible and as part of conversations between you and your employees helps drive accountability. Employees are able to measure their own progress and also gain their own sense of accomplishment when they achieve their goals. And they certainly know what results you expect from them.

✔ **Development:** When performance plans also address areas for professional development or have employees working on areas where they expand their knowledge and skill, employee development is enhanced. Employees are learning and growing as they produce important results.

✔ **Gratitude:** This pillar is influenced less directly than the other four. Nonetheless, performance plans give you the criteria you need in order to give feedback and recognize accomplishments. For many individuals, achieving their goals provides personal satisfaction and a sense of gratitude for a job done well.

Chapter 7

Taking the Blues Out of Reviews

. . . .

In This Chapter

▶ Using performance reviews as a key to success

▶ Utilizing status reviews for managing projects and big assignments.

▶ Conducting mini performance reviews

▶ Applying the postmortem tool

▶ Influencing employee commitment with periodic review tools

. . . .

*T*he practice of doing a formal performance review is common in many organizations, both in private and public sectors. In terms of frequency, managers generally write reviews on an annual basis. Occasionally, some organizations carry out performance evaluations every six months.

The review is certainly the time when, for the record, employees are told how they are doing in their performance. But a lot happens during the 12 months between reviews. How do managers who function as coaches monitor progress and let employees know how they are performing *between* reviews?

Many managers, especially the doer types (see Chapter 1 for more on doer managers), use one of two methods.

✔ The manager knows every detail and frequently checks on what the employees are doing, sometimes to the point that the staff feels smothered. When this approach happens — a *watchdog mode* — employees use the "m" word to describe it: *micromanagement.*

✔ The manager goes the other direction and practices a *laissez-faire* or hands-off approach — assigning work and hoping everything turns out okay. The manager is too busy with his or her own work to pay much attention to how his or her employees are doing until something goes wrong, as in really wrong. Then the manager goes into watchdog mode and ends up smothering the problem employee.

In either case, employees are often not getting direct feedback as to how they are performing. And when completing the annual performance evaluations, you, the manager, go into panic mode trying to write the darn thing without throwing too many surprises at the employees — a time of high anxiety for you.

This chapter tells you how to put an end to that anxiety and how to use three coaching tools — the status review, the checkup, and the postmortem review — to improve your performance review process.

Ending the Anxiety of Reviews

Managers who operate as coaches adhere to the principle that performance reviews are part of an ongoing process of performance management. Coaching managers don't wait for once-a-year reviews to finally tell employees how they're performing (too much is continually happening to talk about it just once a year) or to tell them that something has gone wrong.

Instead, coaching managers give ongoing positive and negative feedback (see Chapter 5) on staff members' performance as events occur. They also use periodic performance reviews — an ongoing process that promotes success and maintains their sanity!

Processing the process of reviews

Using the coaching approach, managers see performance review as a process that falls into three stages in an annual cycle (or sometimes in a six-month cycle).

- ✔ **Stage 1 — planning:** In this stage, manager and employee, in a collaborative effort, set the performance plans that focus the employee on the important results to be accomplished. *Performance plans* are a recipe containing three key ingredients: goals and standards, action plans, and measurements. (See Chapter 6 for the details of the recipe.)

- ✔ **Stage 2 — feedback, periodic review, and documentation:** The second stage involves ongoing two-way coaching discussions about performance with positive and negative feedback given informally along the way. You also hold periodic performance-review meetings — organized, yet informal in nature — to assess progress with projects, key assignments, and overall performance plans, and to do necessary replanning in order to stay current with changing priorities. As the manager, you record the feedback you've given and the important review meetings held so that you don't have to rely on your memory for this information. As an old saying goes, the shortest pencil will outlast the longest memory.

✔ **Stage 3 — wrap-up:** In this stage, you bring the year-long discussions and feedback about performance to a close, and you write the performance review and discuss it with the employee. The performance review serves as a summary of these discussions. The review tells you how well the employee delivered the results expected as set in the performance plans in Stage 1.

The meeting to go over the performance review not only discusses how performance turned out for the past period but also looks to the future as ideas for new goals and professional development are discussed, leading the way for the next period's performance plans to be set (and finalized shortly after). Thus, the cycle gets restarted and on you go. This meeting is also an opportunity to evaluate how your coaching efforts and working relationship with the employee went during the performance review process — with the chance to then make adjustments going forward.

Knowing why anxiety attacks occur

When managers treat performance reviews as an ongoing part of coaching and performance management, Stage 3 of the process (see the stages in preceding section) is no big deal. Because of the efforts to set performance criteria upfront and to informally assess progress along the way with the employee (in Stages 1 and 2), writing the annual or semiannual review is a piece of cake: You know what has happened in regard to your employees' performance, and they know you know. Most important, they know where they stand. No surprises come at review time, and honest evaluations occur as well.

As a result of these efforts, your employees can read their appraisals and say, "That's pretty much what I expected." Comments like this are recognition to you that you've done your job as a manager quite well. Of course, such a compliment is part of the good results that happen when you make Stages 1 and 2 part of the review process.

Waiting until the end of the year to finally focus on employee performance and write the review can be an onerous task. And for many people, the more onerous the job, the more they procrastinate. When you put off doing your reviews in a timely way, you risk sending your employees the wrong message — that their performance isn't important to you. (Oops! That's one sure way to demotivate employee performance.)

In addition, the following can happen.

✔ A lack of effort in Stages 1 and 2 can leave managers not knowing what to write about negative performance, and this situation can, in turn, lead to high stress. As a result of not discussing problems previously, managers may gloss over them. Or the opposite occurs: The manager uses the review as a vehicle for finally spelling out the problems — and the employee experiences what's called the *surprise syndrome* (feeling hammered or shocked). The shock from the surprise syndrome generally leads to counterproductive behaviors — bitterness, anger, subtle or even overt resistance, being demoralized, or all of those reactions together.

✔ The irregular discussions and feedback about performance and the lack of documentation on what has been happening leave managers with a heavy reliance on their memories at review time. Managers in this situation have to write what they remember best — the last couple of months of performance. The rest of the year may get largely bypassed.

To say that people have short-term memories is an understatement. For example, can you remember what you were doing at 10 a.m. on Monday three weeks ago? How about the same hour and day nine weeks or nine months ago? Now, try to remember what or how one of your employees was doing at these times.

A few employees pick up on their managers' over-reliance on memory in place of regular communication and documentation. So a month or two before their reviews are to be done, their performance really excels. After receiving very good reviews from their managers, and often pay raises to match, they go back into cruise mode for a while. Umm . . . would you call this a timely strategy?

✔ Managers may also experience anxiety attacks at review time if they don't set and develop results-focused performance plans with their employees; that is, if they skipped Stage 1 and are stuck trying to fill out a generic *trait-based appraisal form*. A trait-based appraisal usually has a list of characteristics or traits that the manager is expected to evaluate. For example, quality, organization, planning, communications, productivity, and attitude are commonly found in trait-based evaluation formats.

These attributes come with general definitions and usually a five-level rating (evaluation) system, much like a school report card. Managers may be tempted to give out good grades to most of their employees, thereby creating rating inflation and writing general and subjective comments, such as, "Jane Doe produces lots of quality work. She is a quality-driven employee whom you can count on to deliver quality work. Outstanding rating for quality." When this one-size-fits-all appraisal format is used, the focus on performance often gets lost.

Managing by coaching, on the other hand, emphasizes evaluating employees on whether they are delivering the results needed.

Staying on Top of Old Smoky with Status-Review Meetings

If you're like many busy managers, trying to keep track of what is going on with your own work is tough enough, let alone keeping up with your employees' projects and assignments. Yet, you are responsible for what they produce.

Doer managers handle this tracking effort one of two ways: chasing after employees to check on every detail of their work (the dreaded micromanager) or staying hands-off unless something goes wrong, hoping they'll be lucky and nothing will go wrong. Neither method tends to work well for driving results and giving responsibility to employees, both important facets of a coaching approach.

A status-review meeting, on the other hand, is an effective coaching-assessment tool aimed at driving responsibility and results, without driving you or your employees crazy. (Of course, some employees don't appreciate your asking them to take responsibility. Some like to have you take all the responsibility so that they can blame you when things go wrong. But you don't want to let this stop you because, in time and with good coaching, an employee like this will become capable of handling responsibility.)

 You conduct a status review as a one-on-one meeting between you and your employee. If the project is a team-oriented one, you can do a one-on-group review. When the meeting is a group meeting, however, each member's report needs to be relevant to the other members' reports; otherwise, chins tend to drop and yawns increase as the people find the meeting a bore and a waste of time.

Running a status-review meeting

The purpose of a status-review meeting is to review and plan ahead for an employee's progress on current projects or key assignments. I suggest that you use a *tracking sheet,* such as the one shown in Figure 7-1, to set the agenda for the meeting.

The one-on-one status-review meeting usually is brief and can be done in 30 minutes or so. The employee knows going in what to report progress on, as outlined on his or her tracking sheet, such as the one shown in the column named "Deliverables" in Figure 7-1 (a *deliverable* is sometimes referred to as an action item). The employee reports progress on each deliverable on the list, one at a time ("Here is what is done or not done"), and the evidence for it is shown as needed on the tracking sheet. The deliverable is the task that the employee committed to accomplish during a given, short-term period. The

"Due Date" column (refer to Figure 7-1) is usually the meeting date, though it can be a later date, such as a project milestone. In the latter case, for each item, the employee reports his or her progress toward meeting the milestone.

Status-Review Tracking Sheet

Name _____   Meeting date _____

Deliverables	Due date	Status

Figure 7-1:
Status-
review
tracking
sheet.

As the employee goes down the list reporting his or her progress, both you and the employee fill out the "Status" column (refer to Figure 7-1) about the progress to date. Your role in this meeting is to listen, ask questions for more specifics as needed, and provide the appropriate constructive feedback. The employee does the majority of the talking. Responsibility for the employee's performance is shifting to where it belongs, with the employee. Isn't that great?

After the employee has given the status on each item, the two of you set the deliverables for the next status-review meeting. The employee records the action item list and sends you a copy of the list.

Should problems arise as the employee reports progress, the two of you can take time to problem-solve together and to set a course of action for going forward. If a major problem exists and time permits, you can deal with it at that moment. Otherwise, you can plan a separate meeting in the near future to deal with that single issue.

Status-review meetings help you and your employees stay on top of current projects and key assignments. Because of this, they work best if the frequency of the meetings is fairly regular. I recommend holding them once every one to two weeks. Keep in mind that if some of your employees do work that is more routine in nature and less project-oriented, you won't need to use this coaching tool with them very often.

Status-review meetings are most effective for helping to manage projects and key assignments. They are designed to be quick and are organized to focus on the following:

- ✔ Status on each deliverable
- ✔ Brief problem-solving, as needed
- ✔ New deliverables set for next meeting

A good thing to do at the end of each meeting, after defining the next set of deliverables, is set the date for the next meeting with your employee. Communicate the expectation that he or she is responsible for ensuring that the meeting with you happens, not visa versa. In this way, you keep the momentum of status review rolling while driving the responsibility for the meeting to your staff person. Isn't that great?

Realizing the benefits of the status-review meeting

When done as a regular coaching practice, the status-review meeting provides you and your employees with some strong benefits.

✔ Breaks long-term projects into manageable bites for the employee.

✔ Gives employees a tool (the tracking sheet in Figure 7-1) by which to come prepared to report their progress on the important tasks.

✔ Eliminates frustration about grilling employees in order to find out what they're accomplishing.

✔ Helps you and the employee track important output activities, such as in sales, production, or customer service functions.

✔ Allows you the opportunity to focus your employees' attention on the aspect of their work that needs attention. You're able to challenge them if they're being too lax in their expectations about what they can get done, or, on the other hand, you can steer them away from taking on more than they can reasonably get done during a given period.

✔ Builds quality time. The efficient nature of the meeting makes good use of time for you and your employees. You stay more aware of how your employees are progressing and what they're producing. You no longer have to chase them down to get information, and they no longer have to waste their time writing weekly reports on what they've been doing — which they wonder if you ever read anyway.

✔ Promotes accountability — employees can't just look busy; they have to come ready to report results. They commit to the tasks they'll get done, and they take the responsibility for delivering on them. Status reviews allow you to help employees stay successful. If problems arise, you can help resolve them in the early stages instead of finding out about them after they're out of hand.

✔ Lets employees walk away from the meeting knowing what's expected and what their priorities are.

The status-review meeting helps you avoid acting like a micromanager. (Do you hear that applause coming from your staff?) No need to constantly chase after your employees to see whether they're handling every task: Did you get that done, or did you check with so and so? If you want to be informed about a particular task or issue, just have your employees put it on the tracking sheet. Then set the frequency of the meetings based on how often you need to stay in the loop, perhaps once every week or two. This way, you can let your employees do their jobs.

Going to the "Doctor" for a Checkup

When you go to your doctor for your annual physical, the whole idea is to look at your overall health. You don't wait until you're sick to go for your checkup; the purpose is preventive medicine — to evaluate your total health and catch any problems in their early stages. The second periodic performance assessment tool for effective coaching, the *checkup meeting,* operates much the same way as your annual visit to the doctor does.

The purposes of checkup meetings are to review an employee's overall performance and to reset performance plans as needed in order to focus attention on the right priorities as you go forward. In simple terms, this meeting is a mini performance review that's done without written formality and final judgments.

This coaching tool is quite different from the status-review tool. Status-review meetings are done when you need to stay on top of projects or critical assignments that are currently going on. The checkup meeting takes you to the big-picture level. It has you reflecting with your staff members on how they're doing with their *total performance* in working to achieve their goals and standards. Therefore, its frequency is much less than status-review meetings — once per quarter is what I recommend. While the status-review tool is less applicable when employees are less involved in project-type work, the checkup is a must for all managers to use if they want to make their lives easier.

Managing a checkup meeting

You conduct a checkup meeting as a one-on-one conversation between you and your staff member. The meeting is informal in nature and is divided into three steps:

1. **You and the employee review his or her progress toward meeting each goal or standard included in the employee's performance plan.**

   You can often incorporate the tool of self-evaluation as part of this discussion. For example, have the employee go first, providing feedback on his or her progress with each goal. Ask questions to get more specifics where needed. Listen and periodically reflect on what you hear to ensure that you understand the employee's points. Then provide your feedback.

   Here is a snapshot of how you have the employee self-evaluate in this meeting. "George, as it relates to your first goal to grow a greater number of cherry trees, 25 percent, specifically what have you accomplished so far?"

   George replies, "Blah specific, blah specific, blah a little more specific," and you paraphrase back to him saying, "So in other words, George, you cannot tell a lie, you have been chopping down cherry trees rather than growing them. Is that right?" George confirms your response, and then you add your performance feedback about the goal, which in this case is, "That's pretty much how I see it. Now let's hear your assessment of the results so far with goal two."

With this structured and nonthreatening approach to self-evaluation, you may hear employees criticizing their performance more often than you would. Seldom disagree with them when this happens, because employees can push themselves more effectively than you can. When you solicit specific feedback from an employee, in many cases, you won't need to add much; instead, you can briefly reinforce the points made.

If you're stuck with using a trait-based appraisal form (mentioned in the "Knowing why anxiety attacks occur" section earlier in this chapter) for your formal review, before moving on to the second part of the meeting, do a feedback exchange with your employee on each factor. Doing so enables you to tie actual performance into this subjective format.

2. **Collaboratively discuss whether you need to modify the goals and action plans.**

If new priorities have come into the mix, you and the employee develop performance plans to include the new priorities. The objective here is to ensure that the performance plans stay current and continue to encompass total performance.

Sometimes, the goal is fine but the employee, like George, is not on track and the action plans may need to be modified to help him get back on the track to reaching the goal. Ask for his ideas first. "So George, what steps are you going to take to get back on track into growing the number of cherry trees you need?"

3. **Recap the agreed-upon modifications and close with the employee setting the date for when he or she will give you a copy of the revised performance plans.**

The employee types the revisions because the performance plans are his or hers, not yours — which is not a bad deal! You document the highlights of the checkup meeting for your own notes.

You may also find it helpful to summarize this documentation in a memo and copy the employee on it; be sure to let the individual know you'll be doing that. If you write more than one page, you're writing too much.

To gain the most value, I recommend holding checkup meetings on a quarterly schedule. This one-on-one meeting can generally be done in an hour. In an annual performance evaluation cycle, you meet with each staff member three times during the year to look at overall performance. In the fourth-quarter meeting, you conduct the formal review.

Understanding the benefits of the checkup

✔ **Enhances quality time.** This one-on-one meeting for an hour or so puts you in touch with your employees' overall performances, while at the same time lets them know where they stand with their performance. What a great use of time! Both parties step back from their day-to-day tasks to see what progress is being made and where they're headed.

✔ **Enables employees to stay on track in terms of their performance plans.** The discussions focus on the results that are taking place and push employees to take responsibility and minimize excuses. Another great result!

✔ **Builds flexibility into your performance management process** because it allows you to keep performance plans up to date. There's nothing worse than coming to the end of the review cycle and trying to evaluate an employee's performance on a goal that's no longer relevant — and not having a replacement goal on this list of priorities. That's egg on a manager's face. (Eggs are tastier when you eat them off a plate.)

✔ **Helps you eliminate the surprise syndrome for employees and review-writing anxiety for you** (mentioned in the "Knowing why anxiety attacks occur" section earlier in this chapter). When the formal review is given, coupled with informal constructive feedback along the way including necessary status reviews, employees know where they stand in their performance. No surprises. Of course, writing the final evaluation when the time comes is a piece of delicious cake. You're just summarizing checkup meetings and the feedback in between. Goodbye anxiety attacks!

✔ **Helps you eliminate possible discrepancies in how you and your employees see their performance.** As one manager who uses this coaching tool described, "If the two of us see issues differently on how the employee is performing on a goal or an overall level, that discrepancy is gone before the end of the year. The employee knows where I stand, and the onus is on that person to show evidence of results to change my view." Employees quickly learn to adapt and produce. This communication eliminates surprises occurring with the final evaluation.

✔ **Builds a support system.** By plugging in the self-evaluation approach to this meeting, you end up listening more than half the time. This shows that you care and are in touch with your employees' challenges and successes. And by updating the performance plans together, employees walk away with renewed focus. Communication and understanding are enhanced, which is support at its best, and makes this one-hour meeting once a quarter a worthwhile investment for you.

Doing a Postmortem — Or How Did the Surgery Go?

The word *post* comes from Latin and generally means *after*. A postmortem is an examination of a body after death, commonly called an autopsy. Coaching is not into examining dead bodies but is into learning from the past.

So often in business, major events occur, and as soon as they're over, everyone involved takes a deep breath and moves on to other issues. The next event, similar to the one before it, comes up, and everyone scrambles around and ends up repeating the same mistakes they made in the previous event. This pattern occurs with trade shows, product development and launch efforts, and numerous other special projects and events. It's amazing, sometimes, how managers and employees can let bad history repeat itself. The performance assessment tool, the *postmortem meeting,* aims to eradicate this dog-chasing-tail syndrome.

The main purpose of the postmortem meeting is to evaluate results from projects and other key performance events and to apply lessons learned from them to similar situations in the future. The meeting can even be used as a method of debriefing and learning from sales calls, formal presentations, and other important or public displays of employee performance.

"Operating" a postmortem meeting

As a coaching tool, the postmortem is done on a one-to-one basis or on a manager-to-group basis when the event is a team situation. (Generally, most one-on-one postmortem meetings can be done in 30 minutes to an hour. For large team-like projects, the time may be longer.)

While you are one of the participants in this meeting, your primary role, as manager, is to be the facilitator. The meeting is divided into four steps:

1. **Draw key conclusions from the work done on the project or performance event.**

   Two questions are answered:

   - What worked well in the project; what were the successes?

   - What didn't work as well as needed or desired?

   Have the employee respond to the questions first, then you go second — without any comment or discussion so that the initial input comes out unbiased. (If a team is involved in the postmortem, follow the same process by allowing one person at a time to respond, with no discussion.) Have the inputs recorded on a board or flip chart so that they are visible. Then start the collective discussion and focus on determining the key conclusions being reported.

Be specific about the details of the project: Don't overlook the obvious, but at the same time, make your history teacher happy. Thanks to the postmortem assessment meeting, your staff members obtain valuable lessons from the past that help them perform more effectively in the future. In this way, you drive employee responsibility because they are the ones expected to apply the lessons learned.

2. **Shift the meeting focus to future steps or actions.**

   Start with your employee giving ideas and then add your own. Often, you can hold a brainstorming session in which you each throw ideas back and forth, one at a time. Refrain from discussion so that the ideas can flow, and have the ideas recorded so that they are visible. Focus the ideas on two endeavors:

   • Actions to maintain for continued success

   • Improvements to enhance effectiveness in the future

3. **Discuss and evaluate the ideas shared and collectively decide which ones to go forward with for the next event.**

   Have the agreed-upon actions documented along with the key conclusions determined in the first part. Guess who should do most of this documentation? Hint, hint, it's not you. Ain't that grand?

4. **(This occurs in the future!) Pull out the information documented during the postmortem meeting and use it in the planning phase of the new project or special event.**

   You can evaluate past experiences instead of being doomed to repeating them.

Adding up the benefits of the postmortem

The postmortem meeting works best when held at the conclusion of every important project or special event. Have it be a regular part of the process so that it isn't overlooked. When the postmortem is used for learning and training purposes or for other projects of small scope — such as handling a sales call, making a special presentation, or demonstrating new job skills — you may not need to schedule it on a continuous basis. But do use this debriefing coaching tool whenever needed. Just be sure to announce up front, before the performance efforts take place, that you will do a postmortem right afterwards.

The benefits of the postmortem are many:

✔ **Employees gain analytical skills as they evaluate what happened.** Dwelling long and hard on the problem, blaming, and finding fault are not part of the process. They then gain a solutions orientation because the postmortem meeting is not complete until solutions or steps for next time are worked out. This is a very positive and dynamic experience.

✔ **You get to listen and teach.** The employee gives input and ideas first; you play the role of listener, supporter, and, of course, teacher, because you're providing lessons based on past mistakes and successes.

✔ **You gain quality time with your staff.** The postmortem helps you spend quality time with your employees, during which you reflect, learn lessons, and set actions going forward. Thus, you are having productive meetings with your employees to help good results roll on for the future. (Let the good times roll!)

Building the Pillars of Commitment Block by Block

When used as periodic performance assessment coaching tools, the status-review, checkup, and postmortem meetings (all described in this chapter) affect the five pillars of commitment. Take a look at each pillar within the context of these meetings:

✔ **Focus:** All three of these coaching tools help drive focus. Employees come out of these meetings clearly knowing the goals, plans, and priorities on which to focus. No guessing games as to what they should spend time on in order to produce results.

✔ **Involvement:** All three of these periodic performance review meetings are conducted as two-way conversations with the employees doing more than half the talking. The employees' input shapes the action item list in status reviews, their ideas are used to help modify performance plans in the checkup meetings, and their experiences help determine the lessons to be learned and better ways to do things covered in the postmortem meetings. Active participation is encouraged and solicited in these meetings.

✔ **Development:** This pillar is impacted especially hard, in a good way, in the postmortem meeting. Here, employees receive coaching on areas that they can apply in future performance endeavors and thus grow from their experiences. During the status review and the checkup, opportunities often come to light in which employees can gain experience, skills, and knowledge that will help them in the future. Most importantly, they develop self-sufficiency as they begin to take control and drive the results of their own performance.

✔ **Gratitude:** This pillar is nicely influenced in each of these coaching meetings because recognizing the successes underway is an integral part of these three meetings. The informal nature of these meetings gives the appropriate feedback a chance to fly.

✔ **Accountability:** A major emphasis of these *review* meetings is just that: reviewing results. As long as you follow through, holding the meetings and maintaining their organized and collaborative structure, the employees are the ones who carry the primary responsibility to evaluate and report the results of their performance. They also can track their performance and see the progress they make with it — and thus experience a sense of achievement from their own efforts. This is accountability at its best.

Part III
The Fine Art of Mentoring and Tutoring

The 5th Wave   By Rich Tennant

"I think it's time we cut the mentoring umbilical cord, Stacey."

In this part . . .

Much of coaching involves serving as an informal guide to help your employees learn, grow, and perform. The mentoring and tutoring aspects of coaching covered in this part take mentoring from concept into practical application, providing a wealth of tools for you to help your employees perform to their potential.

Chapter 8

The Do's and Don'ts of Mentoring and Tutoring

In This Chapter

▶ Defining what the mentoring and tutoring aspects of coaching are all about

▶ Avoiding actions that create employee dependency and stifle initiative

▶ Exploring tools of mentoring that challenge employees to think and do for themselves

▶ Influencing employee commitment through mentoring and tutoring

Are you a mentor or a tormentor to your staff? Employees often talk about experiencing the latter and wishing they had the former.

Mentors in the business world are often seen as those wise senior-level managers who provide the support and assistance that help advance your career. Some employees have thought that if they were connected to such a mentor, they could go somewhere in their careers. And some employees have viewed these connections as part of a good-old-boy network, with which not everyone was connected. Regardless, the term "mentor" has always referred to the trusted advisor you turn to periodically for counsel in your career. In either case, this figure usually has not been your own boss.

But mentoring, often referred to in this chapter as *mentoring and tutoring,* is also a part of coaching. It is a set of behaviors and skills that managers can and should use directly with their employees. As part of coaching, *mentoring and tutoring* means the following: You're making efforts to challenge and develop your staff to think and do for themselves and grow in their capabilities. This independence and growth allows them to perform to their best potential, which often leads to growth in their careers. This chapter gives you the details.

Helping Your Staff Fish for Themselves

The mentoring and tutoring aspects of coaching are informal in nature and involve efforts to help staff members do for themselves. The emphasis is on employees being able to solve problems, make decisions, and set plans at their own levels of responsibility — versus being dependent on you for all the answers. You want to push this level of responsibility to its greatest heights so that employees perform self-sufficiently — which also means that you can take vacations and go away to seminars and conferences without taking your beeper and laptop.

The mentoring and tutoring forms of coaching follow the old adage (by Confucius), "Give a man a fish, and the man will eat for a day. Teach a man to fish, and he will eat for a lifetime." This form of tutoring is informal; that is, it isn't direct instruction or training (which are explored in Chapter 14), yet it does involve periodically spending time with your employees, time in which development takes place for them and for you.

Mentoring and tutoring take place through two-way conversation. For example, when employees walk into your office with monkeys — problems — on their backs, they still walk out with them. You have not taken on their problems, but at the same time, they walk out of your office with a plan in mind, one that they helped create, for resolving their monkeys. Now, that's monkeying around at its best.

The origins of mentoring

The term *mentor* has its origins in ancient Greek mythology. The war hero, Ulysses, was heading off to fight in the Trojan War. He turned to his trusted friend, Mentor, to be the tutor of his son, Telemachus. He said to Mentor something like, "Yo Mentor. I am going off on a long business trip again, the fighting-wars kind. Look after my boy, Telemachus, and teach him right from wrong, and some other good stuff. I'll check back with you in ten years." Actually, Ulysses didn't know how long he would be away, but it turned out to be a very long time. But with Mentor's help, Telemachus learned to fish for himself. (Pardon me for having a little creative license with the story. Read Homer's *Ulysses* for more details.)

Within this story is the essence of what the mentoring and tutoring aspects of coaching are all about: getting employees to do for themselves. (Not "abandon your children and hope your good neighbor looks after them!") Managers often make the mistake of taking on responsibilities that employees can carry out themselves — from solving problems for their employees to answering questions that employees can figure out. Instead, mentoring encourages employees to solve their own problems and become more independent.

Understand the Ways Not to Mentor and Tutor

What happens when your employees walk into your office carrying a problem they encountered in their work situation? Does it end up on your desk and out of their hands when they leave? Does your day get filled with constant interruptions of questions or comments like, "What do you want me to do now?" or "How do you want me to handle this assignment?" And then, do you end up providing answers over and over to these questions?

Many managers fall into this all-knowing, all-telling, and come-to-the rescue mode of operation, especially doer types (described in Chapter 1). Unfortunately, they become burdened individuals with little time to do their own work. Having control of their time and providing quality time to their employees aren't possible. What they create is a great deal of dependency, with little initiative and problem solving coming from their staff members: Not exactly the recipe for getting high productivity, but great for feeling important.

These actions are the opposite of the mentoring and tutoring tools of coaching. In fact, the following is a list of common management behaviors that create dependency and little initiative — stay away from these!

- ✔ **Telling employees how to do their jobs:** This behavior is different than training. In this case, you tend to direct employees on how to do nearly every step of their jobs. The focus is on methods, not results. Employees often call this the dreaded "m" word, *micromanagement.*

- ✔ **Giving employees solutions for their operational issues without getting their input:** In this behavior, you become the answer-person. If anything sounds like a problem, you have the solution. No need for anyone else to think, do research, or make any effort to help figure out answers. And often, you insist that your solution or answer is the right one. Employees call this imposing your will or authority, another form of micromanagement.

- ✔ **Making decisions that employees could make for themselves:** Besides being all-knowing (see the previous bullet), you're all-powerful. What happens is that nearly every decision, from big to small, runs through you. Employees frequently come to you asking for approval or permission. Of course, when your decisions go wrong, the employees will have no problem blaming you, because they had no responsibility in the decisions.

- ✔ **Giving frequent advice:** With this behavior, you find yourself making statements that start out like, "Here's what you should do," or "Here's what you need to do." You think that you're being helpful by sharing your great ideas and giving advice without waiting to be asked for it — and all free of charge. Of course in doing so, you overlook one important aspect about advice: It's best received when asked for. Any moment before that, and the advice is usually useless.

✔ **Jumping in to handle situations your employees are paid to handle:** When employees make errors, who corrects them? When one of your staff members struggles a bit to deliver a service or perform a task, what do you do?

Do you jump in, usually unannounced and without request, take over the duty, and get it done? If so, you go to the rescue, but no one is saved.

✔ **Criticizing your employees for their mistakes:** This approach may work for training dogs, and it's often used in coaching football and basketball players, but it seldom has a positive effect on employees. Criticism, not negative feedback (which, as you find out in Chapter 5, is a good thing) gets delivered. To supposedly make a point, sometimes the criticizing is done publicly. But even when done privately, it comes with a sting. What the employee is not to do is emphasized, while learning how to make corrections is often overlooked.

Besides creating dependency, what do these common management behaviors have in common?

✔ **They kill initiative and action.** These behaviors discourage employees from taking action. They create a wait-and-don't-do approach. "Just wait until the boss tells you to do something and don't do anything out of the routine until then. Remember what happened to you the last time you tried something and made a mistake?"

✔ **They discourage real conversation.** These non-mentoring behaviors promote one-way communication. You say, "Do this or that," and get lots of nodding and smiling from your employees, but these management behaviors encourage passive responses, not dialogue.

✔ **They stifle thinking.** These behaviors cause employees to do only a small amount of thinking for themselves, so they take on little responsibility for themselves. The staff looks to you for all the answers and solutions.

✔ **They seem quick.** The best thing about these behaviors is they are quick, at least in the short term. One-way communication is generally faster than two-way communication. Unfortunately, speedy communication doesn't guarantee efficiency and quality. What employees understand from all the talking you do is anyone's guess. The more they nod and smile at you, generally the more you are being tuned out. This situation is compounded because of all the sitting and waiting they do — that is, waiting for you to tell them what to do next, which of course consumes even more of your time. So talk faster.

Using the Two Tools of Mentoring and Tutoring

In the approach outlined in the previous section, employees don't think, act, and take responsibility for their performance, which makes your job a lot harder. Now I invite you to take a look at two sets of mentoring and tutoring tools: sharing (offering insights and observations) and challenging (encouraging employees to think for themselves). Both sets of tools stimulate thinking and help guide employee development and performance.

Sharing: The first set of tools

Sharing — that is, passing on thoughts, insights, and nuggets of wisdom — often creates an atmosphere for good dialogue. This dialogue may happen immediately or in the future, after the employee has time to digest and act upon the shared ideas. The following sections explain the key tools in this set.

Sharing knowledge and experience

When coaching your staff, if you have information to share, you pass it on. Let others learn from what you have learned; from your successes and mistakes. With mentoring and tutoring, you share knowledge and experience strategically. No lecturing, patronizing, or handing out lines like some fathers used to. (You know the kind of thing I mean: "When I was a boy, I had to walk five miles to school uphill and in the snow, and no one gave me new shoes.")

You can occasionally use this tool effectively just by sprinkling it into casual conversation or it may come out in conversations about new challenges an employee will soon take on. Sometimes, you can also express it this way: "That's something you may want to keep in mind." Also, you can share in story form. Sharing knowledge and experience through storytelling often encourages positive interaction. People enjoy listening to stories and are encouraged, in turn, to share their own stories — or they may come back later to tell stories about new experiences.

This tutoring tool can provide insight on technical matters and on how to interact with others, make decisions, or adapt to a corporate culture or work environment. It allows experiences to be shared, as in, "That's been my experience. What similar experiences have you had in these kinds of situations?" Tutoring by sharing imposes nothing and allows employees to try for themselves, while arming them with valuable research from other people's personal experiences.

Sharing observations

Observation is a handy tool when sharing. In this case, you pass on what you notice about the employee's behavior and work efforts. You want to share observations occasionally and in areas important and helpful to the individual's development — sometimes to point out their difficulties or challenges and sometimes to point out their successes.

You offer observations as insights and to spark discussion. For example, "I have noticed you becoming more irritable when you deal with Bob in Accounting. What's going on?" Or, "I saw how you handled that difficult customer situation. You stayed calm and focused on the issue and got the situation resolved. In fact, tell me more specifically what you did that worked so well in this instance." Sharing observations invites self-reflection and the opportunity to learn lessons from past performance — both what to continue doing and what to do better the next time.

Providing suggestions and advice

You can use this sharing tool when an employee seeks your ideas or thoughts. In these cases, your advice is asked for, but the key is not to give it like a preacher or dictator — no responses such as, "You must do as I, the all-knowing, tell you." When you suggest and advise, you want to ensure that you don't impose your decisions or solutions upon the employee.

When an employee asks for your advice, try responses such as the following:

- ✔ "If I were in your position, I would . . . ."
- ✔ "Here is something you might consider." The key here is that this is his or her decision.
- ✔ "Whatever you think will work best, you do." Here, you're giving input, not imposing rules or solutions on employees. They keep the responsibility. (Isn't that what you're paying them to do?) At the same time, you're making yourself a resource to whom they can come for counsel or to discuss ideas or issues (and that's what you're paid to do!).

Suggestions are just what the word says; they aren't the absolute answer. You give them to stimulate thought and encourage two-way conversations. As a result, the employee has the chance to disregard your suggestion or advice. And don't attack them if they do so because then you go from suggesting to making rules: "What do you mean telling me that you don't like my advice? Didn't I tell you that it is the greatest thing since sliced bread?"

When advice hasn't been requested but you feel that it's needed, before giving the advice, say something like, "May I give you a suggestion about that?" Then when the employee says "Yes" or even "Okay," give away freely. One sign that managers are shifting from doers to coaches (described in earlier chapters) is that they go from having many rules and few suggestions to having few rules and many suggestions.

Giving the big picture

One of the clichés or buzzwords running rampant in today's business jargon is *the big picture.* For example, "The trouble with management is that they don't seem to know what the big picture is, or at least they don't tell us what it is." Or vice versa, "The problem with some of these employees is that they don't seem to be able to grasp the big picture here." (Do you notice, no one has any problem with the little picture?)

In the sharing tool of mentoring and tutoring, the buzzword is minimized but the concept is maximized. Sharing involves efforts such as providing a sense of where you see your group going in the next six months, highlighting what good results should look like on an important project, or sharing how you see an employee's role evolving if that person works to develop his or her skills and abilities. Sharing in this way provides a sense of direction and a focus on the future. It works to give employees a greater perspective and understanding of their role and performance within the organizational unit.

Mentoring by sharing messages

Messages to share with your staff are most often one-liners that will be remembered and repeated by your employees. In fact, you know the messages sink in when you hear your staff repeat them to you and others. These messages also provide a sense of importance and are stated in positive terms. None start with "Don't do."

To use this mentoring-with-messages tool as a manager, you need to know first what messages you want to impart to your staff. Some may be ones that you've heard over the years that have stuck with you, like the following:

- ✔ When you emphasize what you can do versus can't do to help, you keep customers satisfied.

- ✔ Consistency, follow up, and follow-through are keys to your success as a manager.

- ✔ If you speak in terms that your audience understands in every presentation you make in this job, you and your presentations will go over well.

- ✔ Taking initiative and attention to detail are two qualities that demonstrate success in this environment.

Mentoring with messages is sometimes a combination of pearls of wisdom and performance expectations. These messages give employees lessons to live by, as well as guidance and direction for their performance. The messages are often stated in conversations while setting assignments, giving constructive feedback, or working on solving problems.

Through mentoring with messages, you provide key nuggets of wisdom or direction to your staff. You target these messages to help employees do the following:

- Develop their technical abilities
- Develop their business knowledge
- Understand the organizational culture
- Develop personally and in their work habits
- Develop management skills

Target these five areas. Like rules, keep the key mentoring messages to a few and tailor them to what's important to helping your staff succeed and grow in their performance.

Challenging: The other set of tools

The second set of mentoring and tutoring skills is the *challenge-them-to-think for-themselves* set. This set of tools is used in two-way conversations and in follow-up meetings (see Chapter 7), in which your employees share details of their projects and review their progress. (By following through with your employees, you encourage accountability while still showing interest and providing support.)

The following sections take a look at the four facets of the challenge-them-to-think mentoring and tutoring tools.

Tutoring with questions

You are often far more influential when you ask questions than when you give answers. As a tool, question-asking is powerful and sophisticated — powerful enough so that Chapter 9 is devoted to ways of doing it effectively.

Asking for plans

Asking for plans applies well to the meaty issues or problems that employees often raise. This strategy isn't a brush-them-off-with-a-busy-work-assignment strategy; it's a collaborative effort in which the employee takes the lead doing the research or other legwork, developing the ideas, and outlining a plan.

Your role is to give them direction, provide them with information and other resources they need, and conduct follow-up meetings to give feedback and mutually establish the next steps. With this kind of guidance and support from you, your employees come up with a plan of action. This approach is the new and improved version of "Put your money where your mouth is."

Depending on the scope of the issue, this effort may be done in a few sessions or in one or two meetings. The best aspect of this mentoring tool is that after you and your staff members agree to a plan for addressing an issue, you can often expect the employees to take the lead in implementing the plan.

Asking for decisions and recommendations

This challenge-them-to-think tool shifts responsibility from you to your employees; however, the effort is a collaborative one. When asking for decisions and recommendations, you and your employees evaluate situations and explore options and consequences of actions together — a good give-and-take discussion. Together, you analyze a possible decision, looking at its pros and cons, its advantages and disadvantages, and its benefits and obstacles. If background work is needed, guess who does it? Not you.

You may want to use brainstorming as a way of generating as many ideas as possible. To make brainstorming work when the goal is to come up with potential decisions and recommendations, follow these tips:

- ✔ You and your employee take turns offering ideas, one person and one idea at a time.

- ✔ Don't evaluate the ideas until the brainstorming session is exhausted. Giving commentary as you go bogs down the brainstorming and often stifles creativity. Remember, there are no bad ideas when brainstorming.

- ✔ Have someone record each person's ideas so that they are visible to all as you go. Can you guess who should record the ideas? Not you!

When all is said and done, the employee tells you which recommendation she thinks will work best — and why. In many cases, you let the employee make the decision and run with it, making clear that she is accountable for the consequences of that decision — both positive and negative.

Giving challenging assignments

This mentoring and tutoring tool is really a delegating effort. But more than delegating, it gives employees an opportunity to learn and gain valuable experience. Your role is to assist and support where needed, and to do the follow-ups — but also to let them carry out the challenging project, responsibility, or other assignment.

The idea here is to stretch your employees. (Not physically, as in, "Hey you, get on the rack!") Often, the assignment is a little new and different for them, but not way above their realm of capability. Much of the support you provide is in terms of giving frequent constructive feedback along with much encouragement to plow ahead. Most importantly, you are seeking to challenge your staff to think and do for themselves and allowing them to experience success from it.

Mentoring and tutoring for making tough decisions

Here is a story about a manager who handled a potentially difficult situation by asking questions and asking for decisions and recommendations. At the beginning of his shift one morning, without advance notice, an employee requested the afternoon off to go to a concert. The manager's response was essentially, "You make the decision."

The manager informed the employee that all the other staff members were not working that day, as scheduled, and that the two of them, the manager and employee, were booked up in the afternoon with customer appointments. She (the manager) also said that if he left, she wouldn't be able to cover all the appointments.

She asked him to evaluate what would happen if he left, versus if he stayed. At this point, she let the employee do most of the talking as he evaluated the situation. He knew he couldn't get any coworkers to come in on the spur of the moment. However, even though he didn't have any good alternatives to offer, the employee still asked to leave early.

The manager simply said that the decision was his, to just let her know by 10:00 that morning. Five minutes later, the employee returned and said that he would work his entire shift. The employee also identified the lesson he learned that day: Giving advance notice of a special schedule change is important, and he had known about the concert for over a month.

Now that's mentoring and tutoring at its best.

Impacting the Pillars of Commitment

When the mentoring and tutoring tools are put into regular practice, they greatly impact the pillars of involvement and development, and positively influence the other three pillars (see Chapter 2 for further discussion of the five pillars of commitment). Here is a look at how each pillar is built with mentoring and tutoring tools:

- ✔ **Involvement:** The mentoring and tutoring aspects of coaching heavily involve two-way conversation. They push the employee to actively engage in developing ideas, shaping plans, solving problems, and helping make decisions. That's involvement at its highest level.

- ✔ **Development:** Mentoring and tutoring are about challenging employees to think and do for themselves. They give employees opportunities to learn and grow through a variety of ways: solving problems, creating plans, taking on new responsibilities, and gaining knowledge and wisdom. The more these tools are put into practice, the more your employees increase their capabilities and confidence.

✔ **Focus:** Mentoring and tutoring provide focus because, by their nature, they guide and direct employees. Through mentoring and tutoring, employees gain clarity on how to go forward and handle different situations. The observations and feedback you provide help focus your employees' attention on the areas they can work on for self-improvement.

✔ **Accountability:** This pillar is impacted strongly, too. One emphasis of mentoring and tutoring is to encourage employees to think and do for themselves. Instead of you doing for your staff, you're pushing them to take responsibility. (In other words, they get to earn their paychecks, not just show up for them. Shhh! Don't let this conspiracy of paying employees to be responsible get out.) With your ongoing dialogue and follow-up efforts, you reinforce accountability. Plus, as employees grow and develop their skills and abilities because of your coaching efforts, they experience a sense of accomplishment — a critical aspect of driving quality results and instilling accountability.

✔ **Gratitude:** This last pillar is influenced through mentoring and tutoring a little less directly than the others. But part of mentoring and tutoring, as employees grow and achieve, is to acknowledge successes. And as a bonus, by recognizing their own development and successes, employees often experience a feeling of satisfaction and a new appreciation for their efforts and results.

Chapter 9

Don't Tell, but Do Ask: Tutoring with Questions

*H*ere are a couple of patterns of behavior that often show up in manager-employee working relationships.

✔ The more you, the manager, tell an employee how to do his job, the less he thinks and does for himself.

✔ The more you, the manager, give answers to an employee's every question — many of which have been asked before — the less the employee figures out answers for herself.

As referred to briefly in the Chapter 8, one of the most powerful tools of coaching is mentoring and tutoring with questions, a coaching tool that compels you to ask questions and listen. Its main purpose is to stimulate employees to think and do for themselves — the opposite of the patterns described in the previous bullets.

When employees can think and do for themselves to achieve desired results, you don't have to constantly look over their shoulders (or under them, if you have tall staff members) to ensure that everything is being done. You can be away from the office without having to worry about whether the place will still run smoothly — and you can even take a vacation! (Remember, coaching is one of the keys to having good vacations.)

Many managers tend to overlook or fail to recognize the power of tutoring with questions, perhaps because it requires them to shift from the all-telling, all-knowing mode of operation to a collaborative approach. Tutoring with questions operates under a simple assumption: Employees are adults and are capable of having thoughts and ideas. Therefore, to enjoy this powerful tool, you, as a manager, need to listen first, speak second; ask first, offer second. You also need to understand when tutoring with questions is appropriate and when it's not. This chapter has all the details.

When and When Not to Plug in the Questioning Tool

Tutoring with questions works well in certain situations, but it's not applicable in others. Be aware of when this coaching tool can be plugged in to get value from it and when attempting to use it defeats its purpose. This section gives you a guide to differentiate these situations.

When questions don't work

To understand when you want to use tutoring with questions, first take a look at when not to use this tool. Attempts to use the questioning tool in the situations in the following sections take away from its value and may cause employees to steer clear of discussions with you.

The "20-questions" game

Did you ever play the game of 20 questions when you were a kid? In the game, someone has something in mind, and through asking questions, the other person tries to guess what it is. Is it bigger than a bread box? Is it hotter than a hot potato? If you guess right in 20 questions or less, you win.

However, if you have something in mind and you think it's the right answer or the right way of getting a job done, asking questions and hoping your staff person guesses right becomes *torturing* with questions, not tutoring with questions. Employees generally don't want to play the game to get to "your right answer."

For example, a manager asked his employee to explain how he would handle the day's heavy operational issues. The manager greeted each idea that the employee presented with "No, try again." After three tries, and having gone through this kind of experience with the manager before, the exasperated employee blurted out, "If there is some way you want me to go about handling this work, just tell me!"

If you have something in mind, say so. Avoid playing guessing games.

Telling employees how they're performing

As I mention in Chapter 5, constructive feedback (which includes both negative and positive feedback) is relating your observations to an employee about how he or she is performing.

One of the keys to giving feedback constructively is to be direct and clear, so this is not a scenario in which you ask questions such as "Regarding your work on the ABC project, how do you think it went?" That just doesn't work.

Most managers don't have a problem giving feedback when employees are performing well. However, when the performance isn't up to snuff, many do have trouble giving negative feedback.

Although questions may imply concern, they often create anxiety and adversarial interactions, not collaborative ones. With both positive and negative feedback, be upfront and report what you observe. Then, open up the discussion to hear the employee's take on the situation and when needed, work out a solution from that point.

You want to use tutoring with questions during discussions with your employees, not when you're giving feedback.

Providing necessary information

Part of your role as a manager is to give your employees the information they need to do their jobs well — the little stuff and the big-event stuff. Generally, asking questions rather than sharing news straight out isn't an issue. Communicating enough to keep your employees in the information loop is more often the challenge (although initial questions in these information-providing situations can make for interesting conversations — for example, "Do you know what happened to the company president?" Or "Guess what management wants me to do with your position?").

Giving direction

Giving employees direction is not the same as being directive. *Being directive* is telling people how to do their jobs and giving them orders — usually actions not well received by most employees.

Giving direction, on the other hand, includes things like explaining what target you want to see accomplished, clarifying where the group should be headed, or describing the parameters and boundaries within which your employees need to work. Employees require and desire direction from their managers.

Asking them how they will meet that direction is where tutoring with questions comes into the equation. Clarifying or giving the direction is best when you explain it.

When employees lack the background

When an individual doesn't have the knowledge, skill, or experience to understand or handle a particular issue, asking the person for ideas about how to handle the issue will be met with blank stares. This is a situation in which the employee first needs information in order to proceed effectively. Your role is to explain and teach. After the employee has the essential knowledge or experience, tutoring with questions can work.

When questions work

Now I take a look at where tutoring with questions *is* applicable. The following sections cover four situations in which questions work well. These are the opportunities to challenge employees to think and do for themselves — true coaching opportunities. During these situations, if you tell instead of ask, employees gain little for themselves.

Some of the following situations are also applicable when you have just given negative feedback. In the discussion that follows the feedback, you can tutor with questions and promote a two-way conversation in which positive outcomes result from the feedback effort (see Chapter 2 for more on two-way conversations).

Analyzing and problem-solving

The process of analyzing and problem-solving is one of the best situations for plugging in tutoring with questions. Instead of quickly giving solutions, you're allowing the person with the problem to help create the solution. Solutions often lie with those closest to the problem. Tutoring with questions draws those solutions from your employees.

Problems are a normal part of anyone's job. Many employees think their roles are to bring every problem to their managers for them to solve. You may be one of those managers who faces the wave of everyone else's problems falling into your lap. In addition, you may have employees who complain to you whenever something isn't working well. These are problem situations and are, therefore, opportunities to use tutoring with questions. Instead of feeling the burden of having to have all the solutions, tutoring with questions pushes employees to understand how they might solve these problems themselves. Because they are the ones who are closest to the issues in most cases, have them think through how to solve the problems. Now that's coaching!

Evaluating options and making decisions

Employees are sometimes quick to come to you for decisions about what to do in areas that they responsible for. Tutoring with questions can help them analyze and determine the best course of action. Instead of making quick decisions when you ask for their ideas or recommendations, employees gain decision-making perspectives. The simple question of "What would you do in this situation?" puts employees in the role of thinking about what is best to do.

That's the idea here — getting employees thinking and making decisions for themselves within their own job parameters instead of expecting you to decide for them. In this way, you expand the parameters of their jobs and grow their capabilities in the process. Hello responsibility for them; good-bye dependency on you.

Doing things better or differently

In many situations, such as when mistakes are made or performance efforts don't go as well as hoped, opportunities exist for employees to learn lessons and correct their course. Using questions to explore what happened and what can be done to make matters work better provides experiences for learning and growth.

Sometimes, managers abruptly react when they see mistakes made. They can be quick to chastise or blame for what happened. This behavior discourages the employee from learning lessons. Some managers just step in and fix the mistakes themselves which, of course, means that employees learn nothing for themselves. Other managers, when employees take initiative that doesn't turn out right, jump on that effort with a harsh and quick reaction. ("What were you doing here! Who told you should take it upon yourself to do that effort!") Such reactions mean good-bye future efforts to take initiative.

Tutoring with questions provides good give-and-take conversations in which employees can learn for themselves and improve as they go forward. It allows for the right behaviors to continue with better ways to do them. This approach is much better than blaming, which kills initiative.

Developing plans

Tutoring with questions also is a great tool for helping employees think out plans of action and steps to take in order to tackle a project or assignment. Instead of telling them how they should go about doing their work, you're helping them to think and develop their own action plans.

This situation for tutoring with questions also helps get employees started when they're tackling a tough assignment. Instead of leaving them on their own, struggling with how to get started, your questions help them figure out a plan of action. Questions can help them think through, in a logical flow, ways to organize themselves to get the job done. Now they're ready to act on the plans your questions helped them create.

To Be or Not to Be? How to Ask Tutoring Questions

Questions are either close-ended or open-ended (which isn't quite the same as being close-minded or open-minded!) *Close-ended questions* are designed to elicit short, definitive responses. Here are a few examples of close-ended questions:

- Did you take out the garbage?
- When is the meeting?
- Where is the meeting on the garbage?

Of course, while the answers can be given in one or few words, some people still like to expound or ramble when you ask close-ended questions. Nonetheless, they are designed to get you a specific piece of information.

Open-ended questions are designed to solicit expressions of thought that range from explanations to ideas. These questions must be answered in sentences rather than one or few words. Here are a few examples of open-ended questions:

- Why are you reluctant to take out the garbage?
- What will you do to ensure that the garbage is taken out?
- What will you do to keep too much garbage from coming into the meeting?

When tutoring with questions, most of the questions that you ask are open-ended. Close-ended questions are used only occasionally to confirm or clarify a message or to get a specific piece of information. Otherwise, open-ended questions are the way to go.

The examples in the following bulleted list provide you with a guide on how to ask a question (or a request for explanation) in an open-ended fashion.

- Describe what you see as possible causes for this problem.
- How would you implement that idea?
- What efforts can you undertake to make the situation work better?
- Explain the benefits to using that approach.
- What are the pros and cons of that possible plan?
- Please tell me more of your thinking behind that proposal.

As you can see in the preceding examples, certain key words — such as what, how, tell, describe, and explain — create open-ended questions or requests for explanations. Sentences that start with verbs like tell, describe, and explain actually serve as good starting points for tutoring with questions as they solicit explanations and depth of information — the whole idea when using this coaching tool. Who, when, and where at the start of a sentence generally shape questions so that they are close-ended (as in, "Who? Him." "When? Yesterday." "Where? There.").

Questions that start with *why* are open-ended, but exercise caution with *why* questions. Why? Quite often, questions that start with the word *why* come off sounding accusatory or like you're grilling the person. "Why did you do that?" While open-ended, such questions often put the other person on the defensive, as though something needs to be justified. So if you feel the need to use a tutoring question or request for explanation that begins with why, either manage your tone carefully or rephrase the sentence to avoid the word. "Please explain your thinking on that issue" is much better than "Why would you want to do that?"

When asking questions, keep two words in mind: space and tone.

✔ Instead of asking leading-the-witness questions (that is, close-ended questions such as "Do you think that idea is really going to help?" Or "Do you think that if you try it my way, everything will work out for the best?"), ask questions that give employees freedom and space to express their thoughts. For example, ask a question like "How do you think that idea can help?" When you ask questions of this kind — open-ended ones — you are giving the person space to express thoughts. These questions have no right or wrong answers, which is the whole idea when tutoring with questions.

✔ Tone is critical to asking questions successfully. An inquisitive and nonjudgmental tone works best, and is much better than an accusatory, sarcastic, condescending, or attacking tone — or plain, old-fashioned grilling.

Facilitate and Listen (Don't Dominate or Vacillate)

To make tutoring with questions work in your coaching, you must be an active participant in discussions, playing the primary role of facilitator, which includes actively listening.

A dictionary definition of the word *facilitate* is "to make easy or easier." In a business meeting, a facilitator guides the flow of the meeting so that it achieves the desired outcomes. Your job as facilitator in a coaching discussion with your employee is to guide its flow and allow the employee to easily express his or her thoughts and reach a positive outcome with you. Besides asking inquisitive questions, you need to take a few other steps to effectively facilitate the discussion. The following sections show you how.

Seek positive outcomes

In order to effectively facilitate discussions, you need to know where you want the discussion to go — that is, the *positive outcome* you want to reach. I'm not talking about the specific outcome but a general one. For example, if you are tutoring with questions about a certain problem situation, your positive outcome is to develop a solution. After the general outcome is established, you can then use the two-way discussion to work out the particular solution.

To guide the flow of a discussion, you need to define the direction in which you want to go. At the start of the discussion with your employee, feel free to explain the positive outcome that you have in mind so that the individual can move in the same direction you are moving. (Even in 1492 when sailing the ocean blue, Christopher Columbus told his crew where he wanted to go — despite the fact that he didn't know how to get there.)

The key is that you have a positive outcome in mind. Often, especially in situations in which problems are being raised, managers aren't focusing on a positive conclusion. Here are a couple of favorites that I've heard tossed out:

- ✔ "I want you to see how your behavior is inappropriate and causing me and everyone else here so much pain."
- ✔ "I want you to realize how you should never do this mistake again."

If you want to push guilt or encourage defensiveness, these negative statements will work well. A statement of a positive outcome, on the other hand, is something like this: "Let's discuss what can be learned from this experience and come up with a plan to make things work better going forward." With this positive focus to aim for, most employees will be happy to talk with you about an issue.

Don't forget the four situations in which to tutor with questions (see the "When questions work" section earlier in this chapter). Be sure to phrase your statement of positive outcome around the applicable situation you are working with — solutions, plans, decisions, or doing things better. As you start your coaching discussion with the employee, state the positive outcome that applies to the situation at hand.

Go in a logical flow

The open-ended questions you ask are to help guide the discussion along a reasonable path toward reaching the positive outcome. For example, if your positive outcome is to reach a solution to a problem, follow a systematic approach to get there. Don't explore causes of the problem when you've already developed a solution with the employee. (As in "Hey you screwball, why do you think the system keeps going down on your shift? Next, let's explore ways to put salt on your other wounds.") Or if you're going to discuss the development of a plan with the employee, don't begin by asking questions such as "Now, what would the last step of your plan be?" Instead, move the discussion in a logical step-by-step approach to reach the final stage of the plan.

Certainly, these coaching discussions don't always flow in an organized fashion. And you do want to be flexible enough to explore an unexpected issue that comes up, if needed. The idea, though, is to think about where you're going with the discussion so that your questions follow a direction to get there. Veering off track isn't difficult to correct when you know the track to go on.

Tune in and listen

To effectively facilitate a coaching discussion, you need to be an active listener, not a passive one. A *passive listener,* which is how many people engage in listening, is one who looks at you, sits quietly, and nods his head every now and then to indicate he has a pulse. Little response or interaction takes place. Passive listeners encourage one-way conversations.

In *active listening,* sometimes referred to as *reflective* or *responsive listening,* you work to draw out the speaker's message. More important, you provide nonjudgmental verbal feedback to check your understanding of the speaker's message — herein lies the real key to effective facilitation in a coaching discussion. So the focus is *not* on what you think of the other person's message, but on what the person really means. When you achieve this understanding, you are truly listening.

Here are a few active listening tools to help you in the tutoring with questions discussion:

- ✓ **Paraphrasing:** "So what you are saying is . . . ." When paraphrasing, you summarize in one sentence the main idea of the speaker's message to see whether you understood it correctly.

- ✓ **Reflecting feelings:** "Sounds like what happened has caused you a good deal of frustration. Is that right?" When emotion, either positive or negative, is prevalent in a message, you can use reflecting feelings to check and show understanding of the emotional meaning in the speaker's message.

✔ **Probing:** "Tell me more about how that idea might work." Probing is asking an open-ended question to draw out the speaker's thoughts, like you do when tutoring with questions, but you're also probing when you ask a follow-up question to take the message to a greater depth.

When you're tutoring with questions (not torturing with questions), you're guiding the flow of the discussion with your open-ended questions to reach a positive outcome. To help guide this flow, periodically explore points to a greater depth (probing), and along the way, check to see whether you understand what the employee means (by paraphrasing or reflecting feelings and other messages). When you make these efforts, your active listening allows the staff person to think and sort through thoughts and come up with workable outcomes that he or she can implement. Now that's coaching.

Handling Challenging Bumps along the Road

Understanding when it's best to apply tutoring with questions — that is, when developing plans, creating solutions, learning to do something different or better, and making decisions — is a key part of achieving success with this coaching tool. However, challenges can occasionally happen with some employees. When you hit one of these bumps and quickly abandon the use of this coaching tool by going into the I-tell-you-what-to-do mode, you diminish employees' abilities to think and take responsibility for themselves. You also implicitly send the message, "I only give the appearance of being open, but want you to do what I want you to do or tell me what I want to hear." And if this pattern develops when you have a challenging conversation with an employee, it's good-bye to commitment and hello to the game of torturing with questions.

So you need to stay the course even when you encounter two of the most difficult challenges in trying to make this coaching tool work. In the next sections, I look at two such challenges and give some tips for working through them. (Wiring the chair your employee sits in during discussions with you, and then hitting a button to give electric shock when you don't like what you hear may be fun, but it's not one of the recommended tips. Buzz! Try again. You say you want a raise? Buzz! Say what now?)

The "I-don't-know" employee

Ever have a staff member in your group who no matter how good your question is, automatically come backs with "I don't know?" (Sometimes this response doesn't happen initially, but comes when you are getting into the crux of the conversation and are seeking the employee's ideas for handling a situation.) In such cases, if you feel like jumping in and saying "Just do this and get out of here," I'd understand. Unfortunately, doing so discourages employee thinking and encourages more I-don't-know responses in the future.

Here are some tips to overcome this bump in the road.

- ✔ **Bounce back and wait patiently.** To *bounce back* means to bounce your question back to the employee again or simply say, "Well, what do you think?" Then wait patiently. Your patient manner is the critical factor in stimulating someone else's thoughts. When you wait patiently, as opposed to anxiously, you allow silence to work as a stimulator for the other person. It says to the employee, "I'll wait for your answer. Feel free to take your time to gather your thoughts."

  Silence with patience also applies positive pressure to the person who has been asked the question. "Hey, my manager really wants me to think and wants to hear what I have to say. I'd better come up with something." If you become anxious or irritated, you shut down any possible flow of conversation.

  Use this tip when employees come frequently to ask you what to do, especially if you think they should know what to do (see the upcoming sidebar, "Better coaching by asking questions," for an example).

- ✔ **Simplify the question.** Sometimes your question may come across to the employee as too broad or difficult, so the initial response may be, "I don't know." This response may follow questions like "What ideas do you have for a solution?" Or "What would your plan be to address this issue?"

  So when you get the I-don't-know response, usually accompanied by the deer-in-the-headlights look, simplify the question. Say something like, "Give me one idea that you think will help." The message that you want to impart is that, at this stage, there are no bad ideas. You want your employee to share one that he or she thinks will help.

Better coaching by asking questions

Here's an example of a manager who changed her behavior after she discovered how coaching could help her, especially through tutoring with questions.

The day after the manager introduced a new procedure to her staff, Sally Tell-Me-What-To-Do came to the manager, as she often did, and asked, "About that new procedure we're suppose to use today, what exactly am I suppose to do again?"

Instead of repeating what she had explained the day before, as she often did, the manager bounced back and replied, "What do you think you do?" Then she waited patiently, and after a few seconds, Sally spoke up and explained the procedure step-by-step. The manager then responded, "Sally, you got it," and Sally responded with a beaming face, a reaction that the manager had seldom seen. Letting employees think for themselves is a-okay.

✔ **Draw upon past successes.** Sometimes, you may be aware that an employee has dealt in the past with challenges similar to the one that's currently baffling him or her. If so, instead of asking the employee (who cannot think of anything) to come up with ideas, shift to analyzing a similar past experience in which the employee achieved success.

You want your questions to encourage the employee to figure out what he or she did successfully in the past. You can then offer your insights, as needed. By drawing on these successes and tutoring with questions, you can help the employee see which ones can be used in the current situation. Quite often, what worked well once, but was forgotten, can work well again.

✔ **Consider what the Lone Ranger would do.** When an employee is stuck and can offer little more than a pondering I-don't-know answer, you can try shifting the focus away from the employee. Insert a respected source of expertise that you both know or admire. "How would our hero, the Lone Ranger, handle this situation?" Or more likely, "If Jane were still here and faced with this challenge, what do you think she would do?" This question allows both you and the employee to remove yourselves from the situation temporarily and become creative, focusing instead on what the employee thinks a proven performer would do.

When you don't like their ideas

The second challenge that causes knee-jerk reactions from managers and defeats the purpose of tutoring with questions occurs when an employee shares an idea that you don't agree with or like at all. And to compound the problem, the employee often expresses the idea with a great deal of enthusiasm.

You probably know that rolling your eyes and reacting in a sharp tone with something like "That idea stinks — it will never work!" won't inspire more ideas. What do you do instead? Here are some ideas:

✔ **Explore the rationale and consequences.** Find out the rationale behind the employee's thinking. To do that, have the individual explain his or her thinking directly, by asking or saying

 • "Explain your thinking or rationale for that idea."

 • "What do you see as the pluses and minuses of that idea?"

 • "What do you see as the ramifications of going with that proposal?"

These questions help you and the employee look at the thinking behind the idea and analyze its possible consequences, with the employee, through your questioning, leading the way in the analysis.

By stepping back first and helping the staff person analyze what has been suggested, he or she is able to conclude what will work and what won't — without becoming defensive. At the same time, by letting the employee think out loud and make his or her case, you may realize that something you didn't think would work will work after all. Isn't that the definition of open-mindedness?

✔ **Check your understanding first.** This means, of course, listening all the way through. As needed, ask more questions so that the employee fully explains his or her idea. Then paraphrase what you hear to see whether you understand the message correctly. "What you're suggesting as the best way to resolve this problem is to run a smear campaign to get the manager in this challenging department fired. Is that right?"

Two things often come out of an active listening effort.

- The employee's idea is clarified. And because you may not have fully understood the idea, after it's clarified, you may realize that it's not so bad after all.

- By paraphrasing, you serve as a sounding board for the employee — who now realizes, through the playback of the message, that his or her idea isn't a good one to pursue. Even if the employee doesn't come to this realization, and you don't think the idea is a good one, you at least understand where the person is coming from and can proceed with the previous tip of exploring the rationale and consequences, or use the following strategy.

✔ **State your concern and let him or her address it.** Beyond dismissing the employee's idea outright, the worst thing you can do is to say you like the idea, when you really don't, just so that you won't hurt the person's feelings.

Managing assertively (as discussed in Chapter 2) is a critical part of how coaching works. You don't want to mislead the employee. Instead, constructively state your concern about the individual's suggestion and explain why. Put your explanation within the context of not seeing how the idea will help to achieve your objective or positive outcome. That way, you sound reasonable, as opposed to being biased or an opinionated jerk who can't listen. You also help align the employee with where he or she needs to go in terms of performance.

When you finish your explanation (and don't be long-winded), say something like "Please address" or "With my concern in mind, explain to me how what you proposed would work." Doing so keeps a two-way conversation going and allows for a good give-and-take dialogue, rather than a raucous debate or sparring contest.

This strategy does two things for the employee, as well. It gives the individual valuable input to consider and, if the person still feels the idea has merit, the opportunity to address your concerns and prove the merit of the idea. That's challenging employees to think for themselves at its best — a key part of the mentoring tools of coaching.

The Case of Tutoring with Questions

The following shares a live example of tutoring with questions:

Dick is a capable supervisor who reports to you. He manages a group of five that includes Jane, his top technical performer and his biggest challenge. The two of them clash at times, especially when they have a difference of opinion on how something should be done.

Earlier today at Dick's staff meeting, the two of them knocked heads over a problem in their work process: Dick expressed much concern over what he viewed as a lack of progress by the team in resolving this issue and Jane reacted and commented how he is not seeing the steps she and the team have been taking to resolve the issue. Discussion at the meeting died after their clash with one another.

You learn of this conflict shortly after the meeting, when, on his way to a customer appointment, Dick tells you what happened. Not long after that, you pass Jane in the hallway, who expresses to you her growing frustration with Dick's "dictatorial and reactive management style."

Now, near the end of the day, Dick is back in your office still stewing over this latest incident of Jane's "obstinate ways." He tells you he wants to sit her down and set her straight. "She needs to know who is in charge of this group! Right?"

So how might you handle this challenging situation by tutoring with questions? Follow along:

> **You:** "Let's explore this issue you have with Jane. Whatever we work out, I want it to ensure that you and Jane can work together effectively and that you get the best out of Jane, who is your most talented performer." (Statement of positive outcome.)
>
> **Dick:** "Ultimately, I want the same thing."
>
> **You:** "Right now, I'm hearing a lot of frustration from you about Jane. Is that right?" (Reflecting feelings.)
>
> **Dick:** "Yes, you're right. She's the biggest frustration and challenge among my staff. Life is not easy with her, but she's a stellar worker."
>
> **You:** "Keeping this in mind, what would happen if, in this frustrated manner, and even without it, you sat Jane down and let her know she needs to straighten up because you're the boss?" (Open-ended question for initial analysis of the situation.)
>
> **Dick:** "I would instantly offend her. That would only make matters worse. But I still see the need to talk with her."

You: "Yes. So how could you do so more effectively?" (Open-ended question to generate ideas toward the positive outcome.)

Dick: "I would probably need to give her constructive feedback on the behavior that causes me concern."

You: "That's putting a coaching skill you learned recently into good use. Where would you go from there in your discussion with Jane?" (Words of encouragement followed by an open-ended question to explore further steps to take.)

Dick: "I would probably need to listen to her next. As you and I have said before, I could listen patiently. I'm certain I do things that irritate her at times."

You: "So, in essence, you're going to state your concerns to her and then hear her concerns about you, in a constructive manner. Right?" (Paraphrasing.)

Dick: "Exactly."

You: "What do you see doing next in the conversation to reach a positive outcome?" (Moving the conversation in a logical flow with the next open-ended question.)

Dick: "We likely need to work out how we can better communicate with one another, especially when we have differences. Clashing with one another just creates friction."

You: "Dick, how will you facilitate this problem-solving discussion with Jane?" (Follow-up probing to explore the idea deeper.)

Dick: "Knowing how Jane works, I need to ask for her ideas first. Then I can add mine. Then together we can evaluate what will help us communicate effectively."

You: "Dick, to recap, the plan sounds like you want to take a solutions-oriented and patient approach to addressing your issues with Jane. Am I hearing you correctly?" (Paraphrasing.)

Dick: "That sums it up pretty well. The key for me is recognizing that I should take this tack more often with Jane."

You: "Can you meet with her this week and check back with me to let me know how things worked out?" (Moving toward closure and setting follow-up.)

Dick: "Sure can. I'll talk with her tomorrow and let you know shortly after how things went."

When you tutor with questions, conversations can go in many possible directions. That is the fun of it. But as the preceding scenario with Dick and Jane illustrates, your questions cause the employee to think first and then go perform, which is much better than acting first and regretting it later.

In the scenario with Dick, you, his manager, didn't offer ideas. In many cases, you can and should offer input as part of the flow of the discussion. Yet, in many cases, your questions do the job itself, and often, the employee comes up with better ideas than you might have.

To summarize, here are the key steps you can take to use this coaching tool successfully.

- **Aim for a positive outcome.** It's helpful, of course, to have a positive outcome in mind and to state it at the beginning of the coaching discussion. Doing so puts the employee at ease and gives the discussion a sense of purpose. But make sure the outcome you're seeking is truly a positive one.

- **Go in a logical flow.** With the positive outcome as the guiding light for the discussion, organize the questions you ask so that they reach the outcome. This approach allows the two of you to move together. Even if you get off track, you know the track to get back onto, which is much better than meandering and having fragmented conversations.

- **Ask first, offer second.** Give your input in the flow of the discussion and only when it's really needed. Let the employee think first and take the lead in developing ideas. Avoid starting off by giving your ideas.

- **Keep the questions open-ended.** Only use this strategy if you want to stimulate thoughts from the employee and have a lively, positive discussion. Otherwise, go close-ended and let the torturing with questions begin (just kidding!).

- **Actively listen.** This effort not only helps you understand the employee and have the person feel that he or she is being heard, but it also pushes you to concentrate and stay in control. That's when your facilitation in this coaching effort really comes to fruition. A participating and non-judgmental listener truly stimulates a rich conversation.

- **Be sincere and patient.** When you tutor with questions, conversations can go from brief to lengthy, depending on the issues involved and the individuals attached to them. As long as you're sincere (not grilling the employee) and patient (not anxious), you'll achieve the positive outcome you're seeking and the commitment of the employee to make it happen. In the long run, and sometimes even immediately, you see an employee who can take responsibility and handle situations confidently. That's a great payoff for your patience.

- **Reinforce successes.** When employees walk away from the tutoring discussion with a plan or solution to act on, they're on the road to success. Do your follow-ups and see what has happened. Most likely, you'll see success and when you do, shower the employee with positive feedback. The more you recognize employees for applying what they learn and achieving good results with it, the more you ensure that they perform self-sufficiently.

Impacting the Pillars of Commitment

The tool of tutoring with questions can positively influence the five pillars for building employee commitment (see Chapter 2). In fact, I am going to ask you to explain how each pillar gets impacted with this coaching tool. (A little tutoring with questions for you.) Go one at a time in whatever order you want.

- ✔ **Involvement:** Involvement, you say, gets hit big time. Yes indeed, but how so? That's right, questions greatly involve the employees in developing the plan, solution, or other positive outcome you're discussing. The employees execute what gets worked out in their own performance, instead of the manager doing that for them or constantly telling them what to do.

- ✔ **Development:** You say that this pillar and the preceding one are the two pillars most positively influenced by asking questions? You have a good point. You're saying that this tutoring tool pushes employees to do much of their own thinking for themselves? The purpose of the coaching conversation is for employees to learn and create, and then go perform based on what they created. Well said, that's developing people at its best.

- ✔ **Focus:** What about this pillar? Uh huh, I see — good point. You're saying that this one is influenced through a guiding approach that works towards reaching positive outcomes. In the end, employees walk away with a clear understanding of what they're going to do and how that will help achieve a positive outcome. Nicely put.

- ✔ **Accountability:** You're ready to explain this one without my even having to ask a question? Well, go ahead. You say that tutoring with questions pushes responsibility to employees. Instead of the manager being the all-knowing, all-telling person, the manager's questions push employees to think of their own solutions or plans and act upon them. By holding follow-ups with you as needed, employees own their results. They get to experience the success of their own ideas. Here's accountability at its best. I agree.

- ✔ **Gratitude:** You don't know here? Think about it for a moment. Give me one way that this pillar is affected by asking questions. (You're just trying to test me.) Oh, good answer. You're telling me that if the successes that employees gain from the tutoring lessons applied are recognized by managers, gratitude occurs. Definitely. And the opportunities to do so are numerous.

Now, to close our conversation. You have recognized how tutoring with questions can positively impact the five pillars for building strong employee commitment. So what are you waiting for (rhetorical question)? Go out and put this tool into practice right away. You're welcome; glad you liked my questions and my listening.

Chapter 10

Taking Them under Your Wing

In This Chapter

▶ Understanding "wing taking" and when to use it

▶ Using others to help in the development of your staff

▶ Working with employees who aren't interested in being under your wing

▶ Influencing employee commitment with this coaching tool

*E*ver heard someone say "He took me under his wing" or "I'm going to take her under my wing?" Taking an employee under your wing — or *wing-taking,* as I often call it in this chapter, is an important part of the mentoring and tutoring tools of coaching. Devoted attention is given on an ongoing basis with an employee to help that person grow and gain greater competence, and often maturity, too. It may involve targeting a behavior, skill, or area of responsibility for development.

This chapter shares why and how to take employees under your wing.

Flying in the Right Direction by Taking Employees Under Your Wing

Look at the staff you have today and assess each employee in terms of where you'd like to see them grow in their skills and capabilities — technically as well as behaviorally — that is, their job skills and knowledge, and their conduct and relations with others in getting the job done. Most managers, if they sit back and think about it, can make a list of ways in which developing employee potential can lead to payoffs. The following sections help you do this.

Starting with some reflection

Taking someone under your wing is about taking employees from a decent level of performance and working with them to move to an outstanding level. If you have an employee who has deficiencies and is performing in one or more aspects of her job at a less-than-satisfactory level, coach to improve first, to get her up to a decent level of performance, and then get the wings flapping from there to help her grow. (For the handful of employees who can't improve and their performance is having a negative impact on productivity and other people, you may be working them off the team — more about this in Chapter 16.)

Look at weaknesses not as anything detrimental or negative, but as areas in which a little work can enhance performance.

For example, when Susan, a director, assessed one of her managers, Milt, she viewed Milt's lack of understanding of how other areas in the business affect the operations in Milt's area as a weakness. This weakness, in reality, is an area of development — it had little negative impact on Milt's performance. If Milt could grow his understanding of other areas, it would help him in his interactions with his peers and could increase his promotion potential, which Susan is considering.

Knowing where you can plant seeds that grow

Wing-taking focuses on getting the most out of employees' potential. It is often about helping employees smooth out their rough edges, helping them gain experience and confidence to shine, and, in a metaphoric terms, turning caterpillars into butterflies or planting seeds to become beautiful flowers. It is you playing mentor to your employees, as discussed in Chapter 8.

The following are some examples of caterpillars that can be pushed into butterflies. (No grasshoppers, as in the original *Kung Fu* television show. Although this is the right idea for taking someone under your wing, no one wants to be referred to as "Grasshopper!")

- Develop a technically solid performer to take on project-leading responsibilities.
- Assist a talented and creative employee in developing effective interpersonal skills to work well with others.
- Boost an inexperienced yet eager employee to competently handle higher level responsibilities.

✔ Groom a strong staff member to move up into a management role one day, possibly even to be your successor.

You can often increase your likelihood of moving up in an organization when you have your successor ready to step in and take your place.

✔ Help a new supervisor gain confidence and competence as a manager.

✔ Build a manager's knowledge and perspective of how internal operations or external sales or customer factors affect the business and his area of responsibility.

✔ Stimulate an executive to develop a broader company and leadership perspective.

✔ Prepare an administrative staff person to move one day into a professional level role.

These aren't the only possibilities to take someone under your wing, but the common theme in all of them is that you're taking an employee who performs fairly well and shows need and potential for growth, and working with him or her to help make this growth happen.

Your wing serves as a supportive cover. You're interested in the employee succeeding and are willing to support efforts to help make that success happen.

Putting wing-taking into action

To begin taking employees under your wing, follow these steps:

1. **Assess your employees' strengths and weaknesses in all aspects of their performance and look where areas targeted for their growth can be beneficial for them, as well as for the business.**

   Keep in mind the eight examples listed in the previous section so that you're targeting meaningful situations for your employees' growth.

2. **Share your views with your employees and get their take, as well, through one-on-one conversations.**

   Target the areas in agreement. Generally, stay away from the areas where resistance to work on them exists.

3. **For each employee, set a plan together.**

   The plan should target the area for growth and identify which actions the employee will take and what you will do to support the efforts. Utilizing the buddy system can be a part of the support strategies (see the following section). Keep the plan informal, so that it serves as a guide versus a stringent rule book.

A look at wing-taking in action

Toni transferred to a different office in her company to become the branch manager. Among the eight employees on her team was Julie, technically the strongest performer and also a person who showed leadership abilities.

After being on the job for three months, Toni got to know Julie quite well and saw her strengths and where she could grow in her effectiveness. She called Julie in one day and gave her assessment in specific terms of Julie's strengths — output, quality, technical knowledge, and the respect of her team — and where she could increase her effectiveness, which was in her interactions with fellow team members. Toni's feedback shared observations of how Julie sometimes rolled her eyes, displayed sharpness in her tone, and made sarcastic comments towards other team members in meetings and in one-on-one interactions.

Julie agreed with the assessment and was able to laugh about her interactions, revealing that was her frustration getting the best of her. Sometimes the other staff did and said things that irritated her or weren't focused on the issue at hand. She didn't intend to hurt others or create friction.

They agreed to work on Julie's interpersonal leadership to increase her effectiveness, especially because Julie desired to become a supervisor one day. They outlined a simple plan to do this that defined the key behaviors Julie needed to focus on to stay positive, especially when she started to get frustrated with other staff. In addition, Toni was to periodically share management strategies and plans with Julie to get her input and to give her exposure to these issues. Julie and Toni met every three weeks to share feedback and review Julie's progress.

A couple of months into the mentoring effort, a few of the employees in the office, individually and unsolicited, remarked to Toni how positive Julie had been these days. Whatever she was doing with Julie, they said, keep it up: Julie was certainly someone they could support as a supervisor if the opportunity ever occurred — which happened a short time later.

This is an example of wing-taking at its best.

---

4. **Follow through on the plans with your employees.**

   Do whatever you said you would do to provide support. In many cases, this may mean having conversations with your employees and sharing some knowledge or experience, or it may mean connecting them to resources — people, information, training, and so on — that can be of help to them.

   Much of this effort can be included as part of the checkup-review meeting that's detailed in Chapter 7. No need to create new structures if existing ones serve as useful vehicles.

Using the Buddy System Now and Then

The great thing about taking someone under your wing is that you don't necessarily have to do the whole job yourself. You can use other resources — internal or external — to help in the growth and polish of your employees. Your job as manager is to connect your employees to resources that can be helpful to them and to your coaching efforts.

Staying inside — using internal resources

Wing-takers for your staff members can come from many directions inside your organization. Here are some examples:

- **Fellow members in your group:** Pair a senior level staff person with a junior level staff member or an experienced staff member (not necessarily with higher skills or in a higher position) with a less experienced staff person. This senior or more experienced employee often works alongside your junior or less experienced employee and has knowledge, skill, and experience to pass on to help in this person's development. Because this wing-taker has the opportunity to spend more time on a day-to-day basis than you do with this particular employee, he or she can, in essence, serve as an assistant pilot in your efforts to take employees under your wing.

- **Senior level employees from other groups:** On occasion, a senior-level employee from another group in your organization can help be wing-takers for an employee during a special assignment, project, or task that pairs these two employees together. To get value out of this arrangement, find out which resources outside your group are interested and willing to give attention and to share their expertise and experience in working with your employee.

- **Managers from other groups:** Managers from other groups can be great wing-takers, but be prepared to offer this service in return someday. During special projects, when working on task forces or other special committees, or when given short-term rotational assignments, this manager may play a lead role and your employee may be part of the work group.

- **Staff specialists in the organization:** Sometimes you have people in your organization who, due to the nature of their jobs, perform staff support functions for everyone in the company and thus have expertise in that area. This can be someone in finance or accounting, a human resources representative, or a safety specialist. Sometimes, these resources can be people whom your employee seeks out to gain more knowledge in an area that helps your employee and your department.

For example, Jacob took Sharon, who's on his staff, under his wing. One of the key areas of improvement that they targeted was her knowledge of the company's budgeting and recruiting processes. Jacob looked to Sharon to take on a more lead role for the group, especially as it related to financial management and hiring. So, with Jacob's assistance, Sharon periodically spent time with Greg in Accounting to learn about budgeting and cost control issues and with Kim in Human Resources to learn about sourcing candidates and interviewing effectively.

✔ **Your boss:** In some cases, your own boss can serve as a good wing-taker for your staff. When you need extra support or want your employees to gain technical or business insight, you may want to connect your employees to your boss. Make sure that your boss is willing and available and that he or she knows what outcomes you're looking for.

For many bosses, helping out like this is a great treat. Junior staff coming to them for wisdom and advice means little responsibility and great fun at the same time — not a bad combination.

Opening the door and letting the outsiders in

Outside consultants can often be helpful resources when employing the buddy system to take someone under your wing. Consultants, who often call this one-on-one arrangement with a client *coaching,* can bring expertise that can be beneficial to your employee. The idea of external coaches has been increasing in companies, and is certainly useful.

Because you are the *sponsor* of such a resource — and they do come with a cost — you want to stay in touch with their efforts in working with your employee. With that in mind, do the following with the external consultant or coach:

✔ Have defined objectives for what you want this coach to concentrate on with your employee.

✔ Make sure your employee agrees with these objectives and wants to work with an external resource on them. Don't spend time and money if the target of your efforts, your staff person, is only working with a coach to appease you.

✔ In most cases, set time limits for the assignment.

✔ Check in with the coach and the employee periodically to monitor progress along the way.

✔ Share with the coach what you are seeing in the employee's efforts to add insight to the work that person is doing with your staff member.

> ✔ Find out from the coach what you can do with your employee to reinforce the work the coach is doing.
>
> ✔ Express your gratitude for the good work the external resource does with your employee and give positive feedback to your employee on his or her development successes.

When you're utilizing the services of an outside coach to work with staff members of yours, you want to stay connected. Yet at the same time, to allow the coaching efforts to be effective, you need to respect the confidentiality of the coach-mentor relationship that often develops. Focus on what the employee is working on and learning with the coach, not on what he or she is talking about with the coach. Give your employees the safety to talk freely because that is what you'd want if you were working with a coach for your own needs. By your coming in with objectives about what the coach should put attention to, you can allow the coach-mentor relationship between the coach and your employee to develop its own chemistry without running amok.

You, too, want to maintain a relationship with the coach you hire to help work with your staff. Use the coach as a supplemental guide in your mentoring efforts with your employees.

Choose as an external resource to help out in your mentoring efforts someone in whom you can have confidence: someone who will work with your agenda and who not only brings expertise — which is why you bring such a person in — but also articulates strategies on how to execute your agenda in the coaching work.

> ✔ Talk to other managers and your human resources department for leads on good external resources.
>
> ✔ When you attend outside seminars and conferences, keep an eye out for trainers or presenters as resources for one-on-one coaching.
>
> ✔ Professional organizations are popping up that train people to become coaching resources, too. Publications about professional associations, as well as the Internet, can be sources to find out about these coaching groups.

Getting your money's worth out of wing assistants

When you call on internal resources to assist you in your wing-taking efforts, keep in mind that you aren't looking for those resources to *manage* your employees for you. Think of parenting: While relatives often don't mind taking your children for a day or two or for some fun activity, most aren't interested in becoming parents to those kids.

Calling on the outside coach

Mary was a senior-level manager. She herself had worked with a management coach off and on over a period of time and had found this person very helpful as a source to work through her own management challenges and issues.

When some of those challenges involved developing three junior-level supervisors, especially when they ran into some bumps along the way in their performance, Mary hired the coach to work with these junior managers. All three were talented performers but were inexperienced as managers.

- With one supervisor, the coach worked with her on communication skills so she expressed herself more effectively with her staff and her clients.

- With another supervisor, the coach worked on how to coach his staff and how to set a positive tone in his group, showing leadership by example in his behavior.

- With the third supervisor, the coach was called on to help her work on addressing some performance challenges in her group and gain improvement with them.

In all three cases, Mary outlined what she wanted the coach to focus on with each person. The coach usually had four to five visits with each person, usually about two hours per session over the course of two to three months. In each case, Mary saw the supervisors grow in both ability and confidence. "The good doctor," as she refereed to the management coach, was a great supplemental resource to Mary's efforts to mentor her staff.

You also don't want wing-taking buddies to give directions to your employees that will undermine your efforts and needs for your employees in their jobs. And you don't want buddies to share their bad habits or do other things that can adversely influence your employees.

Therefore, to make these buddy arrangements work effectively, keep the following tips in mind:

- **You take the lead role.** You're the one taking your employees under your wing. When you use internal resources in this effort, it's to enhance your ability to challenge and develop your staff; in essence, to increase your wing span. When you abdicate this responsibility to others, your wing-taking won't work well. But when you lead the effort, you're still involved and connected to your employees and to what they're working on and learning from others.

- **Indicate what kind of help you want and get real agreement for it.** Avoid the common mistake managers make: "Joe, I want you to work with Bob here and help him out." Joe, being the compliant type, usually gives an affirmative nod and smiles, and then you walk away. Joe then wonders what he is suppose to do with Bob and either has him tag around for awhile or tells him, "Look, I got a lot of work to do and have little time to bother with anything or anyone else."

Instead, start with the internal resource by clearly asking for his help and defining where it can be put to good use with the buddy employee. Let him know where you want him to put his attention and target efforts with his buddy.

Say, for example, "Joe, because of your experience with our product, I'd like you to work with Bob to share your insights and to teach him the paths you've followed to success. Please tell me if you're interested in helping and how you can make this work with Bob." Work out the objectives and estimated time for Joe to spend with Bob so that their time and attention is efficient.

✔ **Set time limits.** Avoid leaving the buddy arrangement open-ended. A time limit can be the duration of a project, a few months to help an employee through a learning curve, or an ongoing relationship for particular needs. Setting a time limit avoids locking either party into a situation that outlives its usefulness. If the two work well together, which is your intent, they can call upon each other as a helpful resource when the need arises in the future.

✔ **Monitor progress.** Periodically check with your assistant winger-taker to see how your employee is progressing. Do the same with your employee to see how the efforts are going from his perspective. Also monitor what you're seeing in your employees' performance related to the areas you've targeted with your buddy-system efforts. Give feedback to your employee on this performance and share any feedback you may have received from the buddy. Encourage the buddy to give your employee feedback all along the way.

✔ **Express appreciation.** Show appreciation for the buddy who is helping your employee learn and grow. The buddy is sharing his knowledge and experience and giving some attention to someone else at the same time.

Stay connected with both the employee and the buddy. Keep in mind that you're the one who's leading the wing-taking efforts — outside or inside resources only supplement your efforts.

Wing-Taking Isn't for Pluggers

Many employees, when you take them under your wing, thrive on the interest and support you provide and, as a result, experience much growth. The ambitious employees, in particular, really develop under this coaching tool.

Getting under your boss's wings: A bit on managing upwards

If you're like many managers who make the effort to take your employees under your wing, you may wish you had the same efforts provided by your boss to you. Unfortunately, you may have a boss who shows little inclination to spread his or her wings. If you're willing to manage upwards, however, you can indirectly gain some quality mentoring from your boss. Here are a few tips to help make this happen.

✔ **Recognize strengths, don't dwell on weaknesses.** You can put a lot of wasted energy into fretting about the actions of your boss that may be less than effective. Instead of dwelling on your manager's shortcomings, identify the strengths. What knowledge, skills, or other qualities does your manager have from which you can gain value.

✔ **Initiate actions that allow you to access the strengths.** Create ways to periodically connect with your boss and set the agenda for what you want to learn from him or her. Whether it be occasional meetings, morning coffee chats, or lunch out together, take the initiative and set up the communication vehicle that allows you to have access to your boss on your terms.

Here's an example: A manager once complained that she had little regular communication with her boss and that the only times he ever came to her was to ask her to do something or to criticize her for a problem. To change this pattern, she set up one-on-one meetings with her boss about once every three weeks. She used the meetings to hear about her manager's experiences and to ask questions to tap into his broad knowledge base. These inputs were of great value to the work she did and thus the meetings became very productive for her.

✔ **Make giving support easy to do.** Avoid wishing for your boss to do things that don't fit his or her character. Instead, make providing you with support an easy thing to do. Many bosses will allow you to take time to attend a conference or seminar or will be happy to pass on words of recognition to a staff member of yours when asked to do so. These are examples of simple ways that your boss can support you in your own development and coaching efforts. And as you need, seek feedback on how you're doing in your performance.

Keep your requests for support simple and positive so that your boss can look good without breaking a sweat. That's managing upwards at its best.

✔ **Create your own mentoring plan as if you were the manager of you.** What areas would you target if you were the subject of someone else's wing-taking efforts? If you aren't sure, ask your staff and they can tell you what to work on. Outline the steps you can take to work on your area for development. Also outline simple strategies for accessing your manager's strengths and for getting occasional support. Now you have your own mentoring plan — run with it!

✔ **Access your own buddy resources.** Don't look at your manager as your sole source for wing-taking. What other managers or individuals, inside and outside your organization, can you learn from and have a relationship with? Seek them out and create quality time with them, during which you access their strengths and value. Budget to have your own management coach.

Yet for some employees, called *pluggers,* when you attempt this coaching method, they push back against your wings. They seem resistant to your coaching. And, as coaching goes, that's okay.

What's a plugger?

Pluggers are the "Steady Eddie" employees. They do what you ask them to do and usually do it well, but only do the basics. Ask them to take on more challenge or stretch beyond the basics of their job descriptions, and they say "No, thank you." Career ambition? What's that? Desire to grow professionally? No way!

Yet pluggers are valuable assets. They're willing to do the mundane or routine duties that have to get done and usually do them without complaint. Their interests are different from many other employees, including you, their manager. They show no career ambition nor profess to any.

Many pluggers are satisfied to stay at their current levels in the organization. They aren't seeking new challenges or opportunities. They like their job situations just the way they are and aren't interested in changing anything if they don't need to do so.

For many pluggers, the job is a paycheck: a place to earn a living and pay the bills. Quite often, pluggers have interests outside the job. Their main concern may be with spending time with their families. You can count on them to be reliable and plug right along in getting their assignments done, but to get them to go above and beyond isn't likely to occur.

Plugging in the plugger in the right direction

John was a veteran firefighter who had been on the job for 20 years. He did a good job, yet unlike most firefighters in his department with half his experience, John had never made any effort to seek out the opportunity to move up to the level of fire captain — the first-level supervisory position.

When his supervisor wanted to work with John to help him learn about the role of a captain and then take the exam for the position, John resisted. What the supervisor soon learned, by directly asking John, was that John was satisfied being a firefighter. Anything to do with what a supervisor's job entailed was of no interest to him. The mentoring efforts in this direction then ended.

John's supervisor then redirected his efforts to capitalize on John's experience and knowledge as a veteran firefighter. Instead of working with him to become a captain, he kept John doing the duties he was good at doing, gave him projects that required initiative, and had him share this experience with junior firefighters. By having John work more closely with the less seasoned staff, he was fully utilizing John at his own level — fully plugged in.

Pluggers aren't the same as *ROTJ (retired on the job)* employees. ROTJers do as little as possible and look to blend in and not be noticed. Some call them *slackers.* They are performance problems, because their lack of effort usually creates a negative impact on productivity and other staff.

Getting the best out of your pluggers

Pluggers work hard and get things done. They do what they're asked to do and usually not much more than that. Often, because they're experienced, they require little close supervision. Because their managers see little initiative beyond the basic scope of their responsibilities, as well as little interest in professional growth, many managers tend to leave pluggers alone and ask little of them, which they usually don't mind: When the end of the day rolls around, they are right out the door.

Just because taking a plugger under your wing isn't his or her cup of tea, leaving pluggers alone and avoiding coaching with them isn't the answer. Not everyone is going to become the company president! Here are some tips to maximize the productivity of pluggers.

- ✔ **Recognize their value and keep them busy.** Remember that pluggers can and do perform, but if you give them little, they don't ask for more. Give them as much as possible that fits within the scope of their jobs. This means you can often shift the mundane tasks or the detail-oriented assignments off of others who want to take on more challenges and give them to the plugger in your group to do.

- ✔ **Have others access their strengths.** Some pluggers are quite good at certain tasks of their jobs. Their knowledge and experience, while limited to the tasks of the job they do well, are often assets to others in the group if you tap into them. So while pluggers generally won't seek to learn from others, others in the group can learn from them. Create assignments through which the pluggers share and train others on what they know.

- ✔ **Assign them related tasks or duties, not new ones.** Any assignment labeled as new, different, and exciting, which motivates many employees, often has the opposite effect on pluggers. Safe, routine, and dull assignments may have greater appeal to pluggers. So instead of pushing them to take on new and different duties, give them assignments that are similar to what they have done. Nothing new, just work that may require a little more effort for a short while. This is how you can often enlarge the scope of pluggers' jobs or at least maximize their productivity. Add little bits versus big pieces; go one step at a time versus taking giant leaps.

Spreading wings to develop managers

When Don was promoted to the level of division manager in his organization, an upper middle-management level, he took on a division of over 30 employees with four supervisors. The timing of his promotion worked well as he entered the organization's leadership academy at the same time — a management development program with an emphasis on managing as a coach.

The division Don took on functioned fine but not at an outstanding level. Morale varied among the staff, but also wasn't at a high level. On a division-wide basis, Don began to implement some strategies to build positive change and increase productivity — working with staff to develop a core purpose, setting service standards, defining performance goals, and giving staff substantive performance reviews. (Some of these strategies relate to the coaching tools covered in Chapters 6 and 7.) Don knew that none of the changes he was trying to make would have much effect unless his supervisors' commitment and leadership efforts were behind those efforts.

As a result, Don took each of his four supervisors under his wing, working with them on how to set meaningful performance goals, give constructive feedback, and reinforce teamwork and quality service. He met with each supervisor on a one-on-one basis, usually once a week. At the same time, he enrolled them in the next session of the leadership academy that he had been through.

Periodically, Don exchanged management articles with his staff. In addition, once a month, he held a session with each individual that focused strictly on discussing and learning about leadership issues. When the special session started, Don laid out ten cards on his desk, each with a topic on it — topics such as setting a positive tone, building a team, reinforcing performance, teaching employees, and so on. The job of the supervisor was to pick one for the session, and then be ready to raise questions and to discuss ways to apply the leadership lessons with his own staff.

After one year with his mentoring efforts, the supervisors all reported that their management styles had changed and that morale and performance in the entire division had gone up considerably. One supervisor refused to even be called by that title, preferring to be called a team leader or coach. Commitment was high and respect for Don and his efforts to take them under his wing was even higher.

✔ **Give them the assignment of taking initiative and pitching in to help.** Many pluggers don't seek out and reach out to do or help. Yet pluggers, as part of these habits, tend to willingly do what you ask them to do as long as it falls within the scopes of their jobs. Make clear to them that taking initiative to solve problems and pitching in to help other team members are routine expectations of their job, and then give constructive feedback on how well they take initiative and help out in their scope of responsibilities.

✔ **Don't take them for granted.** While pluggers usually ask little of you and need little guidance, like most employees, they still want to be part of the group and valued as an asset. As such, give them positive feedback when they do something well (not just negative feedback when they make a mistake) and give it periodically to acknowledge that they keep the place running. In particular, acknowledge when you see them stretch: taking initiative to handle a problem or taking on a new task.

Also recognize when something special occurs in their lives outside of work. Build the working relationship with your plugger as you would with any of your other staff. Just recognize that their needs and interests may be different and not job-related. As discussed in Chapter 3, managing people as individuals is true coaching.

Wing-Taking and the Pillars of Commitment

Taking employees under your wing, while informal in nature, is a targeted and ongoing effort aimed at getting the best out of someone's performance potential. It encompasses all of the mentoring and tutoring tools of coaching that are in Chapters 8 and 9.

Does this mentoring tool influence the pillars for building employee commitment, discussed in Chapter 2? You betcha! Here's how:

✔ **Focus:** Taking employees under your wing operates with a plan of attack, not just some ideas you've kicked around or left in the back of your mind. You and your employee know what area or areas to work on with steps identified to make performance happen.

✔ **Involvement:** Wing-taking has a major influence on this pillar. Who helps shape the mentoring plan? Who helps drive the plan? Who is encouraged to push you to follow through on your commitments of support? Who is actively involved, besides you, in helping make this coaching plan come alive? Your employees, of course: the people who benefit from your taking them under your wing.

✔ **Development:** Development is at the core of what wing-taking works to do. Its emphasis is on helping employees grow in their skills and capabilities to reach their full potential.

✔ **Accountability:** The responsibility for driving the mentoring plan is shared between you and the employee with whom you're wing-taking. If both of you follow through on your parts and maintain the ongoing follow-up efforts to review progress, results happen. And your employee experiences a sense of accomplishment through his taking responsibility to help in his own development. When your wing-taking works, he succeeds — and your job gets easier.

✔ **Gratitude:** The pillar of gratitude is influenced a little less directly than the other four pillars by wing-taking. Nonetheless, when you get an opportunity during wing-taking to acknowledge and reinforce employee growth and accomplishments, take it! While getting appreciation and recognition from others, especially you, is important, as your employees experience their own development, a sense of satisfaction grows for themselves too — a sort of self-gratitude.

What employees don't usually know going in (and by all means, don't tell them) is that by being taken under your wing with a focused approach, they end up having to work harder than they ever have before. The reason is simple: Success rides heavily on their own efforts and they respond to your challenging them to perform better. Less effort was required when they worked for managers who gave little interest or attention to maximizing their potential. While providing this attention requires work on your part, payoff does occur for both of you. For your employees, they experience success through the sense of achievement and growth they gain. You, on the other hand, gain greater respect and personal influence, and you have an employee ready to perform better than ever.

Part IV
Motivating and Empowering Your Staff

The 5th Wave   By Rich Tennant

"It's the crew, Captain Columbus. As we appear to be approaching the horizon line at full sail, they'd like to hear your 'Round World Motivational Lecture' one more time."

In this part . . .

This part helps you understand what motivation is all about and explores practical strategies that make a positive difference in stimulating employee performance. You also find how to truly delegate — ways for easing your burdens as a manager that maximize your resources, deliver results, and motivate your staff, too.

Chapter 11

Motivation — Not Inspiration or Perspiration

. . . .

In This Chapter

▶ Defining motivation

▶ Investigating motivators and rewards that have a positive effect

▶ Examining the big issue of motivation and pay

▶ Exploring theories on motivation at work

. . . .

*I*n the public-speaking world, in which people get paid to talk to people, some speakers and celebrities refer to themselves as "motivational speakers." They appear at professional association conferences, conventions, and company-wide meetings, address large audiences with all the enthusiasm and energy they can muster, and hope that you leave the session feeling motivated.

In the same way, some sports coaches like to give hard-hitting pre-game or half-time speeches to rally their players. The effort usually conjures up an image of Knute Rockne, the famed Notre Dame football coach, exhorting his players to "win one for the Gipper." The players get excited and charge out on the field, screaming the whole way.

Evangelical clergy in the religious world and charismatic candidates in the political world may also give rousing sermons to stir their congregations or fiery speeches to rally their political supporters. (But you know what people say about religion and politics, so enough on this.)

Regardless of the arena, these situations are all about inspiration — not motivation. "Motivational speakers" in business and other arenas are really inspirational speakers. If they're able to entertain and excite you, they make you feel good. (Movies often aim to do the same thing; they move you or stir your emotions, although for me, the price for the tickets to the movie is enough to stir my emotions!)

This thinking is that, if you as a manager can get your employees excited and pumped up — and maybe even perspiring heavily — you've motivated them. But you haven't. Motivation is something altogether different: This chapter explains what it is and how you can use it when coaching your staff.

Calling for Action: Understanding Motivation

The focus of motivation is on action. Specifically, look at motivation as meaning something that causes or influences a person to act or perform. As a coaching tool, *motivation* is the creating of conditions that stimulate an employee to achieve a highly productive level of performance.

As a manager, you can influence the conditions that stimulate performance. You can affect people's *motivators*, intrinsic as well as extrinsic factors that drive a person to act or perform. You can also provide *rewards* to motivate employees, things people receive for achieving something in their performance.

You may have heard the saying that the end justifies the means: As long as you get the results desired, who cares what you did to get there. The manager who uses motivation as a coaching tool, however, cares about both, the means and the end. The emphasis is to stimulate good performance, not just for the short term but on an ongoing basis.

The beatings will stop when morale goes up

You may have seen signs or bumper stickers that are similar to this heading. They give you a good chuckle. Unfortunately, it is sometimes the essence of a strategy that managers practice, knowingly and unknowingly, to motivate employee performance.

The core of the figurative beatings strategy is fear. Instilling fear in others and having them be intimidated by you can be a powerful motivator. Here are a few examples — don't try these at home!

- Argue and browbeat a staff member who expresses a disagreement.
- Terminate an employee or two suddenly and without warning to send a message to the rest of the group.
- Chastise employees every time something goes wrong.

✔ Cut employees off when they raise concerns and give orders telling them what to do.

✔ Publicly lambaste someone for a mistake or error in judgment.

✔ Say belittling remarks in an arrogant tone to employee suggestions that aren't seen as worthwhile.

✔ Display loud outbursts of anger when problems are brought to the surface.

If you've been in management, you've probably seen these tactics — and may have even done a few of these yourself.

In the history of human-kind, instilling fear has often attained stunning results, especially for life-threatening situations. In business, where life-threatening situations usually don't exist (although job-threatening ones do), instilling fear in employees may also appear to yield good performance results. The problem with this motivational strategy is that few people like it and few respond to it in a favorable way.

Motivating by fear tends to breed compliance, not commitment; silence opposing views, not stimulate thought-provoking discussion; extinguish morale, not light it up; and create deference to authority and disrespect to you in the position of authority. Its effect, while often immediate, tends to be short-term. So if you have to scream, threaten, or bark orders to get employees to perform, your ability to influence their motivation in any sustaining manner is rather limited.

Why do managers do that?

When well-intentioned managers exhibit harsh behaviors towards employees, the source driving the manager is quite often a stressful, challenging situation. Such situations may be any of the following:

✔ Employee resistance to your direction.

✔ Pressure to meet revenue numbers or other output targets.

✔ A demanding boss not satisfied with your group's results.

✔ High volume of work with limited resources and tight deadlines.

✔ A struggling new employee not coming up to speed fast enough.

✔ An employee performing at a subpar level.

For some managers, when they talk about facing these difficult challenges, they often mention that sometimes you have to "lower the boom" or "come down with your hammer" to deal with these situations — actions of managing aggressively instead of assertively (as discussed in Chapter 2). When managers do so, they often instill fear and intimidation in their employees.

Motivating employees in tough times

Larry and Mary were two managers faced with similar situations. Both managed sales-related functions where group performance was less than expected targets. Here is how each dealt with their challenging, stressful situations.

✔ Mary called a team meeting and outlined to her staff the problems at hand, including her observations of where effort was lacking. In a straightforward manner, she noted that attention to detail, follow through, and hustle were inconsistent in people's efforts, and as a result, the office's numbers were below target.

The group then brainstormed with her on strategies to bring the numbers up. Solutions were developed that clarified goals, promoted teamwork, and identified areas for training. The group's morale picked up, and Mary did the necessary follow-up with individual staff to ensure that plans were carried through and progress reviewed.

✔ Larry took a different approach than Mary. He abruptly terminated a couple of the low performers in the group. The next day, he called each staff member into his office one at a time and gave them a contract to sign. The contract spelled out what goals each person had to meet, even though the targets were at levels few had ever achieved, and stated they would be terminated if the goals weren't met in the next couple of months. The issues of lack of training and inefficient systems were not addressed. From these two back-to-back events, the group's morale took a sudden dip.

While both strategies could yield the desired results, whose do you think would most motivate your performance and build your commitment?

Forsake intimidation, go for positive ways of motivation

When faced with a stressful or challenging situation, step back and determine the results you want to achieve. From there, determine the means to getting to the results desired that will rally your employees *with* you, not against you — for example, collaboratively solving problems, setting goals, clarifying expectations, or conducting progress reviews while staying positive and firm. That is when you use the coaching tool of motivation.

So what are some motivators or rewards that can act as a positive stimulus to employee performance? I've asked groups of managers this very question over the years and let them brainstorm some ideas. Here is the ever-growing list of positive examples of motivators and rewards.

- ✔ A good performance review
- ✔ Accomplishments recognized by top management
- ✔ Article in newsletter recognizing good work, service to customer
- ✔ Autonomy
- ✔ Being kept informed
- ✔ Candy, flowers for appreciation
- ✔ Care and concern from others
- ✔ Cellular phone, laptop computer
- ✔ Challenging work
- ✔ Chance to be creative
- ✔ Chance to create solutions and help overcome obstacles
- ✔ Chance to lead desirable project
- ✔ Chance to learn new things
- ✔ Chance to travel
- ✔ Choice of work schedule and vacations
- ✔ Company T-shirt or other clothing
- ✔ Conducting training
- ✔ Control over how your job gets done
- ✔ Cross training
- ✔ Education benefits
- ✔ Enjoyable assignments
- ✔ Extra time off without using vacation
- ✔ Family-friendly environment

- ✔ Flexible schedule
- ✔ Getting an office or a better office
- ✔ Good communication with your boss and a trusting relationship
- ✔ Good incentives or commissions
- ✔ Good pay raise
- ✔ Group barbecue or potluck
- ✔ Group recreation or social activity
- ✔ Having ideas listened to
- ✔ Influencing decisions and direction
- ✔ Involvement in higher-level meetings
- ✔ Involvement in important decisions
- ✔ Involvement in planning
- ✔ Job enrichment
- ✔ Letter of recognition with a copy to the personnel file
- ✔ Lunch or dinner at the company's expense
- ✔ Making presentations that provide visibility
- ✔ Manager going to bat for you or improvements
- ✔ Mentoring
- ✔ New equipment or tools
- ✔ Paid health club membership
- ✔ Paid membership in professional association
- ✔ Parking place
- ✔ Party to celebrate success

- ✔ Personal note for special occasion
- ✔ Positive feedback
- ✔ Profit sharing
- ✔ Promotion
- ✔ Prompt response to proposals
- ✔ Public recognition
- ✔ Publication of group sales or output results
- ✔ Represent company at special events
- ✔ Sabbatical
- ✔ Seeing ideas put into action
- ✔ Seeing improvement in performance
- ✔ Service recognition award

- ✔ Showing interest in someone's career development
- ✔ Special projects and assignments
- ✔ Spot bonuses
- ✔ Staff support and resources
- ✔ Stock options
- ✔ Support to resolve problems
- ✔ Telecommuting
- ✔ Tickets to sporting event or concert
- ✔ Trophy or plaque
- ✔ Weekend trip at company expense
- ✔ Working with talented, caring people

This wonderful resource list contains both intrinsic and extrinsic motivators and rewards, and, while not all-inclusive, it contains many ideas that managers have some influence or control to use. If you come up with other useful motivators or rewards, add them to the list.

Draw upon the list. Put it in the forefront of your consciousness! When managers look for ways to positively stimulate employee performance, they often become surrounded by motivated employees and positive performance.

Show Me the Money: Pay as Dynamo or Dynamite

The list in the previous section focuses on creating conditions that positively motivate performance. A few of them involve pay, which begs the question: Is pay an effective tool for motivating employees to perform? Get a group of managers together to discuss this question, and often a great debate begins.

To do the coaching tool of motivation justice, you cannot ignore the issue of motivation and money. Scholars and behavioral psychologists who study motivation often have strong opinions on the subject but not usually consensus on their views. In the following sections, I share a collection of views, including my two cents.

All in favor, say "Aye"; all opposed, say "Nay"

When I ask managers if money is a motivator, those who say it is bring up the following points:

- **People perform at what they get paid to do.** Employees don't volunteer to work. They look for opportunities that will pay them well or have good earning potential. If people got paid to play, not many would be showing up to work.

- **The top performing sales people are driven by the commissions they can earn.** They want to beat their quotas to earn their pay rewards.

- **Money is a form of status.** It gives people their sense of importance. If someone feels he is earning less than what his skills or experience call for, he is demotivated in his performance. If he gets what he feels he's worth, he feels satisfied and desires to do a good job. This is why organizations look to set up competitive salary systems in line with the labor market. They want to avoid having employees feel that their value is not fairly compensated.

- **In a materialistic society such as ours, money is a form of sustenance.** People desire it because of the lifestyle it can afford them. They also need it to survive. Thus people are motivated to perform to receive the benefits their pay can buy for them.

- **Money is a form of recognition and reward.** When they get a good raise or receive a bonus, it is a tangible way to recognize contributions of good performance. The financial reward is proof of the good performance delivered, and one many seek to earn.

For all the managers who feel strongly that money is a powerful and important motivator, just as many comment that it really isn't. Here are the comments most commonly said in support of the opposing point of view:

- **People want more out of their jobs than just a good paycheck.** They want good work and good people to work with. If they had lousy working conditions, a nasty boss, boring work, and other negative factors, you couldn't pay people enough to stay in such a job. Satisfying or fulfilling careers are far more of a motivator than money.

- **Money breeds contentment and security.** If employees feel they're paid well, they feel more happy and safe in their situation, but that doesn't mean you get any greater performance out of them. Some professional athletes, as an example, when they earn long-term contracts that give them security, no longer perform at the same level they did prior to earning the big contract.

✔ **Surveys taken on the subject of what employees find motivating in their jobs usually report pay as low on the list.** Factors like recognition, challenging work, and a good company atmosphere often rank higher in importance.

✔ **When you find employees who do a good job and take pride in their work, you also find that money isn't what's driving them.** They like their work and the sense of accomplishment in it. Those are the motivating factors, not money.

✔ **When people only perform for money, they aren't really motivated to perform with quality.** They become like spoiled children whose hands are sticking out waiting for you to drop money in it. They only act when you give it; otherwise, they don't care. The drive to produce and deliver quality performance for the sake of doing a good job gets lost when the focus of jobs is all on money. That's not motivation; it is more like greed.

A few pennies for my thoughts

Here's how I see it: Money has great potential to motivate employee performance — no one usually turns down money or an opportunity to get it. However, money is often very difficult to use in motivating performance. Here are some reasons why.

✔ For most employees, getting a regular paycheck doesn't qualify as something that will greatly influence their performance or productivity. It is much like breathing. You expect it to happen and notice it only when something impedes it.

✔ The importance of money isn't the same for everyone. For some, it may serve as the driving force that pushes them to perform. For others, especially when you see a strong level of dedication, money is often not the reason why. Wanting to make a contribution, wanting to support a good cause, and getting satisfaction out of one's work are factors that push this commitment to excel. For these people, the intrinsic motivators, not money, are what motivate them.

✔ Most salary systems in organizations are designed to pay people more on their position and power within the organization than on their level of competence and quality of performance. The company president is usually the highest paid employee and because of that position of power, has a greater compensation package than the outstanding widget maker in production. The great widget makers at the line-worker level may do a far better job than the bigwig at the top, but that won't be reflected in their pay. (Keep in mind that in some cases, the employees of the company miss the great widget makers, should they leave, much more than they would miss the company president!)

✔ In many organizations, how people move up the salary ladder, based on policy or actual practice, has more to do with time on the job than performance in doing the job. More often than not, people at the top of their salary ranges are the ones who have been with the company the longest.

✔ When pay issues come up, they quite often create more distraction than motivation. When employees feel, whether based on perception or reality, that their pay is not equitable to either other employees at their own company or to similar positions at other companies, you will often see a lack of focus and outward signs of discontent. If correcting the inequity is justified and you're able to do so, you've most often removed the distraction but are still left to figure out what's needed to motivate that employee's performance.

✔ Money can often be a big part of what lures someone into a job, but is less often a significant factor as to what motivates them to stay. Research done on issues of retention and turnover more often report that the quality of manager, the growth potential in one's career, the challenge and fulfillment in the work, the amount of recognition, and the culture and values exhibited in the organization play a much greater role than compensation as to the reasons why employees stay or change jobs.

✔ For the vast majority of employees, what they earn is mostly through their base salary. In most organizations, managers' opportunity to affect someone's pay occurs only once, and at best twice, a year. Therefore, your ability as a manager to use money as a tool for motivation is fairly limited.

✔ Where you have the most opportunity to use money as a tool to motivate employee performance is if you can use a variable pay plan. *Variable pay* is earning potential above a person's base salary that varies based on how well certain performance targets are met. Unlike base pay, it's not a set amount each payout, because a person's results may not always be the same. Variable pay plans come in the form of commissions, bonuses, and incentives. The word *incentive* is sometimes used as the umbrella term for all these kinds of variable pay approaches. (See the "Some incentives for incentives" section that follows.)

When examining factors that motivate performance, you may notice that only about ten percent have to do with pay. So if you decide to stay away from pay as a potential source of motivation, you still have at your disposal, a profusion of ways to motivate performance. And in many cases, you have more control over the non-pay motivators, anyway. (See the "Forsake intimidation, go for positive ways of motivation" section, earlier in this chapter, for a list of motivational ideas.)

Some incentives for incentives

Traditionally, *incentives* or *variable pay plans* (earning potential above a person's base salary that varies based on how well certain performance targets are met) have existed for sales people and executives: Sales people are tied to commission plans and executives receive bonuses. In both cases, while payouts have varied, these have been standard parts of their compensation packages.

A growing trend in the private sector, and even some in the public sector, is the use of incentive plans for all sorts of positions. In some circumstances, employees from these plans have the potential to earn an additional 10 to 20 percent more than their base pay. For those in management roles, the incentive ranges often begin well above 20 percent. As part of this trend, some companies are increasing base salary at lower rates than in the past and emphasizing more opportunity for employees to earn on the variable pay side. Regardless of the plan or the total pay structure associated with it, the intent by more and more organizations is to create a greater link between pay and performance.

If you're a coach who has an incentive plan for your employees in place or are thinking about getting one put into place, here are a few guidelines to help:

✔ **Establish clear targets or goals.** Define what employees need to achieve to get the incentive payout. "Good performance," as determined solely by manager discretion, is too vague to work.

✔ **Make sure the goals are challenging, yet attainable.**

✔ **Attach measures to the targets or goals.** If the means of measurement take some work, that can be okay as long as the task isn't onerous or irrelevant for the business. For example, creating and administering customer surveys to measure customer satisfaction is worthwhile.

As often as possible, you want your employees to be able to track their own performances so that they clearly see their results.

✔ **Establish a *clear line of sight* for the participants in the plan;** that is, be sure that employees understand the relation between their performance efforts and the incentives they can earn. They should see the direct link. Discretionary or arbitrary incentives then go away.

✔ **Communicate the amount or scale of amounts that employees can earn in terms that are simple to understand.** If you don't tell them what the plan is, they won't know how well they can do. Stay away from secret compensation plans that make how much employees get in their incentive checks the clue in the mystery game. Also, if the plan is too complicated, it defeats its own purpose. Confusion doesn't motivate.

The incentive to leave

The new executive management in the Highly-Motivate-Them-Corporation (HMTC), saw many of their sales reps earning high levels of commissions. While delivering great revenue results for the company, management was worried, nonetheless, that such commissions were too easy to earn and costing the company too much money.

So management raised the quota levels but not the commission payout levels. The sales reps referred to the plan as the deliver-more-and-we'll-pay-you-the-same commission structure. At the end of the year, some of the sales force had met their higher targets but no one exceeded them and some didn't reach the stiffer targets — although no one brought in less revenue than the previous year. Turnover among some long-time sales reps began.

The following year, management added more guidelines to the commission plan that complicated it and made getting payouts harder to understand and achieve. This was all done, management announced, with the intent to build a highly motivated sales force. By the end of the year, revenue for the company had taken a sharp dip and over half the highly dedicated sales force that were with the company before this new management started had departed. Management viewed their changes in the incentive program had worked because they were able to get rid of some veteran sales staff who had grown complacent — motivation at its best.

While the story is fictional, HMTC exists in many places around the country. Do you work in one?

- ✔ **Target important behaviors or factors for business success.** If the goals are too narrow, you may be rewarding one behavior and ignoring other important behaviors that end up creating problems. If, for example, you create incentives around an individual's production levels but ignore quality, you'll likely see more widgets getting produced but also more defective widgets at the same time. Some target areas to consider are outputs, revenue generated, cost savings, accuracy, customer satisfaction, timeliness, and safety.

- ✔ **Make the amount of incentive pay earned for reaching target levels meaningful and rewarding for employees.** Good riddance if all one gets is a pittance.

- ✔ **Make the incentive payout functions relatively timely, from once a month to once per quarter.** The longer the time cycle, the less impact the incentive will have on performance.

- ✔ **Only create team incentives for situations in which a connection exists between the work everyone does on the team and the combined efforts contributed to the group results.** If your employees work more as individual specialists, a team incentive is less appropriate.

One other point to keep in mind with a variable pay plan is that, if you change plan guidelines frequently or make the targets harder to reach, all with the effect of making the incentive payout less likely to be earned, you create a *disincentive plan*. Employees likely will view such an incentive plan as a management cost control measure, not a tool for motivating performance.

Accentuating What Motivates and Eliminating What Demotivates

Many ideas exist as to what motivates employee performance. One of the psychologists whose work has most influenced my thinking, Frederick Herzberg, focuses on motivation in the workplace. His theories are referenced in this section.

To begin to understand what motivates and demotivates, follow these steps and answer each question for yourself:

1. **Review the following factors that can affect people in their job situations:**

   - Benefits and compensation
   - Interesting, challenging work
   - Job security
   - Meaningful responsibility
   - Opportunities for learning and growth
   - Policies and their administration
   - Recognition
   - Sense of achievement
   - Working conditions and physical environment
   - Working relationships and being part of good team

2. **Evaluate for yourself what factors would most motivate you and your performance.**

3. **Evaluate for yourself what factors would demotivate you or cause you to have the most dissatisfaction with your job situation.**

4. **Categorize the list in Step 1 into the factors that motivate and those that demotivate.**

   While responses may vary, common responses are found in Table 11-1.

Table 11-1	Motivators and Demotivators
Factors that Motivate	*Factors that Demotivate*
Recognition	Working conditions, physical environment
Sense of achievement	Benefits and compensation
Opportunities for learning and growth	Policies and their administration
Interesting, challenging work	Job security
Meaningful responsibility	
Working relationship and being part of good team	

5. **Looking at the list in Table 11-1, determine which of these factors you would label as more influenced and controlled at the organizational level, and which of these factors would you label as more influenced and controlled at the managerial level?**

   Organizational level here means the policies and decisions that are made, usually by executive management, that affect the organization as a whole; *managerial level* refers to the practices and decisions that you make that affect how your group operates.

   Looking at the set of factors on the right side of Table 11-1, you see factors that demotivate, and these are items that are most impacted and set at the organizational level. When not in good shape, these factors cause employees to be demotivated in their jobs, and serve as detractions from performing well. Yet, if these factors are at a satisfactory level or are corrected to be in good shape, they still don't motivate performance, although they may minimize dissatisfaction.

   The organizational-level factors in the right hand column, when they are of good quality, certainly help people feel better about their jobs and workplace. They are not, in most cases, stimulators that drive performance. And you, as a manager, have less control over making good things with them happen.

   The message here is that the factors that motivate people's performance are tied to the jobs they do, more than to the places they work. If they have opportunities for challenging work, for growth and learning, for recognition, and the other factors on the left side of Table 11-1, their performance is greatly impacted. Interesting enough, these factors are the ones over which managers have the most control and impact.

Managers can provide staff members with challenge in their work and responsibility to make the work happen so that they experience achievement in doing the job well. They can also encourage and support opportunities for employees to learn and grow so they expand their skills and capabilities, if not their careers, and thus strengthen their possibilities to achieve success. Managers can also recognize when the job has been done well and can work to build a team where people work cohesively and productively together.

When coaching to motivate by enacting changes at the managerial level, keep the following points in mind:

✔ Put attention to the issues that motivate employee performance as opposed to the ones that cause dissatisfaction. This follows the keep-it-simple principle: Focus your attention on the matters with which you can make the most positive difference for your employees.

✔ If problems arise for any staff member in the factors that demotivate, manage upwards to the executive level as best you can to get the problems corrected. Then focus back on the job at hand with the employee.

✔ Work with your employees on matters that provide enrichment in their jobs and a sense of inclusion in the group — all with the focus on getting good performance.

Understanding Yourself as a Manager

What motivates you in how you function as a manager? In this section, you get a chance to reflect on yourself as a manager and discover what motivates you. I use these ideas when I give coaching seminars, and they often spark quite a discussion with managers. (The following ideas about what motivates managers are a takeoff from work done by David McClelland, a psychology professor.)

To assess yourself as a manager, look at three needs or desires that motivate managers in their performance to varying degrees. Here they are with a brief description of each:

✔ **Desire for personal accomplishment:** If this is a high need for you as a manager, it means:

• You like to have personal responsibility to achieve success with a work effort, such as with a project or important assignment.

• You like challenge in your work and the hands-on aspects of getting things done.

✔ **Desire for quality relationships:** If this is a high need for you as a manager, it means:

• You like the social aspects of work — the interactions with other people.

> • You want people to bond with you, and you want to get along well with your staff. You reason that if people like you and visa versa, people will work well together.
>
> ✔ **Desire for influence:** If this is a high need for you as a manager, it means:
>
> • You like to assert your leadership influence and have a positive impact on others to get things done.
>
> • You like to give people responsibility and prepare and develop them to handle it, and then firmly hold them accountable to produce results.

How strong are each of these needs for you as a manager today in terms of what motivates you in your job? Using the worksheet in Figure 11-1, rate on a scale of one (lowest) to ten (highest), how strong each of the three needs are for you. You may also want to list your reasons. Then take a look at the following interpretations of your answers. McClelland discovered these kind of findings in his research, and I have seen much the same in my work with managers and executives over the years.

> ✔ **If you're a manager whose strongest need is in the personal accomplishment category, you're likely a high achiever.** Your greatest satisfaction comes in checking tasks off your to-do list as you get them done. You like to be hands-on with projects and the one who delivers much of the work that makes the projects successful.
>
> You may also fall short in effectiveness as a manager because often you try to do all the important aspects of the group's work yourself. Delegating, getting others involved, providing guidance and direction are not so much part of your *modus operandi.* Getting a group organized and focused are where you run into trouble, but you're a hard worker. Sounds like a doer-type manager, doesn't it (see Chapter 1)?
>
> ✔ **If you're a manager whose highest need is in the quality relationships category, you're certainly a people person.** Staff may often find you quite likable. You enjoy having a social feeling in your work; the relationships with people are where you often get much pleasure.
>
> As for your ability as a manager to pull people together and set direction, make tough decisions, and hold people accountable for high standards and results, you may tend to fall short. You worry about people feeling bad if you take these actions. As a result, you may get along well with your staff but at the same time frustrate many of them as you shy away from tackling problems and taking charge of your management responsibilities.

The Motivators For Managers

	Personal accomplishment	Quality relationships	Influence
Strong	10			
	9			
	8			
Moderate	7			
	6			
	5			
Not important	4			
	3			
	2			
	1			

Your reasons:

Figure 11-1:
The
motivators
for
managers.

✔ **If you're a manager whose strongest motivator is the influence category, you fit closest to what makes an effective manager.** You're willing to exercise your influence through others to make performance happen. You get satisfaction by asserting your personal influence, as described in Chapter 2, and not by pushing your authority or coercing people to perform. Achieving popularity or doing more than anyone else are not your goals; influencing employees to perform well is. When you see individuals and the group achieve their goals and have success, you find that rewarding.

Thus you seek to develop your staff and maximize their capabilities to the fullest in order to produce the results the business needs. You know that motivating staff to get the best out of their performance requires positive leadership. All of which sounds, based on the definition in Chapter 1, like a coaching manager.

Managing as a coach is not a panacea, and doing so doesn't make you a superhero who can tackle all the management challenges you face today. The point to keep in mind, as you have probably seen in your own experience, is that managers who have a strong personal influence and work to assert this leadership influence in positive ways tend to be very effective. They are able to focus everyone on the work that needs to get done and involve them in figuring out the best ways to do so.

Most managers are motivated to some degree by all three needs described in this section. Don't lose sleep if the personal accomplishment or quality relationship needs are currently greater motivators for you. For success in getting the best out of your people's performance — the heart of what motivation is about — you can slowly change your focus in order to increase your ability to motivate your employees.

As you reflect on your own motivators and use that insight to coach others, consider the following observations:

✔ How technically brilliant and achievement-oriented you are isn't enough to be an effective manager. A great sales person doesn't guarantee a great sales manager; a great engineer doesn't always turn into a great engineering manager.

✔ How nice you are and how well you like people aren't critical to management success. Far more useful for success is being able to be sincere, direct, positive, and firm — that's managing assertively.

✔ Management, regardless of one's style or motivations, is about making others effective and delivering results through them — and hopefully keeping them around for awhile so you don't have to start all over so soon.

✔ Coaching skills can be learned. As you grow in your coaching skills, you can increase your ability to positively influence employees while maintaining high results.

Chapter 12

Seven Practical Strategies to Motivate Employees

▶ Keeping your focus on motivating performance rather than emotional well-being

▶ Using recognition and passion about work as effective motivators

▶ Tuning into your own behavior and seeing how it can help motivate

▶ Matching individual needs with business needs

Motivating employees is a coaching tool that focuses on creating conditions that can stimulate high levels of performance. Performance, the focus of coaching, involves *behavior* — yours and your employees' — in the workplace, not in people's personal lives. While work life and personal life sometimes converge (and occasionally crash) when people come to work, motivation as a coaching tool concentrates on job performance. Thus you have no need for a degree in psychology, a license to practice therapy, or experience as a parent. All you need is to be a manager who wants to positively influence employee commitment and performance.

Understanding the Magnificent Seven

Chapter 11 explores motivation more on the theoretical side. In this chapter, I move fully to the practical side and share seven strategies for motivating employee performance in your coaching efforts. These strategies for motivating employees, which I call *the magnificent seven,* work hand-in-hand, often in conjunction with other coaching tools mentioned throughout this book.

Don't make them say "cheese!"

Give me an M — M. Give me an O — O. Give me a T — T. (The word is too long for my energy level to last in leading this cheer, so I'll cut to the chase.) What's it spell? Motivation! Motivation! Rah, rah, rah! Two, four, six, eight, what do you motivate?

The answer is employee *performance,* not *happiness.*

Too many managers have a misguided focus when motivating employees: They judge how motivated employees are by the emotions they display. If employees are smiling, they must be motivated. If the staff members are complaining, they aren't motivated any more. You may hear laments from managers along this line such as , "So what needs to be done here to get the employees happy?" or "We gave them a great holiday party, how come the employees are still groaning and moaning?" (Maybe being a manager who provides little support and appreciation for all the hard work your employees do has something to do with their dour mood, but they do like the free food at the party.)

The emphasis in this misguided focus is on happiness and not on performance. While no one wants to create unhappy employees, the happiness or unhappiness of a group of staff members isn't central. Instead, motivation works best when its focus is on enhancing and sustaining performance.

Which of the following two groups would you want to manage?

- ✔ Group X is highly productive. In fact, when the pressure is on to produce and meet deadlines, they kick in and produce quantity and top quality. Of course, they do have their grumpy moments.

- ✔ Group Y has the happy-go-luckiest group of people you'd ever want to meet. They are friendly and really like each other, and they get little done on the job. Quality work — what's that? Meeting deadlines — what are those? Take responsibility — some other time. Don't worry, be happy.

Most people would gladly take Group X. They are top performers. They may have their moods at times, but they produce and do the job well. Group Y is full of non-performers. (Now, who would you want for a party? Group Y, hands down.)

Happiness is an emotional state — it's a personal thing and shown by people in a variety of ways. The person who is most responsible for your own feelings of happiness is yourself, not someone else, especially not a manager.

Reward the right behaviors

How you reward positive behaviors, whether through financial or non-financial means (see Chapter 11), is less important than the fact you do it. In whatever way, shape, or form you use, acknowledging good performance increases the likelihood you'll see it again.

Positively reinforce the behaviors shown that you want to see continued. When good behavior is recognized, it becomes a regular practice. Fail to encourage good performance and you encourage the rise of poor performance. Reward undesirable behaviors and you motivate them to continue.

Don't be inattentive

Sometimes, when you're getting the positive behaviors and performance that you want from your staff, your lack of attention to them can give them a sense that the good performance doesn't really matter. Here are some examples:

- ✔ When you point out an important behavior that you want to see out of an individual or whole group, do you do anything to acknowledge that behavior when they do it?

- ✔ When one of your staff does something outstanding in their performance, although not spectacular or flashy, do you do anything to acknowledge it?

- ✔ When your employees have been working long and productively to help the group through a tough period, do you do anything to acknowledge this behavior?

In fact, what message do you send as a manager when you say or do nothing when positive employee behaviors occur? In effect, you're saying, "Good performance doesn't really matter around here." While few managers intend this message, these are often the messages that employees receive when little attention is shown towards important acts of performance.

Don't discourage the right behaviors

Sometimes managers discourage behavior that they really want to see. Here are a few examples:

- ✔ When staff members attempt to inform you of some bad news, you verbally lash out at them because you're upset at what you are hearing — referred to as *shooting the messenger*.

- ✔ When employees attempt to seek your help or counsel with a problem, you react like the situation is a crisis and create stress for everyone near you.

✔ When a staff member points out a mistake you made or disagrees with an opinion of yours, you harshly attack this perceived insurrection.

✔ When employees attempt to offer ideas that you don't like or find contrary to your own, you cut them off before they finish their explanations or react with a comment such as, "That will never work here."

In cases like these, you may have asked for your staff members to let you know when something isn't going well, to come to you when they have problems, to speak their minds about an issue, and to offer ideas. When they do, however, your behavior punishes them for doing so. Then you wonder why you never hear about problems until too late in the game or why your employees never have any ideas when you ask for them.

Behavior that's rewarded is repeated, so reward the right behaviors that produce good performance.

Don't reward the wrong behaviors

Sometimes managers go one step further and, usually unknowingly, reward the wrong behaviors. Here are a few examples:

✔ Every time Melody Mistake-Maker in your group makes an error, you say little and correct it yourself.

✔ Every time Ollie Outburst has a temper tantrum, you say little because you don't want to upset him further.

✔ Every time Esther Extension misses a deadline, which happens often, you say little or even say, "That's fine and do your best to get the job done."

✔ Every time you raise an issue with Walt Wiggle-out-of-Responsibility about how he's not taking responsibility for an assignment, you end up in long discussions about all the challenges Walt has and work out no plan for correction.

When you avoid dealing with performance issues directly, you encourage the wrong behaviors to continue. When you don't let the employee take responsibility for correcting mistakes, controlling behavior, meeting deadlines, and getting work done — regardless of your intention — the message sent is that non-performing behavior is okay. Coaching to help employees know what to do, and holding them accountable to do those tasks, are how you start to motivate behavior to move in positive directions.

Keep your rewards short-term

Time plays an important role in making motivation work. The longer a person has to wait for good performance to be acknowledged or rewarded in some sort of way, the less likely the reward has much lasting effect. For example, if once a year you tell your employees about all the positive contributions they make in their performance and say nothing the rest of the time, your efforts of positive feedback, while nice, mean little to them. Where were you when they were delivering those good results?

In the same way, if once per year you give your employees a raise, it has little effect on their performance the rest of the year — you're not giving them any compensation when the actions occur. A year, as in these examples, is a long time to wait for good performance to be rewarded.

A case of misguided focus

Jane managed a group of four who provided internal services for the employees of their company. Jane's staff was quite frustrated because a sister company in the same large corporation, responsible for processing payroll and personnel information that affected the employees in Jane's company, ran an inefficient operation, made numerous mistakes, and often took weeks or months to correct their errors.

When employees came to Jane's staff with their problems, her staff could do little to help because the corrections of the problems were out of their control. Every time an employee presented a problem, Jane's staff sent off a nasty letter or made a harsh phone call to their counterparts in the sister company with little effect, other than to annoy the staff in the sister company. In return, Jane's staff voiced their frustrations more and more and didn't come across as very professional doing so.

The sister company's operation was located in a different state. Jane had attempted on occasion to talk with managers there about the problems but had not been met with a friendly reception — something related directly to the way her staff

acted. Jane didn't persist and began to put her attention to what she could do to ease the frustrations her staff felt.

To attempt to motivate this group, Jane started leaving notes, small gifts, or other tokens of appreciation on the desk of each staff member about once per week. She also verbally let them know as well that she appreciated them hanging in there under such difficult circumstances and wanted them to feel good about working in this group.

But the group grew less effective at providing internal customer service and more effective at acting unprofessionally with their concerns. How come? Because the motivation had been mismanaged.

Jane's focus had primarily been on trying to make her staff happy. Her focus got away from performance, so the problems that the group faced stay unaddressed. Jane's group was also good at whining, ranting, and raving because that behavior had, through the small gifts and notes, been rewarded. In this case, the wrong behaviors were being rewarded.

Instead, keep the time frame for acknowledging good behavior relatively short. If the reward is given long after the behavior has occurred, the motivating effect that the positive reward could have is lessened, if not lost. The idea, instead, is look for ways to reward as close as you can as to when it happens. Here are a few ways to reward performance in the short-term:

- ✓ **Incentive programs:** An incentive program provides monetary reward for good performance. Link the incentive to performance and have the payouts occur at a reasonable intervals. The reasonable interval to be most effective is from once a month to once each quarter.

  The shorter the time frame for getting the incentive payout, the more the incentives can help motivate performance.

- ✓ **Spot bonus:** A spot bonus is a discretionary bonus that can range from small amounts to over a thousand dollars. The idea is that when something significant is accomplished in an employee's performance, that person gets hit with the bonus (figuratively speaking) right on the spot — or close in time in to the event. The spot bonus is a surprise — it's not given at set intervals the way incentives are. If budgeted for and given periodically, employees appreciate the financial acknowledgment for a job done well.

- ✓ **Gift certificates:** Like spot bonuses, these are given when good events of performance occur and not at any set time. Instead of cash, they are a cash equivalent payment that allows the receivers to enjoy something in their leisure time. Gift certificates for dinner, hotels, or purchasing merchandise at stores are often well received.

- ✓ **Positive feedback:** Positive feedback is cheap and is immediately at your disposal. No permission from higher management nor planning for it in your budget is needed to give it out, which means that you can be quick and timely in its use and have a motivating effect while doing it.

  The key is to give positive feedback, not praise. State the specifics about what you've noticed in performance as opposed to general comments. Be sincere and acknowledge good efforts and outcomes of performance rather than just saying something nice. See Chapter 5 for more tips on giving positive feedback.

- ✓ **Public recognition:** Public recognition, being verbally acknowledged in front of your peers for some achievement you did, can be a powerful motivator. Many companies and organizations have formal recognition programs, operated monthly or quarterly, for which employees are nominated for good service, teamwork, quality, or other important aspects of performance. In addition to being recognized in front of the other employees — nothing like the applause of your compatriots to put an extra bounce in your step — the recipient sometimes gets a plaque, clothing with the company name, a gift certificate, or even a little bonus.

  If you have a formal recognition program in your organization, it provides you a vehicle to recognize outstanding performers in your group. Get those nomination forms in right away.

Public recognition can even be done informally within your own group. It can be a simple form of congratulations for a job done well. "Hey everyone, before we start today's meeting, I wanted to take a moment to recognize Sue's persistent efforts that won us a major account. Let's give her a hand."

Be careful to avoid resentment and embarrassment. If you reward one employee and don't mention another who assisted on the assignment, you may have a resentful employee on your hand. (This can be a problem for winners at the Academy Awards ceremony. As many people as you try to thank for helping you win the Oscar, invariably someone doesn't get mentioned.) In addition, if public adulation is a big turn off for the employee you're trying to motivate, your public recognition, even if well received by the group, may have a demotivating effect on the employee.

✔ **Private recognition:** You usually can't go wrong if you recognize an employee's outstanding performance privately. This may include writing a note of appreciation, giving the employee a day off that doesn't against vacation time, or taking the staff person out to lunch to express thanks for a job well done (avoid fast-food restaurants on this one). In addition, getting your boss to say or write something to the employee recognizing what was done has a very positive effect.

Remember that one size doesn't fit all

Motivation is an individual thing. The issue of motivation and pay discussed in Chapter 11 is an example of this: Some employees may be driven by money while others say it's not important to them in their job situations. Assuming that a certain strategy works to motivate all of your staff is misguided thinking. In addition, be careful not to base how you motivate your staff on what motivates you, as in the following example.

Jim came in with much enthusiasm as the new manager of the Operations Support group. He wanted his three staff members to feel challenged and motivated in their jobs. Although he never asked what each person's interests were, he knew what had motivated him when he was at their level in his career. So Jim started arranging training sessions and special cross functional projects for his staff to get involved in. Two of his three staff members really enjoyed these opportunities, but not Bob.

Bob found the training sessions and projects as extra work. They were taking him away from his daily responsibilities and backing him up in getting his work done. Instead of adding spice to his job, these motivational activities left Bob frustrated. Jim picked up on Bob's dissatisfaction but was puzzled as to why Bob felt the way he did, especially when the other two team members were enjoying them. For Jim, these activities helped him move up in his career.

What interests you — or the majority of your team — may not be the same as to what interests every staff member. Seeing the world from your own point of view, even under the best intentions, may blind you to what motivates your employees. (Emphasizing the importance of recognizing individual differences, a key part of coaching, is discussed further in Chapter 3.)

When you get to understand every employee as individuals, you can understand what motivates them in their jobs. Of course, to know how to individually motivate each of your employees, you have to observe, listen, and ask questions, as opposed to assume, tell, and impose your own ideas.

Tap into your employee's passions about work

Think of passion as an intense feeling about and a strong desire for a particular activity. The term "passion" is used a lot when people talk about what they wish for in their love lives, but passion certainly extends far beyond that. When you see people who are passionate about some interest or work in their lives, their enthusiasm is often so infectious that it causes you to gravitate towards them and listen to them talk of their activity — even if the activity isn't interesting to you. Passion for something can often drive people to great feats of performance.

Passion at work doesn't have to be a burning desire, nor does it have to be expressed with enthusiastic outbursts and singing in the hallways. The key to tapping into people's passion at work is to find out what gives them that extra oomph or bounce in their step — an activity or opportunity they really enjoy that drives them to perform.

Many employees are passionate about one or more of the following areas:

- ✔ **Becoming an expert:** In some employees, you'll find a thirst for learning. Whether the learning is done through research or training opportunities often doesn't matter. What matters is the opportunity to expand knowledge and have it tapped into as the expert resource.

  Being an expert often means being the one that others turn to for advice or who represents the group in special events related to the subject of expertise. In whatever way the knowledge is called upon, being able to learn and share that knowledge with others is what stimulates passion. As a manager, you want to tap into this passion.

- ✔ **Teaching others:** Some employees love getting in front of a group, small or large, to conduct training. Sometimes coupled with the passion to become an expert, the passion comes from being on the stage as the center of the training activity. For others, often among senior-level employees, the opportunity to teach newcomers and help them come up to speed is of great enjoyment. Formal or informal, working with a group or working with an individual, the chance to teach others is often what gives some employees passion in their jobs.

✔ **Being creative:** Having a chance to use creativity is another area that may stimulate passion at work for employees. Sometimes, the creativity comes from being able to take ideas and act upon them, design new products or processes, develop a campaign to rally or interest others, or to write important material that others enjoy reading.

The opportunities to apply creativity are often boundless in people's jobs. For you as a manager, the trick is to encourage — not stifle — staff members who can think and implement efforts that are somewhat new or different, especially when they can have a positive impact. For those who get turned on by the chance to be creative in their work, let them have at it. Set the parameters as needed and hold the employees accountable to act upon their good ideas, but you don't need to have the ideas. You just need to let them run with theirs and acknowledge the improvements they make with those creative actions.

✔ **Solving problems:** Some employees thrive on taking on tough problems and working them through to solutions. Call upon their troubleshooting skills and the passion flies. You often see this among technical employees who work hours on end until they can come up with the right solutions for problems, but the desire to solve problems is a passion that transcends all positions. The key for you as a manager is to recognize the need to have problems tackled, and then let the employees who want to go into fix-it mode have at the issue — kind of like a dog chewing on a juicy bone.

✔ **Helping others:** For some people, the chance to help others in their work is very gratifying. In such cases, you see employees dedicate themselves to their work because they see others gain from what they do. Sometimes, tapping into this gold-mine of passion is as simple as asking a staff person to help a new employee, to lend an extra hand in a project, or to represent your group at a service-to-others function. Whatever the need or occasion, the good feeling that comes when others say thanks for the assistance becomes the reward that fuels this passion further. Seeing others benefit from the service provided is reward in itself.

✔ **Making a contribution:** This area sparks a passion for people who want their work to make a positive difference: contributing to an outstanding team, creating a better way for something to be done that benefits others, or doing work that supports a worthy cause. For many, when they see they've made a good contribution, a sense of achievement for a job well done kicks into high gear.

Sometimes, creating an opportunity to spark one passion may spark a few others at the same time. For example, when you ask one member of your staff to contribute to a special project team, and her work is outstanding, the team is successful. Jane is motivated not only because of the great contribution she made to the team but also because her supportive help made a positive difference.

✔ **Taking risks:** Employees who find passion in their work through taking risks are the ones who like to work as change agents or tackle new ventures in which the chance for success can be as great as the chance for failure. When others say, "We never have done it that way before," or "I don't know if that could work here," they're ready for action. When given such opportunities, they may perform like fearless mountain climbers.

Clearly define your parameters with such employees, and then give them the freedom to go make something happen. They may run into an obstacle or two along the way, but their passion to take a risk and make success out of it helps them not be deterred along the way. Your role, when you tap into this passion, is to provide support and keep the bureaucracy out of their way.

Keep in mind that your role as a manager is to first learn what creates this passion for each of your employees, work with them to create opportunities to tap into this passion, and then give them the support needed along the way. When you do, look out! Motivating in this way will lead to outstanding performance.

Walk the walk, talk the talk

The relationship between managers and employees is important in motivating employee performance and influencing employee commitment — and it's often overlooked.

Generally, the better the boss, the more motivated the employee. Sure, a handful of employees can perform well despite having lousy managers, and great managers can still encounter a few lousy performers on occasion. But the more self-aware you are, the more in tune you are with your conduct and words, the better chance you have of motivating better performance from your staff.

The following actions, grouped into three distinct sets of behaviors, set good examples for your staff and will motivate them to perform:

✔ **Show care and respect for the individual.**

- Respond timely to employee requests and inquiries.

- Follow through and do what you say you'll do.

- Make management by walking around (MBWA), as highlighted in Chapter 4, a regular practice so that your staff finds you approachable, and you become aware of the person behind each employee.

- Be patient — and truly listen to understand — when an employee comes to you with a concern.

- Give negative feedback, not criticism, and then coach to correct the issue. Always do this in private, never in public.

- Send cards or notes to acknowledge a special occasion such as a birthday, anniversary, loss of a loved one, or other event.

- Share information and keep your staff in the information loop so that they know what's going on in the department and organization.

- Stay in control in difficult or pressure situations. Become solutions-oriented in your manner to tackle the problems.

- When you want an employee to do a task or assignment, request what you need as opposed to giving orders.

✔ **Show appreciation for good performance.**

- Provide ongoing positive feedback for behavior and work done well.

- Nominate the employee for your company's recognition program due to an outstanding performance.

- Take the staff person out to lunch as recognition for good performance.

- Allow an individual to leave work early or take a day off, without using vacation time, for productive work that has involved long hours.

- If you can, give a spot bonus or a gift certificate. (See the "Keep your rewards short-term" section, earlier in this chapter, for more information.)

- Reward the employee by providing the opportunity to take on a favorable assignment.

- Say thanks as a regular practice for the little things employees do that keep your organization running well.

- Write a favorable performance review that specifically itemizes the contributions of good performance.

- Send a letter to your boss and copy the employee and the employee's personnel file about that person's efforts in doing a project or event well.

- When you receive a compliment from an internal or external customer about what your employee did, share it quickly and note it on your significant events list (as described in Chapter 5).

✔ **Show a desire to consider and develop employees' ability to think, as well as their capabilities.**

- Discuss career interests. Together, map out a development plan for every employee.

- Delegate a challenging project or assignment the employee is ready to take on.

- Help the employee get the opportunity to attend in-house as well as outside seminars and conferences.

- Seek the employee's input on plans and issues you're tackling.

- Mutually set performance plans where the employee actively shapes them with your guidance. (See Chapter 6.)

- Mentor and tutor your employee, from sharing your experience to tutoring with questions, to help that person develop in areas of greatest benefit. (See Chapter 8.)

- Include the employee in higher-level meetings for exposure and upwards visibility.

- Have the employee teach or share expertise at a group meeting.

- Help create opportunities for cross-training through which the employee teaches other staff to help do his function, and they do the same with their functions.

- When opportunities arise, have the employee participate in a special committee or project team that involves staff from different departments.

- Let the employee take an idea for some change or improvement, propose recommendations for how to make it work, and lead the effort for its implementation.

When the actions in the previous list become regular practices, you will motivate employee performance. Your personal influence grows tremendously, and that creates a desire for employees to perform well.

How will you feel if you have a manager, who as a regular practice, carries out actions that show care and respect towards you, show appreciation for the good performance you do, and show interest in your development and the ideas and abilities you have to offer? Most likely, this will be a manager for whom you will have great respect and with whom you'll feel challenged, stimulated, and appreciated.

Match business needs to employee needs

In any kind of business, the employer has needs that it hires employees to meet and employees have needs that they seek to meet in their employment. The employee and employer both have expectations about meeting those needs of one another, but those expectations often go unstated.

One motivational strategy involves getting these two sets of needs known and building bridges between them. When you do, you have a powerful effect on employee motivation while helping the business accomplish what it needs.

But first you have to understand what motivates each of your employees. What are their needs? What is important to them in their job performance? When you can specifically answer these questions, you know what motivates each staff person and you can then tune them into the needs of your group and the business. Whenever you have this overlap occurring — that is, individual needs are being met at the same time that business needs are being fulfilled — high levels of motivation are stimulated, resulting in good performances.

You won't be able to meet each person's needs — your job as a manager isn't to cater to each person's needs or to try to meet them all yourself. The responsibility is a two-way street. What you want to be able to do is understand what needs each employee has.

While you'll get a sense, through your interactions and observations as you spend time with them, of what's important to every employee in their job situations, the most direct way to truly find out about each employee's needs is to *ask*.

What do you want to ask about? Find out about your employees' needs related to the key issues of their work and job performance — from what they like to do to where they need improvement, from recognition to needs for guidance and support. Here is a list of questions to ask (questions that I refer to as the *motivation questionnaire*) that help you uncover those needs in all these areas:

- ✔ What duties and assignments do you find most challenging?
- ✔ What do you most like doing in your job, and what do you least like doing in your job?
- ✔ What working relationships and work situations with other people do you like?
- ✔ In what areas of your job would you like to
  - Have more guidance?
  - Receive training?
  - Gain autonomy?
- ✔ In which kinds of decisions would you like to have input?
- ✔ When you do good work, how do you like to be recognized for it?
- ✔ What gives you a sense of passion, challenge, and/or accomplishment in your work?
- ✔ In which areas do you think you could use some improvement?

✔ Based on the needs of our business and of our group, in what skills or areas would you like to gain development and experience?

✔ In our working relationship, describe the kind of communication efforts you would most like to see happen.

✔ Describe a situation or two (tell the whole story) where you performed at a highly productive and effective level.

Keep the following tips in mind when putting this motivation questionnaire into action:

✔ Schedule a time to meet with each of your direct reports. Allow time for an in-depth conversation. A lunch meeting can work quite well.

✔ When making the request for this meeting, tell your staff members that you're sincerely interested in exploring their job-related needs and desires.

✔ Conduct the session as a conversation rather than an interview. You want the feel of the meeting to be relaxed and informal.

✔ Use the questions only as a guide. Probe beyond the given question so that you come away with in-depth knowledge.

✔ Listen without judgment and periodically provide verbal feedback to confirm your understanding of what you are hearing.

✔ Have a good time.

After asking probing questions, you can develop a motivation plan with the employee. The plan serves as a guide to create opportunities for individual and business success. In developing the plan, follow these steps:

1. **Together with the employee, draw conclusions on the important needs of the individual and develop strategies on how to best meet those needs.**

   This can often be done in the meeting in which you ask probing questions or as a follow-up meeting a short time later if time doesn't permit.

2. **Using Table 12-1, list the key needs of the employee.**

   Use the left-hand column of the motivation worksheet. To be realistic, target only two or three needs. You also want to go after needs through which the greatest possibility exists to create matches with the business needs.

Table 12-1	Motivation Worksheet
Employee:	*Date:*
Employee's Needs	*Strategies to Motivate*

Matching needs and firing up passion

Brian was a senior engineer who had been with his company for a year when Roy, his manager, met with him to complete the motivation questionnaire. The conversation went extremely well, and he learned some things about Brian he didn't know before.

As a performer on the job, Brian did a decent job, but nothing outstanding. He was knowledgeable and got his work done, but showed little initiative or creativity in his technical project work.

In his conversation, Roy discovered Brian had been working as a part-time college instructor and loved the opportunity to teach others, even in job assignments. He enjoyed learning and sharing his knowledge with others. Doing project work was fine, but not something that greatly excited him.

Roy then shared with Brian a challenge he was wrestling with for the group. He saw a need for

someone who could stay on top of all the latest technical changes in their field and, in particular, who could train new engineers in the group and help keep the experienced engineers up to date with these findings. These functions would likely constitute a half-time role.

Brian jumped at the chance. Together, he and Roy targeted a motivation plan that adjusted Brian's role to become the group's researcher and trainer on a half-time basis.

Brian thrived in his new role and his performance excelled. Everyone enjoyed their workshops with Brian. He was an outstanding trainer and became a valuable resource for expertise. Even in his project work, he took initiative to mentor junior engineers. Roy, by matching individual needs with business needs, tapped into a passion of Brian's — and the benefits of now having a highly motivated employee really paid off.

---

3. **After identifying the key needs together, list the strategies or action plans to meet the needs.**

   Use the right-hand column of the motivation worksheet.

   Don't confuse a strategy with a need. A need is something important or desired in the job situation; a strategy is the action to take to meet the need. For example, if your employee talks about wanting training in certain skill areas, the need is not for training. Training is a strategy or action to be taken. The need is to learn and develop skills.

   As you and the employee develop the strategies for the motivation plan, do the following:

   - Write them in specific, action-oriented terms.

   - Include target dates as to when the actions are to happen.

   - Ask the employee what steps you can take to help meet the need.

   - Ask the employee what support he or she needs from you in order to meet each targeted need.

4. **Do a periodic follow-up, perhaps once per quarter in your checkup-review meeting (see Chapter 7), to see how the motivation efforts are going.**

   Also, annually update this information with the employee, perhaps at your performance review meeting. Ask the probing questions again to see what other needs come up. Employees' needs and interests do sometimes change as they move along in their careers.

The employee is the driver, the one to take responsibility to make the plan happen, and your role as the manager is to provide the necessary support, not to do the motivation for the employee. Your role is also to let the employee know the departmental and business needs, and to then work with him or her to create the matches — opportunities for individual needs that help meet business needs to be met. Table 12-2 shows you a motivation plan for John Doe.

Table 12-2	Sample Motivation Worksheet
Employee: John Doe	*Date: 01-11-01*
Employee's Needs	*Strategies to Motivate*
1. Strong interest in sharing experience and the knowledge gained from it.	1a. Outline a training program for new hires who come into the group. Finalize by 3-1-01. 1b. Deliver training for recent hires and new hires thereafter. Start 3-1-01. 1c. In biweekly, one-on-one meetings, manager will share plans and seek John's input and feedback on them. Start immediately.
2. Have skills expanded, get new challenges.	2a. John will mentor Sue and Bob to cover half his day-to-day responsibilities. Start immediately. 2b. John will assist on half-time basis as project manager for ABC Project. Start when Sue and Bob are ready, estimated to be 3-1-01.

Shaking Those Pillars of Commitment

The five pillars for building a strong level of employee commitment, covered in detail in Chapter 2, are greatly impacted when you apply the magnificent seven strategies for motivation:

✔ **Focus:** Creating a motivation plan targets efforts to meet employees' needs. The efforts provide a focus for your employees as to what steps to take to make good things happen in their performance. They know what direction to go and, as a bonus, are motivated to do so because they benefit from it.

✔ **Involvement:** For many of the motivation strategies in this chapter, you seek your employees' input or ideas, and then involve your staff in taking on the responsibilities they want to have. Employees help shape their motivation plans and truly own what happens with them. Your role is one of support.

✔ **Development:** This pillar of commitment is greatly impacted by your motivation efforts. Much of the work you do in your motivation efforts seeks to develop your employees' skills and capabilities. You're stimulating their desire to grow — that's development at its best.

✔ **Gratitude:** Behavior that's rewarded is repeated. When you apply the motivation strategies of giving positive feedback and utilizing various forms of recognition to acknowledge good performance, the gratitude pillar is influenced tremendously.

✔ **Accountability:** This pillar for building employee commitment is impacted when you proceed with your follow-up efforts to review progress with your employees on their motivation plans. Because your employees own the plans, the sense of accomplishment and motivation is in their hands. This is accountability at its best.

Chapter 13

Don't Try to Do It All Yourself — Delegate

*W*hen you struggle with not having enough time and not getting as much done as you would like, the advice you may often hear is, "You need to delegate better." While you may agree with this often-unsolicited advice, the *but* kicks in (this is different than kicking butt!), as in, "Good idea, but . . . ," and all the reasons you can't delegate better start pouring out:

✔ "Good idea, but I don't have enough time."

✔ "Good idea, but I don't have enough resources."

✔ "Good idea, but my staff isn't skilled enough."

Quite often, at the core of this delegating dilemma is the difficulty of letting go — the belief that your staff won't do the job as well as you need or as well as you could, or that your employees will mess up the job and make matters worse. For some managers, the difficulty in delegating is that employees will do the job very well, which may leave others to wonder why the manager's job is necessary.

But ultimately, most managers find that delegating is a great tool to empower employees and increase productivity — their staff members' and their own. This chapter gives you all of the tips and tricks you need to start delegating effectively.

Delegating 101

A big part of the misconception many managers have about delegating — misconceptions that fuel apprehensions about it and create a reluctance to do it — is the thinking that by delegating you're completely letting go of control. But giving others a share in the responsibility extends influence and creates commitment to the cause. Control isn't lost; you're just letting go of the burden of doing everything yourself.

Think about it. If you're the only one who can get important work done to maintain daily operations in your group, you bear a heavy burden. If instead, through effective coaching, you delegate some of this responsibility among your staff, and they get the work done with good results, what's happened for you? Less burden — and more control of the operations and of your use of time. (Less filling, tastes great!) That's the whole idea with delegating: You can better leverage your time for higher-level work and extend your influence to greater levels in the organization.

Gaining a definition of delegating

Delegating as a coaching tool is assigning and entrusting assignments and responsibilities to others. Delegating isn't about giving people tasks to do. Tasks are the simple and short-term items of work to be done. As a manager, you probably ask your staff to do tasks nearly every day. "Joe, can you get me the report on last week's sales figures?" or "Sue, would you check with the vendor on what his volume rates are for discounts?"

Delegating is about having staff take on juicy or meaningful work — projects, duties, and other important assignments. For example, "Joe, I would like you to take on the responsibility of creating the weekly sales analysis report" or "Sue, I'd like you to tackle a project involving vendor relations and how we can maximize discounts with each one with whom we do business." Don't stop asking your employees to do tasks when needed, just recognize that's not real delegating.

Entrust is a key word in delegating: It means that you care about the results of what you delegate and you're willing to provide the support needed to help the employee achieve those results. But you're going to let the employee do the assigned job. You don't have to be hands-on for the right outcomes to occur, but neither are you uninvolved and unaware of what's occurring.

Along with providing the right support comes spelling out clear expectations and maintaining employee accountability. This is what effective delegating means and (hold your buzzword buzzer) what empowerment is truly all about. To *empower* your employees is to do three actions:

✔ Give them the freedom to get a job done (no breathing down their necks).

✔ Provide them with the right level of support to get the job done well, including information, training, resources, and so on.

✔ Hold them accountable to produce the outcomes needed.

All three actions go together as part of the process. Thus, when you delegate effectively, you empower your staff. (Holy cow, this stuff could be dangerous!)

Understanding delegating perils and pitfalls

Delegating is far more than just assigning work for people to do. It is being involved at a support level versus doing the work hands-on yourself. In addition, to make delegating efforts work, a key is to build on successes with employees, not on failures. Here are the common reasons that lead to delegating failures.

✔ **You don't communicate the expected results.** Most employees don't have the ability to read your mind. While most managers tell what they want done when they attempt to delegate an assignment, they don't directly articulate the results they need to see from the completed assignment.

Employees may learn of the real expectations through trial and error, in a comment like, "That's not what I was looking for on this project. That's not how this is supposed to look."

✔ **You tell the employee how to do the job.** When you tell your employees how to do assignments but don't define what results need to be produced, you stifle people's desire and ability to take on responsibility and think for themselves. Managers who function as doers often fall into this trap (see Chapter 1). They focus on the methods of how to get a job done instead of the quality results needed. The following story demonstrates this point well.

Sheila was given a project to develop the company's new marketing brochure. Based on her past experience and her creative flair, she was excited to take on this assignment in her new role. Getting involved in work like this was one of the reasons she took this job. Then, however, her manager, Mel, started to explain what this project entailed. In great detail, he described each step to take in getting the brochure developed and the proper ways to do it. Attempts by Sheila to let Mel she knew how to do this kind of work were brushed aside as Mel insisted on not being interrupted with his delegating initiative. The more Mel continued to lecture, the more Sheila sat by passively. By the time he was through explaining how to do this job, Sheila's enthusiasm for the project was gone.

✔ **You, the delegater, don't let go — and even get in the way.** In essence, you're still trying to do the delegated assignment yourself — often under the guise of just trying to help out. This so-called help is neither asked for nor needed.

For example, through every key step the employee needs to take to complete the assignment, you're there, unannounced, hovering over the person's shoulder to check on how things are going. Or you jump in at times and do tasks the employee hasn't gotten to yet. Or with every decision the employee needs to make, you help make or even overturn them. As a result, good performance and employee commitment are inhibited.

✔ **The assignment you delegate is beyond the person's capability level.** The assignment or responsibility you delegate is one that the individual isn't ready to handle. It is greater than the person's knowledge, experience, or skill level, and it leaves the employee unable to competently perform and produce the right results.

Employees are often willing to take on duties they aren't really ready to handle, and many are reluctant to speak up even if they know the job is beyond their capabilities. After all, who wants to admit he or she isn't ready enough to do something? So the employee is given the job with a sink-or-swim approach — throw the person the job and see what happens — which usually leads to the employee drowning.

✔ The project you delegate is beyond the person's capacity level. In this case, the issue isn't one of competence level but one of workload. You have a maxed-out employee on whom you pile another critical project. While many such individuals don't outwardly complain or, when they do, aren't listened to, they suffer with the burden and stress to try and keep up. Overload the machine (your employee in this case) without consideration of its capacity level, and eventually, mechanical failure sets in.

✔ **You don't provide any review during the process.** In this case, you give the assignment and that's it, abdicating taking any responsibility for what gets produced. While you let the staff member have total autonomy for handling the assignment, no progress review is given along the way to help the employee and to see how he or she is performing. You may then wonder why the employee runs into difficulties and why the end results don't turn out very well.

✔ **You give responsibility without giving support.** When you delegate, support takes on many forms: initial guidance and training, information, equipment, a budget to work with, decision-making authority, or access to staff or material resources.

When support is lacking, you may assign a project, saying "Here, get this project done," and then end the conversation. The lack of support becomes an obstacle that the employee has to expend energy to overcome.

Use this list as your checklist of what not to do when delegating. Note that these reasons for delegating failure are all manager-driven. The manager is the source of the problem, which also means that the manager can correct the problem.

Knowing What to Delegate

Knowing what to delegate (and what *not* to delegate) is a two-step process:

1. **Make a master list.**

   Think of this as a brain dump. List all of the projects, duties, tasks, and activities that you perform and are involved with — daily and periodically. You want to keep tasks as small as possible, so list all the activities and work assignments that use up your time — from big to little, from really important to less important. Most managers are able to list from 20 to over 40 items on this pre-delegating analysis list.

2. **Categorize the list.**

   Label each item on your list following these guidelines:

   - Items you can completely reassign.
   - Items you can share or reassign in part.
   - Items you need to keep.

Ask yourself this question: If I delegate this item to one of my staff, will the time spent up front to provide the guidance and support needed pay off later in productivity, in how the group functions, or in better use of my time? If yes, delegate it. If no, keep it.

You need to keep some items because they truly fall into the manager's domain. Writing performance reviews, negotiating your group's annual operating budget with your boss, and handling personnel issues are some of the responsibilities you can't give to others to do — even if you want to give them away. Your time and attention are best spent maintaining productive operations and good morale in your group. If not you, who is going to take the lead in the following endeavors?

✔ Pushing forward initiatives to improve processes or tackle big operational problems

✔ Getting people and material resources that your staff needs to get their jobs done

✔ Organizing staff training needs so that they perform effectively

✔ Providing technical direction to the group

- Charting the group's future path
- Clarifying key work priorities for the group
- Representing the group's needs with management
- Challenging and developing staff to perform to their best

The problem for many managers is that these critical and strategic issues often receive little attention. They get so caught up in their daily tasks, projects, and meetings that a leadership void in the group occurs. Delegating properly helps you begin to focus on more important tasks and fill this void — one so vital to your group's success.

What many managers overlook when figuring out what to delegate are the items to share or reassign in part. Items related to the day-to-day operations of your group, which some managers tend to hold onto, are where your greatest potential exists to delegate wholly or in part to people on your staff. Here are some examples:

- Solving fairly routine customer problems
- Setting the daily work schedule and work flow
- Preparing agendas for your regular staff meetings
- Making decisions on situations that employees face in carrying out their responsibilities
- Completing functions you're less qualified for or not too good at doing
- Handling technical duties
- Compiling data
- Composing regular administrative reports
- Researching issues that come your way
- Training new employees or others in the group
- Carrying out important functions for which little staff coverage exists, meaning there's no back-up support for day-to-day operations
- Handling vendor-relations issues
- Seizing opportunities that build upon others' creative talents or desires
- Answering questions you're frequently asked
- Dealing with new functions that come about due to change in the workplace

Understanding the returns you get for your investment

What do you gain when you learn to apply this coaching tool of delegating? Here is what managers who have done so report:

✔ **Increased productivity:** Ultimately this is the main reason you delegate. It is about maximizing the human resources you have in your group to the fullest. The more others can get work done, the greater the productivity you see.

✔ **Staff development:** In many cases, the assignments and responsibilities you delegate provide your staff members opportunity for growth. As they gain success in them, their skills and abilities strengthen. Competence — and often confidence and motivation — grows.

✔ **More assistance and coverage:** Delegating often serves as a useful mechanism for filling holes. Sometimes you're vulnerable because you're the only one who can do a function that affects day-to-day operations, or one of your staff is that key solo performer. Delegating to utilize more people in the operations gets you more help and better coverage in return.

✔ **Good creativity and solutions:** Delegating assignments that allows staff members to have autonomy sometimes leads to more and better ideas from your group. Better solutions are often produced as the delegatee is able to give more attention to the problem at hand. In fact, in some cases, you're tapping into expertise that's better equipped to handle certain issues than you are. That's why you hired them in the first place!

✔ **Better use of your time:** By shifting some of the day-to-day operational work to staff to handle, your attention and time get to shift elsewhere — to the big-picture stuff. You can spend more time with key people you need to be in contact with and to take on more leadership in addressing problems or moving initiatives forward. This better use of your time elevates you to become the leader that others need you to be.

✔ **Less stress for you:** This benefit often comes as a result of the other benefits you gain from your delegating efforts. When you're increasing productivity, putting your time to better use, and maximizing and developing your resources, you're no longer the one person who has to handle and worry about most of what goes on in your group.

In many cases, the items you partially delegate can become items that you completely delegate in the future. You do this by adding one piece of the responsibility at a time. Each time the employee masters the new part delegated, another piece is given to handle. You delegate one step at a time in manageable increments and build off of that success.

If you assign the whole responsibility or project today — for instance, handle the whole set-up and preparation work for an upcoming job fair — the employee could fail. Delegating in increments reduces the chances of this.

Matching Employees to Tasks

When you know what you want to delegate, you determine to whom you will delegate. Which person will be good for which assignment? Here are some important questions to ask before initiating a delegating effort:

✔ Where does the assignment best fit functionally within your group?

✔ Who has capacity in terms of time and workload to handle the duty?

✔ Who has the interest?

✔ Who has the skill and experience level best for the job?

✔ Whose capabilities do you need to expand to fill coverage gaps in the group's day-to-day operations?

✔ Who is in need of a new or different challenge?

✔ To whom do you want to give an opportunity for growth?

Notice how one of the factors not listed is "Who has the best track record?" Sometimes managers have a tendency to delegate mostly to their reliable performers. As a result, they don't distribute the workload evenly among all the staff in the group. This has an effect of punishing the good employees. It may also create resentment: among the star employees who wonder why they have to carry the workload for others in the group, and among other employees who feel passed over for the most challenging and growth-oriented work. Instead, develop and challenge everyone in your group.

Sometimes, resources to delegate work to can be staff outside your group. For example, one manager had limited staff resources within his group. Nonetheless, he went ahead and delegated some administrative-related duties he had to a couple of secretaries in his office. While not his direct reports, they were willing and able to provide the help and enjoyed having the chance to have some variety in their jobs. He followed through in using the delegating tool (see the following section), and the employees involved performed the duties with good results.

Putting the Delegating Tool into Action

Time to walk you through how to use the coaching tool of delegating to empower and achieve positive results. The tool has six steps to it, as outlined in this section. Steps 1 through 5 are done when you introduce the assignment; Step 6 is done along the way and at the completion of the delegated assignment.

1. Describe the assignment to be done.

Kick off the delegating effort by informing the employee of the work you want done. But you go further than that: Tell the *purpose* of the assignment, spelling out why this assignment is important and what you want to see accomplished. In particular, spell out these three aspects of your performance expectations:

- **Deliverables:** These are the work products, the tangible items to show from the work done.

- **Quality:** This is providing the picture of what good results in producing the deliverables should look like. You're articulating the standards of performance you want to see happen, not the details of how the job should be done.

- **Manner:** This expectation applies when the delegated assignment involves much interaction or work with others. State the positive conduct that others should consistently see from the employee in getting the assignment done.

Provide background information and other pertinent news so that the employee has an overview of what the assignment or responsibility entails.

Avoid getting overly detailed as you introduce the assignment in this first step. Stay away from telling the person how to do the job, which can be discussed in Step 3. Focusing on how to do the job overlooks that people have their own styles of work and may stifle creativity. Stress the results you want rather than the methods of doing the job.

2. Define parameters.

Parameters mean boundaries or limits — the worst thing to have happen is for employees to go off in a certain direction or exercise a level of authority and be told afterwards that they shouldn't have done what they did. Understanding the boundaries to work within through trial and error can be a painful way to find out what is acceptable and not acceptable to do. It often has an effect of killing initiative.

Here are four areas of parameters to consider:

- **Budget:** A budget is a spending limit. If the assignment involves making purchases or other expenditures, what are the dollar limits for what can be spent?

- **Timeline(s):** A timeline is a deadline for any milestones and for the completion of the job. Sometimes when you're delegating an ongoing responsibility, a schedule must be maintained.

- **Feedback or information you need:** This information is what you need to be kept in the loop as the project or assignment progresses. This may include certain reports you want or news of certain kinds of situations or problems of which you want to be kept abreast.

- **Level of authority and decision making:** This is the line for employees at which they can act and decide for themselves and beyond which they need to bring you in to the situation.

3. **Provide resources for support.**

   Collaborate with the employee on what he or she needs to help ensure success in the project. Sometimes little is needed because the staff person is ready and competent to handle what you're assigning. Other times, what you're delegating is a big step forward for the employee, and some up-front investment of your time and help is needed to put the person on the road to success.

   Here is an overview of items to discuss:

   - **Expenses:** As you get into discussing with the employee what is needed to do the assignment, you realize some money to cover costs will be needed, and you then make arrangements to allow for that.

   - **Materials:** Materials are the equipment, tools, or supplies needed to get the particular job done.

   - **Access to information, resources:** Often, to do the assignment, the delegatee needs to be given certain information or needs to know where to go to find it as well as who to talk to on issues related to the assignment. Your role in this is to connect the employee to the "what" and "who" factors needed to get the job done.

   - **Staff:** Sometimes, especially if you're delegating a project in which the staff person is to play a lead role, you want to work out with your employee the human resources needed and their roles for assistance in getting the job done.

   - **Adjustments in priorities and duties:** For the delegatee to take on the project or responsibility you want done, change is sometimes needed in that person's current workload. Such adjustments include shifting current schedules with projects or priorities or assigning some tasks or duties to others on the team.

   - **Training:** Sometimes you need to teach new skills to employees so that they can complete the responsibilities you delegate to them. This may consist of walking them through the job once or twice before you give it to them to handle. It may consist of bringing in someone else who has expertise in the area to do the training.

   Whatever the case, after you complete the training, let the employee carry out the delegated duties in his or her own style. Not everyone does a job in the same way. After they learn how to do a job, allow employees to have the freedom to do it in their own style. That's when the best performance comes. Put your focus less on methods and more on the results you need to see.

- **Informing others of the employee's new role:** Sometimes, when others don't know that this person is now the responsible party, their tendency is to not give much cooperation or attention until they hear from the horse's mouth (meaning you) about the change. You can provide support by telling everyone that the delegatee is now handling a certain project or responsibility, and ask them to give that person full cooperation. This usually removes potential obstacles, and provides the authority to go with the responsibility.

Before you move to the next step in the delegating meeting, ask the employee the following question: "What else do you need in terms of support in order to handle this assignment successfully?" This question serves as a safety net for you. You may not think of all the support issues needed. In addition, asking this question provides an opportunity for the employee to raise any concerns — concerns that you two can address more easily now rather than later.

4. **Check understanding.**

Before sending the delegatee off to get to work, make sure the person understands what you want. Far too often, you think you've clearly covered everything the person needs to know, and by that person's conversation with you, you think the employee understands too. But what happens then? The employee goes off in a different direction or produces results different from what was needed, and then you find out that person's interpretation and your interpretation of what was to be done weren't the same.

To check understanding, ask an open-ended question in a clear and direct fashion. For example, "To see if I was clear on all this, please recap your understanding of what you're being asked to do here and the expectations for it." Such a question helps you see if there you need to clarify any misunderstandings *before* the employee gets started on the assignment. It also helps you know if you left any important details out of your discussion.

The worst question you can ask is "Do you understand what I am asking you to do?" Of course, almost every time the answer comes back "Yes," usually with a nod and smile. Unfortunately this close-ended question tells you nothing about the employee's understanding.

5. **Establish checkpoint meetings.**

This is the last step of the coaching discussion that you cover with the employee before the person gets started on the assignment. *Checkpoint meetings* are progress-review meetings — times set when you and the employee get together to see how the project is progressing. By setting them up front, you're planning together and, as a result, building in milestones and time frames for the assignment instead of leaving timelines vague.

A good rule to follow in setting the checkpoint meeting times is the more the assignment is new to the employee's skills and experiences, the more frequent the checkpoints. The more the employee has the skill and experience to run with the job, the less frequent the checkpoint meetings.

The checkpoint meeting helps you get the following benefits, which makes them worth your while:

- **Allows for course correction:** If the employee is off-track or is having problems, you're able to work with the person to get problems resolved. The meeting gives support and helps employees not get derailed from completing their assignment. You're increasing the likelihood for good results and employee success.

- **Builds accountability:** The checkpoint meeting prevents employees from running and hiding or procrastinating terribly in getting the assignment done. The meeting is also an opportunity to reinforce the good job your employees are doing in taking responsibility for completing the project.

- **Minimizes nagging disease:** I can think of nothing worse than being delegated a project and having a manager checking up with you daily to see what you have done. Employees usually call this behavior *micromanagement;* I call it *nagging disease.* You're nervous about letting go and want to make sure everything is being handled well. While this is understandable, the constant checking up is a major nuisance.

  Scheduled checkpoint meetings give you the opportunity to be fully informed of what is happening without having to chase after your employees to find out. Set the meetings at the frequency level that meets your needs and the needs of the employee, and then leave the person alone to get the job done.

- **Maximizes your investment:** Checkpoints allow you to emphasize quality time with your employees, as discussed in Chapter 4. The meetings allow you to be involved with what is going on without being too hands-on. They allow you to show interest without having to have daily contact. They allow you to see how spending time getting the employee started is paying off. In essence, checkpoints are the step to ensure that you get a good return on your investment of time and trust with the employee.

When you hold a checkpoint meeting, consider using the status review format as outlined in Chapter 7.

6. Provide feedback and positive reinforcement.

The last step of the delegating tool is carried out at each checkpoint and at the completion of the project or assignment. At the checkpoint meetings, give both positive and negative feedback (see Chapter 5).

Recognize the progress the employee is making and the good results being delivered. This positive reinforcement is a critical element of building success for the employee. Remember, delegating works best when you build upon success, not failure.

Steps 1 through 5 of the delegating tool are done when you initiate the assignment. Step 1 is when you do most of the talking — you know what the project entails and what outcomes you need. Steps 2 through 5 are best if done interactively. Discuss and negotiate each relevant issue as a two-way conversation. You want the employee involved and helping to shape the project specifics, for that person is the one who must own and drive the assignment. Step 6 is done along the way — the assignment is in progress, so this step involves feedback exchange. Make sure you get your feedback stated directly — especially the positive feedback to acknowledge the successes.

The end of the delegating woes

Doris was an executive vice president who ran a large department of over 100 employees. In her role, she depended on her group directors to carry out her business and leadership initiatives and to keep day-to-day operations running efficiently. As such, she often delegated — well, attempted to delegate — to her directors.

Doris found that delegating efforts with her managers didn't go smoothly and often involved much rework before getting the final products in place. After taking a coaching seminar, Doris tuned into the delegating tool, and as she put it into practice, she recognized where some of her delegating mistakes had come from.

✔ **She didn't always spell out her expectations.** When her directors turned in work to her, she often found herself saying comments like, "That's not quite what was needed," or "That's not what I was really looking for." Of course, these comments were usually met with frustration by her staff members. After the seminar, this changed for the better as Doris clearly defined the results she expected up front. Sure enough, the products and projects that came back were of higher quality.

✔ **She didn't effectively review progress.** Doris had checkpoints in her mind but she didn't articulate them. She knew that when her directors would turn in their assignments, she would review the work and ask them to make changes. The directors viewed their work as final products, not drafts for review. So when the work was sent back for revisions, frustration came out again. Doris set up clearly defined checkpoints with her directors when assignments were introduced. Having work reviewed and revised became a normal part of the process. Frustrations were gone and work was done more timely.

Doris now found delegating to be an easy coaching effort. She pulls out the six-step delegating tool to guide her discussion when she initiates an assignment and away she goes.

Here's an example of the delegating tool in action:

John was the vice president of human resources (HR) in his company. He had been having recent discussions with his fellow members of the executive team about developing and implementing a telecommuting program, in which employees work at home for some to all of their normal working hours rather than coming into an office. They looked at it as a practice that could help attract and retain employees, if it could work for the business. From these discussions, John was asked to put together a program that the executive team could review and implement.

John turned to Anne, an HR analyst on his staff, to be his point person for the research and development of a telecommuting program. This project was something Anne had wanted to do, and she had recommended to John that the company should look at implementing such a program. They met, and John utilized the delegating tool in getting Anne off to a good start in the project. Here is what they worked out.

✔ **Step 1:** The project was to involve both research and program development — interviewing some employees and managers within the company, visiting other companies, and researching periodicals to learn about telecommuting programs and what might work best for their organization. The purpose of the project was to recommend a cost-effective telecommuting program. John outlined the results he expected:

  • **Deliverables:** Two reports, one summarizing the findings from the internal interviews and one summarizing the research from the external sources; a recommended telecommuting policy; and an implementation plan for its rollout. At the end, John and Anne would make a joint presentation to the executive team on their recommendations.

  • **Quality:** The recommended policy needed to be clear and concise, addressing cost considerations, what positions would participate, and how the program would work.

  • **Manner:** Maintain responsive listening efforts in all the interactions and maintain confidentiality of all findings until they have been reviewed with the executives.

✔ **Step 2:** One parameter was for Anne to do no out-of-town travel for her research on other organization's practices. Incidental expenses that occurred in doing the research were acceptable. The other parameter was that in her fact-finding, she was to give recommendations and let employees know that she talked only of the possibility of a telecommuting program, not of the assurance of one.

John and Anne negotiated a three-month deadline. By the end of three months, all of Anne's deliverables would be written, and she and John would be ready to deliver the joint presentation. This project was also a good development opportunity for Anne, especially the opportunity to present to the company's executive management.

✔ **Step 3:** John would send out an announcement to all the employees and managers so that they would understand the project. He would also shift some of Anne's hiring activities to Bill, another member of the group. In addition, because Ann was nervous about making formal presentations, John would be involved in the presentation. He also agreed to coach Anne in making presentations as part of their preparation work.

✔ **Step 4:** Almost without asking, Anne summarized to John the essentials and expectations for this project. She was excited by it and took good notes during their dialogue.

✔ **Step 5:** Together, Anne and John set up the checkpoints around the key milestones in the project. For the first checkpoint, they would meet in one week to review Anne's draft questionnaire for the interviews and her proposed list of employees and managers to survey. The next checkpoint was set at a month-and-a-half, the midway point in the project, during which Anne would review her two fact-finding reports. This meeting would also be used to plan what the policy might look like. The last checkpoint was set for one month after the second one, and Anne would come ready with her drafts of the telecommuting program and a plan for its implementation. This would allow enough time to make necessary revisions and prepare the presentation to the executive team.

Handling Employee Resistance

Sometimes despite the best of efforts, employees don't want to do the work you want to delegate to them — no matter how nicely you ask or plead. What then?

Low interest is most often the source behind the resistance. Discover what's effecting the low interest and you uncover what is driving the resistance against what you want the employee to do. This is the key to overcoming resistance and getting performance moving forward.

This lack of interest sometimes is displayed outwardly, "Do I have to do this assignment? Can't you get someone else to do it?" Sometimes it's displayed more quietly, in which the employee nods and smiles when you make the assignment, but little effort follows. Some even take the approach to produce the opposite of what you asked to be done. Others get the job done fine but with a lot of moaning and groaning along the way.

However the low interest gets expressed, the reasons for it most often stem from employees' past experiences. These experiences may have come from working with you, while others have come from managers of long ago. Some people hold on to emotional baggage for long periods of time. No matter who the source has been, here are some experiences in delegating-type situations that have turned employees to the low point on the interest scale:

- ✔ Was given much responsibility but no authority with it
- ✔ Had an annoying manager who kept insisting on the job being done her way
- ✔ Was given assignments to use skills that aren't strengths and received no training support to develop them
- ✔ Was offered an interesting project but had it pulled away by the manager because the direction the employee took didn't suit the manager's taste
- ✔ Had a bunch of new duties dumped on the employee with no help to figure them out
- ✔ Took on a challenging project and got chastised on every little mistake made
- ✔ Was assigned a difficult project in which cooperation from others was needed but wasn't forthcoming, and the manager didn't want to be bothered with it

When you come along ready to delegate a new assignment, you encounter resistance. Reminders of the past, plus apprehensions of what could happen now, add up to a lack of interest in your project.

Managers often don't explore the reasons behind the lack of interest. Which employee would be easier for delegating an assignment to handle?

- ✔ Employee A: High interest in the job, but skill less developed to do it
- ✔ Employee B: Low interest in the job, but has high skill level to do it

Most managers select Employee A because developing skill level, especially when the person is eager and willing, is easier than motivating someone with low interest. Don't give up on that disinterested employee, however. Keep at him!

The past experiences that are blocking staff members from wanting to take on what you wish to delegate indicate, in most cases, a lack of effective guidance and support with previous delegating attempts. The key, then, to overcoming the employee resistance so they will perform is to reverse the problems that previous managers created. In particular, here are some actions that may help:

1. **Listen patiently and responsively to discover the employee's concerns.**

   Through your active listening efforts, you may discover a simple reason for the employee's disinterest in what you want to delegate: The individual just doesn't like that kind of work — no apprehensions or past experiences of suffering involved. So even though the assignment is something the person can handle, it is just not something the employee likes to do.

   In these cases, take the *such-is-life approach:* Oh well, such is life that on occasion something has to be done in your job which isn't something you're fond of doing. You don't say these thoughts, but with this approach in mind, you can acknowledge the employee's point, nod and smile, and then proceed to working on the delegating plan with that person. In simple terms, don't dwell on an area that isn't that important.

   Keep what you learned in mind for future assignments. But if this is the best resource to take on an assignment you need help with, proceed. It's all part of work and why your employees get paid to do it.

2. **Plan with the employee steps to take to ensure that the right level of support is given for success to occur.**

3. **Explain the importance of the assignment and related big-picture stuff as you develop the plan together.**

4. **If the assignment has meaningful benefit to the employee, spell that out.**

   Only do so if it is truly the case; otherwise, you're selling broccoli to someone who hates vegetables.

5. **Reassign the job to someone else only when you see that truly is the best option under the circumstances.**

   If you do give the project to someone else, off-load something from the other person to this employee. Be firm about your expectation that everyone helps the team and is to pull his or her fair share of the work.

6. **Follow through on the support efforts you agreed to and be receptive when the employee comes to you with any questions in doing the assignment.**

Using Delegating to Build the Pillars of Commitment

One major benefit you get from delegating effectively is having a positive influence on employee commitment. Here is how this coaching tool affects each of the five pillars for building employee commitment, discussed in Chapter 2.

✔ **Focus:** By spelling out your expectations and setting parameters when you delegate, you give employees a clear direction and the sense of importance they need to get the job done well. When employees know the high standards you expect, they're more likely to focus on meeting them.

✔ **Involvement:** Shaping the initial course of the delegated assignment is done collaboratively between you and the employee. When you use this tool right, you're not assigning work; rather, you're planning together to get work done. The employee takes over from there and works to bring home success. This is involvement at its best.

✔ **Development:** Many delegated assignments or responsibilities provide staff with opportunities to grow in skill, abilities, and experience. Through training provided, employee's capabilities develop for the better.

✔ **Gratitude:** This pillar is especially impacted through your follow-up efforts in checkpoint meetings (discussed in the "Putting the Delegating Tool into Action" section earlier in this chapter). As you delegate, you positively reinforce the progress your employees make, building on experiences of success.

✔ **Accountability:** The progress review nature of the checkpoint meetings serve to reinforce employee accountability. In addition, because you let employees handle assignments when you delegate (your role is to give support), they know from the fruits of their own labor when they're doing well. Self-sufficiency is promoted, and that's a key driver for accountability.

Part V
Grooming and Growing Your Employees

The 5th Wave   By Rich Tennant

"I think Dick Foster should get the promotion. He's got the vision, the drive, and let's face it, that big white hat doesn't hurt either."

In this part . . .

This part focuses on developing employee skills and capabilities. From training your employees to helping them actively manage their own careers to jointly creating plans that guide efforts for growth (or guide improvement when performance isn't up to par), this part is jam-packed with ideas and tips.

Chapter 14

Knowing When — and How — to Train

. . . .

In This Chapter

▶ Determining in what areas you need to train staff

▶ Preparing and organizing the instruction

▶ Keeping the trainees involved in their own learning

▶ Using others to deliver the instruction

▶ Reinforcing what your staff is taught

. . . .

*E*mployees frequently ask you how to do aspects of their jobs or ask you to show them how to accomplish a task step by step. Questions like these are the signs that some form of training needs to happen. If you leave the questions unanswered, employees fumble in their performance. On the other hand, by quickly answering them — telling employees to just do this or just do that — employees don't learn to do the task or skill themselves.

Sometimes, as a coach, you need to stop and teach. This means actually taking time to train a staff member or your entire staff in some aspects of their jobs that will help them perform better. This is direct and guided instruction, different from the mentoring and tutoring aspects of coaching that are covered in Part III. Mentoring and tutoring take place through conversation in an informal manner and through allowing employees to learn from their experiences and share them with you. With the mentoring and tutoring tool of coaching, you share insights and challenge employees to think and then do for themselves, but you're not telling them how to do their jobs.

When you need to train (the focus of this chapter), the effort is somewhat more formal in nature. In this case, you're actually showing and telling employees how to do something in their jobs.

In every job from widget maker to company president, training needs to happen. Some training happens informally and through experience on the job. But some of it, if your objective is to get the best out of each employee's performance, needs to happen through direct instruction. This chapter shows you how to train your staff effectively.

Come One, Come All: Time For Training

Sports coaches recognize that sometimes before you work with your team to execute a strategy or game plan, you first have to teach the fundamentals. (Oops, couldn't help throwing in this sports analogy in this coaching book!)

Managers often have the same need. Before the staff can carry out certain duties or functions, they need to be taught how to do them. But how do you know when such training for individuals or the group is needed or what to teach if it is? The following sections can help.

Knowing when to train

Certain signs and situations indicate that one or several employees will benefit from staff training:

- ✔ **New employee:** Consider this an automatic. Regardless of the person's previous experience, recognize that this individual has not yet worked in your organization. Tossing the person into the job without any instruction slows the learning curve and makes the initial adjustment much more difficult.

  New employees usually need to learn procedures, tasks, special job skills, and the workings of the organization. Look at these areas as starting points for organizing training for new employees.

- ✔ **Operational changes:** Operational changes can involve a variety of factors that affect the way employees are to do their jobs going forward. Changes may come from implementation of new work standards, new computer systems or applications, new products or services, or new procedures or policies.

  Introducing changes without any instruction tends to increase errors, reduce efficiency, and convince employees that the changes are no good anyway. Training not only speeds up employees' abilities to do the new skills required but increases their comfort level and adjustment time with the changes made.

- ✔ **Questions you're asked:** Sometimes, one or more individuals in your group come to you fairly often with similar questions about a subject, and the nature of their questions point to not having skill or knowledge in that area. When such patterns are showing, you're getting a sign that training is needed.

  Such time will be time well spent. After employees know how to do something, time that was spent being interrupted with how-do-I? questions is freed up. Employees also have better use of their time because they are not sitting and waiting until they can get their questions answered. The training increases their self-sufficiency.

✔ **Sharpening skills:** Employees are like bread. Leave them sitting there for awhile and they grow stale. Sharpening employees' skills may actually mean retraining — training again on skills and procedures taught before. Look at the important duties, tasks, and procedures in your employees' jobs. Training them once, if at all, in those areas and expecting them to be top notch and proficient in them is wishful thinking. Employees constantly need to keep their skills current and sharp. Don't let the bread get moldy.

✔ **Mistakes and quality problems:** What errors are some individuals (or the entire group) making from time to time? What are problems you see in your processes that keep quality from being as strong as you need? What difficulties do employees encounter in trying to perform their job functions well? Quite often, these patterns of mistakes and problems can be corrected through organized teaching efforts.

Leaving these quality issues unaddressed keeps them lingering and sends the message that high standards of performance aren't that important. Behavior that's rewarded is repeated: Training helps employees correct mistakes and improve quality and thus reinforces high standards of performance.

✔ **Important behavior skills:** One of the amazing feats performed in businesses today, a Ripley's-Believe-It-or-Not feat, is that when employees are asked to take on critical responsibilities that require some important behavior skills, they receive little or no training on how to exhibit these behaviors. This feat often shows itself in the areas of management, teamwork, and customer service, to name a few.

These behaviors are usually incorporated into the regular duties of the job; employees are living them, often on a daily basis. So their importance may not be fully recognized and they're taken for granted. Working on the development of these skills with your employees goes a long way toward increasing their success on the job.

✔ **Grooming:** Nothing to do with hygiene or dog care on this one. Sometimes you have an individual or two whom you want to grow and prepare to take on greater responsibilities. Hoping that the individual figures everything out on his own is akin to locking him up in a dark room and asking him to find the light switches that happen to be outside the door.

When such needs exist, you want to provide training that develops employees for these bigger duties and opportunities. Training also serves as a sign of support and indicates to employees that you want to prepare them to succeed.

✔ **Promotions:** Preparing for promotions is similar to grooming, except that the person has arrived — often without any grooming to get there. Many new responsibilities and skills needed to do the higher-level role face people when they get promoted — and may overwhelm them and smack them in the face. In many cases, when people get promoted, as into management roles, they feel like new employees all over again.

The sink-or-swim approach; that is, you're now on your own to figure out your new job, does little to help employees make fast and effective adjustments. While providing instruction isn't all that's needed, teaching efforts help greatly and give employees a feeling of support.

✔ **Coverage needs:** Perhaps you or another person on your staff is the only one who can do a task or duty that affects the day-to-day functioning of your group's operations. In this case, a dependency exists that can leave you vulnerable. What happens if that person gets ill, moves away, or gets called away for a special space mission? And how do you allow vacations to occur?

When such dependencies exist, you can provide training so that others can cover the functions, expanding the number of people who can do the task or function, and providing you the coverage you need. Customers appreciate this, too.

Tune into these signs and situations. They indicate that you need to take the time to teach. Leaving employees to figure things out for themselves doesn't enhance professional development and productivity. Coaching is about getting the best out of employee performance, and sometimes you need to provide training to do so.

Recognizing what to teach

The emphasis in coaching is to maximize your resources. To do so means you need to develop employee skills, knowledge, and abilities that enhance their performance. This emphasis on growth and development is done on an ongoing basis with coaching, and training is a tool to help in the effort.

By having this ongoing emphasis on development, needs that arise that call for training are easily recognized. You don't have to wait until the crisis moments hit to decide that training may be helpful, as in the following case: "We are losing dozens of customers each month and have been for many months because our employees don't understand the products we have or how to best service customers. Maybe if we did some training, now, that would help!"

The areas where training needs most often arise fall into five main categories, covered in the following sections.

Job-technical skills

Every job has technical aspects to it. "Technical" here doesn't refer to a certain field but rather to the core skills and knowledge needed to perform the essentials of the job. If you're a plumber, plumbing is your technical area; if you work as an accountant, accounting is your technical side; if you work as a city government building inspector, construction and building codes are your technical areas; if you work in human resources, personnel functions are your technical areas; and if you're a software engineer, your technical side is computer programming. These skills are what carry out the tasks and responsibilities in employees' jobs on a daily basis. They are essential for keeping the operations running.

Some job-technical skills even require some formal trade or college education as a base to performing the job.

Literacy skills

Everyone is supposed to learn skills to read and write in school. Yet multitudes of people who have passed through the basic levels of formal education — elementary through high school — are in the workforce with limited abilities to read and write. Referred to as *functional illiterates,* such individuals often get by in unskilled positions but are limited in how far they can go and in what they can truly perform on the job. Adult literacy programs have been growing in the United States to address these problems, and more and more employers are bringing such training services into their organizations.

In other cases, basic literacy isn't the issue — employees can read and write at functional levels — but business writing skills leave much to be desired. The ability to write work-related correspondence, memos, reports, and other important documents are the focus of the teaching, from using grammar to writing thoughts with clarity — all with the intent of helping people do their essential duties more effectively.

English-language skills

Training may also be needed to help employees speak more effectively. For those who have limited English speaking skills, *ESL* (English as a second language) programs have sprung up to build the speaking skills of the new workers. Employers may contract these services to be done in-house or send their employees to get training through outside services.

Other employees may have the need to increase their confidence and skill in using the language. Advanced language-skills programs and specialists exist to help your staff increase their use of vocabulary and enhance their ability to clearly pronounce words.

Computer-application skills

Today, computers are a standard tool of the job, just like a pencil. Few jobs now exist in which the people in them don't have to touch a computer for some work use, even if it is just entering simple data.

More and more jobs require employees to use some form of computer application — including word processing, spreadsheets, graphics, databases, data entry and manipulation, and using the Internet — to get their work done. Teaching employees these various applications and the systems that go with them is necessary to maintain work demands and productivity.

Professional-behavior skills

Sometimes called *soft skills,* in actuality, these are hard skills to learn because they deal with people's behavior and making changes to that behavior. These are the areas employees need for interacting and working with others effectively to get their jobs done. Some critical areas include the following:

- ✔ Customer service
- ✔ Interpersonal communications — active listening and assertive speaking
- ✔ Management development, including coaching
- ✔ Teamwork and shared decision making
- ✔ Problem solving
- ✔ Conflict resolution
- ✔ Running meetings
- ✔ Managing and adapting to change
- ✔ Formal presentations
- ✔ Sales

Because most jobs involve people working and interacting in some way with other people, opportunities for using these behaviors are plentiful and the need to develop skills in these areas vital. Unfortunately, helping employees develop professional behavior skills is often overlooked — akin to having a group construct a building but not giving them any tools to do the work.

Preparing Before You Teach

You may know what areas to go after for training staff, as well as the situations to pay attention to when trying to determine when training is needed. But before you call in your staff to teach them what they need to learn for their jobs, get yourself prepared and organized first.

Creating a lesson plan

Figure 14-1 provides you with a lesson plan to help you prepare your training, whether you're going to work with an individual or conduct a seminar for your entire staff. Like a teacher in a school classroom, coming ready with your lesson plan helps you have a plan of attack for carrying out your training efforts.

Learning objectives:

Time allotment:

Outline of subject matter:

Methods of instruction:

Materials:

Figure 14-1:
The lesson
plan.

The following list describes each of the key ingredients in the lesson plan in Figure 14-1. The idea is to fill it out before you start your training session and to use it as a guide when you deliver the training.

- ✔ **Learning objectives:** These are the outcomes you want to achieve from your teaching effort. They answer the question, "What you want the participants to accomplish?" Consider having one, no more than a few, for any training session you do so that no one is forced to learn everything at once. Learning objectives give the training a focus.

   Write the objective statements in one clear sentence. Here are a few examples:

   - To build the skills to resolve difficult customer situations.

   - To reinforce the department's quality assurance procedure.

   - To develop skills to proficiently use the new accounts payable system.

- ✔ **Time allotment:** How much time are you going to spend for the training session? If this is a subject you wish to cover over a few sessions, how much time will you devote to each and over what period? The answers to these questions help you manage your time more efficiently and let your staff know how long to plan to be in training.

   Nearly nothing is more painful than going into a meeting and seeing it run on and on with no ending time for it. The training session with a staff member or the group is a form of a meeting. Set the time for it so you can use the time together wisely.

- ✔ **Outline of subject matter:** The outline is the listing, in order, of the key topics you're to cover in the training session. For example, suppose your subject for a training session with your staff is delivering quality customer service. Your outline could be as follows:

   I. Introduce key learning objectives

   II. Two key principles for delivering quality service

   III. Listening to customer needs and issues

   IV. Resolving customer problems

   V. Close: your take-away points

   The outline goes to the content of what you're planning to teach. It serves as an agenda to guide the flow of the instruction. Certainly, you can be more detailed by listing subtopics under each main topic, but avoid creating a script. You're not delivering a major political speech for which you want every word written out. Instead, you're organizing the flow of your instruction.

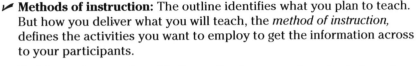

✔ **Methods of instruction:** The outline identifies what you plan to teach. But how you deliver what you will teach, the *method of instruction,* defines the activities you want to employ to get the information across to your participants.

Feel free to be creative with the methods you use in order to keep learning fun. The key is to use instructional strategies that involve the learners in the experience of learning. People retain better and apply more of what they learn when they have some kind of active engagement in what they are taught.

The following gives you a variety of ways to deliver training to your staff. In many situations, you may want to use more than one method of instruction for a training session. Many are explained in the "Shaping active learners" section later in this chapter.

- **Ice breakers or warm-up exercises:** Introductory activities that teach a simple point and loosen up participants for more instruction to follow.

- **Model:** Demonstrate a method and the trainee follows your example.

- **Trainee does task hands-on with verbal guidance:** The trainee completes the skill or task hands-on by following your verbal explanation of what to do.

- **Inquiry:** You guide the participant to perform the task or skill being taught, primarily by asking questions.

- **Explanation followed by structured practice:** You verbally tell how the task or skill is to be done and allow the individual an opportunity to try it a few times to get the hang of it.

- **Presentation followed by trainee summary:** The trainee explains back to you the highlights of the information you explain to him.

- **Role-play:** Acting out a skill to get the feel of how to do it.

- **Simulation:** Creating or reenacting a life-like situation in which participants perform what they have been taught.

- **Self-study:** The trainee reads and completes worksheets or does the same kind of thing online.

- **Lab activity:** Hands-on application for trying out or experimenting with what was taught — especially useful with technical skills.

- **Discussion:** Group-wide give-and-take dialogue about the subject being taught.

- **Participants present to each other or demonstrate:** Participants teach one another in a formal way on a skill or subject that needs to be learned.

- **Self-assessments:** Participants fill out questionnaires and reflect on how well or how often they employ certain behaviors.

- **Experiential exercises:** Exercises that create an situation from which people can learn.

- **Presentation and analysis of bad and good examples:** Participants see what not to do and what to do by contrasting how each works or doesn't work effectively.

- **Games:** From board games to quiz-show games, trainees play while applying what they've learned.

- **Case studies:** Examining stories and discussing the lessons they teach.

- **Sorting, decision-making exercises:** Exercises that participants use in order to make judgment in different situations.

- **Group brainstorming exercises:** Trainees providing and sharing ideas as a way to learn about a topic.

- **Audiovisual aids:** The use of media — from compact disks to audio cassettes and good old-fashioned overhead slides — to help deliver the instruction.

- **Lecture:** Old-fashioned and common way of teaching in which you talk and the audience receives.

✔ **Materials:** *Materials* defines the learning aids you plan to use to support your instruction. They may be in the form of handouts, workbooks, manuals, slides, flip charts, tools, compact disks, or whatever other tangible items you need for the delivery of instruction.

In most cases, try to provide some kind of written material or other learning aid that reinforces what you're teaching and gives the employees a reference they can call upon when back on the job.

The lesson plan serves as your guide for delivering the instruction. It gets you prepared. Sometimes you find, when writing up the plan, that you need to do some research first. You need to get your facts or other information in order. Consider this research an important part of the preparation.

Going easy, step by step

People learn best when what's being taught is broken down in a step-by-step fashion. In preparing your training, do a *task analysis,* which is the breakdown of the task, procedure, or skill you're going to teach into a step-by-step approach.

In many cases, this means having a written document that spells out the how-to's of the content that the employee is to learn. It walks the person through the task in an orderly fashion from start to finish.

Here are a few tips to follow in writing up your task analysis document:

1. **State what the task or procedure is.**

   This identifies what the employee is to learn. State it as the heading of the task analysis document.

2. **List each important step in sequence.**

   Next, write out each step of how one does the task, in order, from start to finish. Get the key steps down. While you don't want to overkill with detail, don't leave out any important steps.

3. **Translate and be clear.**

   Define all terms and acronyms the learner needs to know. Clearly explain each step as if a beginner were to read the document.

4. **Provide learning aids as necessary.**

   If a diagram, picture, or some other aid goes with the task analysis, be sure to include it for your trainee and refer to it in the document you write.

The concept of task analysis is what the term says. Analyze how tasks are carried out in a logical flow. This guides you to carry out your instruction in a logical and organized manner.

Keep in mind, when you're teaching an individual or a group, you're doing so because they're less familiar than you on how to do something. The beauty and value of doing task analysis as part of your preparation is that it forces you to not take anything for granted and to be organized in delivering your instruction.

I often make this point in my coaching seminars with managers by having them write a task analysis for tying their shoes. This seemingly simple task is something funny to watch as the participants struggle to write a logical explanation of how to tie shoes. People have come up with anywhere from four to twelve steps in the process. I then have them follow what they wrote and explain to me live how to tie my shoes. Quite often they edit along the way, with other participants jumping in to fill in the gaps.

Keeping Your Class Involved

When you're ready to deliver your instruction, you want to find ways to keep your learner actively involved. People learn best when they're involved in the effort to teach them. This tip often is overlooked by many managers and even by professional trainers. The tendency is to talk at people and hope they get it: Give the employees a clear explanation and if they have no questions, you've done your coaching job well, right?

Well, no. When many people receive training, they're good at sitting and smiling. This passive approach to learning tells you nothing about what the trainees are comprehending and what they can truly go out and perform. In fact, if you look at the list of instructional methods and activities in the "Creating a lesson plan" section earlier in this chapter, you notice the last two — audiovisual aids and lecture — are quite different than the other 19 activities on the list. Lecture, a common method of instruction and one used frequently in schools, and audiovisual aids, sometimes used to spice up the presentation, are forms of one-way communication. They don't seek or invite involvement from the receivers who are to learn what you have to teach. The other 19 items in the list have the trainees involved in some way with their own learning.

Shaping active learners

In your coaching efforts, you may have to teach a group. Group training is most applicable when a subject or skill is something you want everyone to learn and doing so together is the best way to get the training done. Other times in your coaching efforts, when the need to teach arises, it is on a case-by-case, individual basis.

When you need to teach in a one-on-one setting, use the following half-dozen strategies from the "Creating a lesson plan" section earlier in this chapter. These methods involve the trainees in their own learning, helping create active, not passive, participation.

Model

To *model* is to demonstrate how to do something. You show the other person first, and then the trainee tries the task as you watch. This I-show-you, you-show-me method usually goes back and forth in the learning session a number of times. You keep doing it until the trainee begins to get competence at doing the task taught.

Modeling is especially effective when you have a hands-on type of task for the employee to learn, such as assembling a piece of equipment, operating a piece of machinery, or performing other kinds of procedures that usually involve some kind of physical activity. The individual is forced to perform as part of the instructional effort — active and involved learning at its best. No nodding and smiling. You really see how the person is getting what you're teaching. Keep the back-and-forth practice going until the individual is truly performing the task — then you've made modeling work.

Trainee does task hands-on with verbal guidance

This method takes learning by doing to the ultimate. The trainee's hands do all the walking and performing, not yours. You provide the guided tour by verbally taking the person through the task step by step. Sometimes you may want the individual to take notes as a reference for later. The written and the hands-on work together — all done by the trainee — often to strengthen the retention of what was taught

This method of instruction is useful when teaching a computer application. The trainee's hands are on the keyboard, not yours. In fact, give the person permission to slap your hand if you start interfering to do the task in an effort to help the learner.

Nothing is more frustrating in my learning experience than to have someone hit all the keys to show you how to work something on the computer while you sit by watching passively. Avoid falling into this trap. It is easy to do because you think you're being helpful by showing off your expertise. But the minute you create a watch-and-do-nothing learning situation, you encourage your trainee to check out and maybe not come back.

Inquiry

The primary thrust of inquiry is to use questions to guide the instruction. The individual figures out how to do what's being taught by answering each question along the way.

The idea with inquiry is to not to play a mystery game with your employee but to challenge the person to think. This works well when the individual has a knowledge or experience base on the subject or task being taught — such as learning the latest version of a software application or figuring out how to do a revised job procedure. Don't use inquiry otherwise. Quite often, you want to refer to that background in your questions to help your trainee draw upon this past experience. It helps the new task seem more familiar and, for your employee, creates excitement as the new task is figured out — the positive energy from feeling a sense of accomplishment.

Explanation followed by structured practice

With this method, you start out by explaining how the task or procedure works. Sometimes you use other methods such as modeling or verbal guidance to give the explanation. But the real learning takes place by having the employee go off and practice what was taught until the skill is ready to be put into action.

This is the key for this method — what is taught is practiced before it is ever applied in real-life situations. The idea is to give the employee safe practice; that is, what is tried causes no harm.

Suppose you instruct a new employee in how to handle customer calls related to servicing the company's products. What you don't do after giving the explanation about handling calls is have the person get right on the phone and deal with the next customer call that comes in. Instead, you have

the staff member work from a tape recorder with simulated customer situations. The trainee practices responding to such situations and then reviews those calls with you afterwards.

So this instructional method goes in steps: instruction, then employees practice on their own, followed by review with you of how the practice went. The practice may get repeated a few times until the employee is ready to perform live.

Presentation followed by trainee summary

Sometimes, the simplest way to teach something is to just talk about the process and explain how it is done. But with this instructional method, you don't stop there; otherwise, all you have is a boring lecture approach.

What you do up front is tell your staff person to let you explain how to do the task at hand, to ask you questions along the way and even take notes as applicable, and then be ready to explain how to do the task back to you. This method is especially useful when what is being taught is more informational than hands-on in nature. Your effort to explain upfront what will happen in the instruction creates the setting for interactive learning.

Here are a couple of examples of this training method in action (and there are multitudes of other examples!):

- ✔ You explain the key steps to follow in handling customer requests, and the employee summarizes back to you what to do.

- ✔ You explain how the purchasing process functions and the employee verbalizes back to you the highlights of how the process works.

Role-play

Role-play is a learning activity that involves acting, although no acting skills are required. Role-play usually works well as a way to practice a skill or process that has been taught.

For example, suppose you're teaching a staff member how to handle difficult customer situations. After walking through some tips and strategies to use in such situations, you re-create one: You play the difficult customer and the employee has to apply what was taught to resolve the situation.

Sometimes you may want to take on the staff person's role first as a way to model how to handle an interaction, and then switch roles so that your learner goes on the firing line. You may also want to have a debriefing after the role-play scenario during which you review together how the situation was handled. Role-playing is meant to be fun, but also helps teach a lesson.

Combining the six instructional methods

The six instructional methods described in the previous sections can be used in combination. For example:

1. **You present how to handle some customer interactions, and the employee gives feedback to show what was comprehended.**

2. **As a form of practice, you role-play some scenarios to give the employee a hands-on feel of dealing with such interactions.**

The key is to use the method or methods that best help the trainee get involved and learn effectively.

Adopting a few tips for delivery

There's more than meets the eye when training your staff effectively. The following sections offers a few additional tips to help in the delivery of your teaching efforts.

Encourage questions

When employees know that asking questions is a good thing to do, they're more likely to do it. Of course, when asking questions, they're more involved in what you're teaching and the quality of their learning goes up.

The best way to encourage questions is to let the employees know they are welcomed. Say so from the start. "Don't hesitate to ask any questions as we go through this training. Remember, there's no such thing as a dumb question." Periodically, throughout the instruction, pause and ask for questions. "Are there any questions about what we just covered?" Or even better, "What questions can I answer for you on what we have done?"

Be receptive to questions asked

While you may say that you're open to questions, what happens when they get asked? If your responses are something like, "We don't have time for that now," or "You're going to have to look that one up yourself," then goodbye future questions and hello "I don't learn much from you."

Questions not only come up while you're doing the teaching but often come up afterwards as the employees are putting into practice what they were taught. In either case, respond to questions that employees raise as if they are gifts of gold sent to you from Fort Knox. Sometimes saying remarks like "That's a good question" or "I appreciate your asking" gives your trainees the feeling that they're truly appreciated. Directly answer all questions or work with the employees to figure out answers.

When you encourage questions and are responsive when you receive them, you create the atmosphere that makes learning safe and enriching. Your behavior is key to all of this. By creating a coaching situation in which questions flow freely, you make your job of teaching easier and often explore issues in greater depth, which benefits both you and your trainees.

Give lots of feedback

As you carry out your teaching efforts, you want to give feedback along the way. Sometimes you give a lot of little feedback and sometimes you give some big feedback.

- ✔ *Little feedback* includes the helpful comments of encouragement and correction you give while the training is happening: "That's good. You got it. Well done. Not quite, try again. Look out for that obstacle."

- ✔ *Big feedback* is the specific feedback, both positive and negative, that you give to review a learning effort or practice.

Constructive feedback, from little to big, provides positive reinforcement and guidance to help your employees learn and do the job right. Therefore (as covered in Chapter 5), make sure your feedback is sincere, helpful, and direct, as well as specific and observations-based for the big feedback moments. No one gets chastised for mistakes, and everyone gets a positive boost for good efforts.

Take the time needed

When the need exists to teach one or more of your employees a task or skill, their familiarity with the subject is less than yours, so you have to allow the time necessary for your learners to truly learn. Sometimes, especially for practical reasons, you may have a few sessions together before the individuals master what you've taught. Sometimes, you may walk them through how to do a procedure a few times before they're ready to do the job on their own.

Gauge how long to take by how well your trainee is progressing. Ask the people you're training to evaluate their own progress, and be open to their feedback for you. You don't have to accomplish the training in one shot.

Do follow-up

After completing a teaching session with your employees, check back to see how they are doing on the job. You're training them on something they are expected to use, so set and hold a follow-up meeting when the training time is finished.

When you do the follow-up review, share your observations of the person's progress and ask the individual to do the same. By knowing you're going to do a follow-up, you're often tuned in to watching how the employee is performing. The progress review also reinforces accountability to apply what was taught, and helps you gauge whether any additional training is needed.

Learning to teach as a coach

Mary is a sales manager who manages a fairly large group of inside-sales associates. People generally hired in the role aren't expected to have that much technical or sales experience because this is considered an entry-level sales position in the company. The new inside-sales associates have much to learn in the beginning — the company's services, its inventory, the computer system, and ways to make telephone sales calls. They also have to learn to coordinate their efforts with the sales professionals out in the field.

The training is one of great struggle for most new inside-sales associates. They have a lot of technical information and sales skills to learn, and after three months on the job, most are not usually up to speed. Over the course of a couple of years, Mary has been going to her human resources director expressing frustration over the slow efforts of her new hires. She is often tempted to fire some of the new employees before they complete their probationary period.

After this problem occurred for the fifth time in two years, the HR director decides to analyze the training efforts for the new hires with Mary. In careful evaluation, they realize that Mary's expectations are not matching reality. Most new hires take six months to really grasp the job, not the three months that Mary expects. At the same time, most new hires aren't receiving consistent and organized training efforts. Mary's time with them is often scattered, and time that senior staff spends with them is much the same. So while the new employees are getting exposed to all the right areas, they're often left on their own to figure everything out.

With the help of the HR director, Mary starts to think like a coach to evaluate what is really needed. This leads her to establish a consistent, organized training process for new hires, with feedback and progress review along the way. Her time is now more structured with them as well. Sure enough, after implementing the new training process, Mary is finding that her new hires do come up to speed in three months, and her frustrations have disappeared.

Plan for it and have fun

You can often find yourself trying to squeeze in some time to teach your staff the skills and tasks they need to know. The squeezing effect often means that you don't devote the time needed, and end up postponing your training efforts. Employees pick up on this and infer that learning isn't a priority and neither are the employees — a fine way to demotivate employee performance.

A coaching manager views the need to teach employees as part of a manager's job, not as something extra you try to squeeze in when you can. When the need to teach exists, time is scheduled and planning is done so that time together will be fruitful.

In addition, a coach approaches the teaching effort with the desire to see employees achieve success through their learning, not as an onerous task to do. For your staff, learning can and should be a positive experience, so have a good time doing it. Allow for a sense of humor. By encouraging questions and using activities that invite participation, both you and your employees have fun during the learning experience.

Using Others for Instruction

When you view helping employees learn and grow in their skills and abilities as an important part of your job, you're shifting to managing as a coach instead of a doer (see Chapter 1). Getting your employees the training they need is part of this effort, but delivering the training isn't a one-person job that you must always fulfill. In fact, in some cases, you don't have the expertise, let alone the time, to provide all the training your staff needs.

Your role here is best served as resource facilitator. While this sounds like a fancy function or title, it simply means that you're the one who works with your employees to find the appropriate resources who can help meet their training needs. As part of this role, you may help organize the training efforts that take place. In sum, you help get the resources needed and ensure the training happens but aren't necessarily the one to deliver the teaching.

Using reinforcements

Sometimes, outside services can be great sources to help meet your employees' needs for training. The key is to plan with each staff member what training will be of help. You're then able to be on the lookout for what these outside sources can offer.

Here are some external resources to which you can send your staff to receive training.

- **Public seminars:** You probably get a lot of flyers in the mail advertising various types of public seminars. For a fee, you go to a conference facility, such as a hotel, along with employees from many other companies and organizations who have signed up for that particular topic. Topics offered at these public seminars are of a wide variety from time management to people management, from using WordPerfect to writing perfect words and sentences. Think of a job-related subject you want to learn about and sooner or later you'll see a flyer for a public seminar advertising it.

  Training organizations, some national in scope and others locally based, usually sponsor these workshops — occasionally, individual consultants offer them, too. Such seminars often run from a half-day to several days.

Sending a staff member to such seminars gives the person a chance to get exposed to the outside world while picking up some helpful tips and techniques at the same time.

✔ **Companies:** More and more companies who develop software, hardware, and various engineering products offer technical seminars or courses for their customers or other interested parties. This usually means that the person you send gets to travel somewhere to attend the training — a nice perk for many employees.

These training sessions sometimes run for a week or more and often also give the participants certification in a particular skill set. Talk to your vendors or the makers of the applications your employees use to find out more about what training courses they offer. Tune into companies that specialize in offering computer-applications training to find out what courses are slated.

✔ **Professional and trade associations:** Nearly every occupational field has a professional or trade association attached to it. If you work in that field, you pay a fee to join as a member and then get access to a variety of resources for professional growth, including educational ones. Like professional associations, government and educational sectors offer much the same type of resources and educational opportunities for people who work in those areas.

These associations offer a variety of workshops and sometimes major conferences for their members — some even allow non-members to sign up, usually for a higher fee. These training sessions usually give the attendees useful information and skills for their job-technical areas and also provide good opportunities for employees to meet with others from the same profession to forge relationships and share ideas.

✔ **Colleges:** Higher institutions of learning, from community colleges to universities, have also become resources to service the training needs of employers and their employees. They have the regular programs for their students, but they also offer day-long workshops or multi-session certification programs to non-students.

Some schools refer to these seminar and course offerings as part of their *extension programs.* They are usually taught by outside professionals who look to bring practical and real-world flavor to the classes. (Sorry, no academic flavors in this ice cream.) Most such colleges publish catalogues with schedules of classes that your employees can sign up for.

✔ **Training departments:** Larger business organizations often have their own internal training departments. These departments usually offer and conduct a variety of training classes that you can send staff members to when a course fits your need. You can also give the internal professionals input on courses you want to see offered when needs aren't yet met and can turn to them for information on outside courses taught through other resources.

Bringing the outside resources in

When many members of your staff have a need to learn something, bringing an outside expert in to teach is far more cost-effective than sending a large group out to various public offerings. Having the whole group go through training together often creates a common experience of sharing and learning. It serves as a form of team building and gives everyone the same song sheet, so to speak, to work from when back on the job — an extra boost for your training effort. Also, by having a paid outside expert come in, and by allowing time away from the job devoted for the training, you give the sessions an extra sense of importance.

Community colleges, training companies, and individual training consultants are usually the outside services that can do in-house instruction for you. They give you the expertise that you're not likely to have in terms of both subject matter and (hopefully!) training skills.

Because you're spending time and money for such resources, the next two sections offer tips to get the best out of these trainers.

Be a part of the course design

Spell out the needs and issues you want to see addressed for your group in the training sessions. Review course materials in advance and discuss activities or instructional methods that the trainer is planning to use. In fact, refer to the lesson plan worksheet in Figure 14-1 to guide your discussion with the trainer as the workshop is being created.

You know your group best. Share their issues and challenges with the trainer, and then make sure that what the instructor designs for the seminar meets the needs you've spelled out.

✔ **Insist upon having take-away materials.** You want your staff to come away with reference materials — books, manuals, learning guides, or other instructional aids. Life isn't a closed-book test. When employees experience the workshop and then have some kind of reference guide to go back to for future situations, you increase the ease of applying what was taught in the course. Have the reference materials be a guide for what was instructed or some kind of reinforcement of the key points taught.

Good instruction is important, but leaving the learning to people's memory alone is asking way too much. Make sure your employees walk away from the training with some kind of materials they can refer back to in the future.

✔ **Emphasize practical and interactive.** Some public seminars you could send staff to have 50 to over 100 people in attendance. When you bring the outside expertise in to deliver training, you get the advantage of having a more intimate setting. As such, avoid having trainers who only know how to lecture and pontificate on certain concepts.

You want your staff to be actively involved in what they are learning — just as you do when teaching as part of your coaching efforts (see the "Keeping Your Class Involved" section earlier in this chapter for more tips). You also want them to get tools or how-to's for use back on the job. Thus, emphasizing the training be interactive and practical is just asking for a bang out of your buck.

✔ **Treat the sessions as a priority.** Because you're spending money to have this training put on, you want everyone the training is for in attendance and giving their best effort. You lose this value if people schedule other meetings at the same time, take long breaks, or pop in and out of the room during the training.

Communicate this importance to your staff. Insist that calls and other work issues be handled after the training session. If need be, hold the training away from the office so that distractions can be eliminated. While no perfect time exists to have training, set it at times that can best fit work schedules and let everyone involved know in advance, with the expectation they should work to get the best out of the training sessions.

✔ **Participate wherever applicable.** A big part of leadership is just showing up. When you set aside time and money for training on subjects you want your whole group to learn, your showing up communicates to your staff that you're participating. It shows you have the need and desire to learn like everyone else and that this kind of training is of great importance. Participating in the session also gives you a better opportunity to reinforce what was learned after the training is over. Turn your cell phone off and participate positively and fully just as you want your staff to do.

Ralph organized a communications and customer service seminar for his staff. He worked with the training consultant to have the course customized to fit his employees' work situations. And he participated in the training session right along with the rest of the group.

A few days after the seminar, one of his staff members came to him with a problem she saw with a co-worker. Because of his going through the course, Ralph tutored with a couple of questions. He asked what she learned in the training that could help her communicate the issue to her co-worker and how she would go about doing that. Instead of him handling the situation, the training served as a coaching tool for him to have the employee handle her own issue.

Afterward, the employee let Ralph know what success she got from the skills learned in the seminar. For Ralph, a great investment of money and time, especially his own, was realized.

Reinforce what's learned at the training session

When you send staff to outside seminars or have them participate in internal training sessions — from within your organization to within your group — don't make the mistake of saying nothing to employees after they return from these sessions. Because the staff received formalized training, often put on by outside experts, some managers think that those employees should instantly apply what was taught back on the job. Wrong!

How you work with your staff upon their return from a training session is where your coaching can be most effective. In coaching, your role is in reinforcing what was learned. *Reinforcement* is asking employees to do something that commits application of their learning back on the job.

Whatever skill set the training targeted, reinforcement is helpful and is especially important when the instruction involves professional behavior skills — the hardest, yet often the most critical, skills to put into application back on the job.

Here are a few ways you can build reinforcement into the training your employees receive:

- ✔ **Sharing with you:** Have the employee share with you materials and key points learned in the workshop. Then ask the individual what will be applied back on the job and agree upon (and stick to) a follow-up time, usually within a month, to check progress. This tip works well when what was learned is more for an individual's use than relevant to others in the group.

- ✔ **Presenting to the group:** When the training is relevant to others in the group, and because you often can't send everyone in your group to an outside seminar or conference, have those who attend come back and report on what they learned. Have them pass on materials and present key points for the group, such as at a staff meeting.

  As relevant, have them be the sources of expertise in the group that others can turn to for assistance.

- ✔ **Putting the entire group into action:** The following works well when your whole group participates in a training session or series together. Here is a three-step organized approach to such reinforcement efforts:

  1. **Each person sets a learning plan.** The learning plan identifies the one or few goals the person plans take away from the training and apply on the job. The plan also identifies how the goals will be put into action and the ways that progress will be measured. It follows the goal-setting format described in Chapter 6. Work with each individual to ensure that meaningful learning goals and plans are set.

  2. **One-on-one progress review.** A couple of months later, meet with the employees individually to review progress on their learning plans. Of course, make sure the plans were written when first set in Step 1.

3. **Group get-together.** Bring the whole group back together for a session about a month after Step 2. In the meeting, have each person report on the learning goals, efforts made to implement them, and results gained from these efforts.

   The sharing of stories and efforts at this last session allows for people to be recognized for their learning successes and builds accountability: Applying what was learned is expected.

Of course, if you participated in the training your group received, follow through and be part of the reinforcement program.

Avoid using the book-report approach to reinforcing learning. In this approach, you have the employee who went to the outside seminar come back and write a report on what was learned. This sometimes painful homework exercise doesn't reinforce learning as much as it creates busywork. The idea with reinforcement is to encourage practices that put learning into application back on the job.

Help, help, is just around the corner

Beyond outside resources that can help deliver training to your staff, you have resources not far away, as well. In fact, sometimes the most effective and cheapest training you can get your staff is from people right within your reach.

Experienced staff and managers from other groups within your company may have a particular expertise they can teach your staff. Or, your boss may be that person. Your role is to organize the training and then reinforce the learning afterwards. When these resources are around you (many of whom like to teach on occasion), don't hesitate to call on them.

In addition, sometimes you can get help from within your group. Senior or experienced staff can often be helpful in training new staff members, especially on a one-on-one basis. They often can be more available than you and are more familiar with the job duties.

To ensure that using your own staff to train others in the group is effective, follow these tips:

✔ **Coach them first on how to train.** Just because they have skill and experience and are willing to help train doesn't mean they know how to train. Coach them first using this chapter as a reference guide with an emphasis on two of the most critical tips covered here — get the learners actively (not passively) involved in their own learning and conduct the training in a step-by-step approach.

✔ **Prepare the trainer on what you want done with the trainee.** Collaborate on outlining what is to happen in the instruction. Refer to the lesson plan form in Figure 14-1 to help you. In particular, communicate the following:

- Objectives for the training

- Subject matter to cover

- Time and schedules to devote to training

- Nuances to hone in on with the trainee

✔ **Have the trainer be a coach.** Inform your staff trainer to give constructive feedback to the trainee on that individual's learning efforts all along the way. Periodically set times with the trainer to review progress on how the trainee is doing.

✔ **Provide or have reference materials created.** Most often, you use experienced staff to train new employees on job-technical skills and on computer application skills to carry out job functions. If no documented procedures are in place for these functions, have the experienced staff create them.

Review the materials to ensure clarity and completeness and let the trainee serve as the true test of their quality. If the materials serve the trainee as a handy desk manual or reference guide back on the job, they're working well.

✔ **Check in with the trainee.** Periodically follow up with your staff person about the training. Evaluate together that person's progress and get feedback on how the training is going. Also, as the individual progresses and uses the new skills and knowledge back on the job, meet periodically to reinforce how they're applying what has been taught.

Even when you're not the direct teacher, reinforce the training being received.

Impacting the Pillars of Commitment through Training

Sometimes in your coaching efforts, you need to teach. In this chapter, you have explored when such efforts are needed, what skills the teaching should focus on, how to carry out meaningful instruction, and how to use other resources to help in the training effort.

Spending time, let alone money, to help staff learn skills and knowledge to do their jobs more effectively is best seen when looked at as an investment. Will training time and effort given get you a return on your investment?

To answer that question, compare these two scenarios:

> ✔ **Group A:** Staff members are thrown in to do a job with no training whatsoever. They are left to figure things out for themselves and serve customers in the best way they can.

> ✔ **Group B:** Staff are given training and reference materials on how to do some key skills needed for their jobs to help them service their customers. The time necessary to master those skills is given in the training with reinforcement after.

Which group is more likely to perform the key functions of the job better? Not hard to figure out. If you're a customer, you want to deal with the staff in Group B.

That's why coaching efforts involve training. Managers who function as coaches view having well-trained staff as part of the job. They know that the more skills, abilities, and knowledge employees develop, the greater the likelihood for good performance. They also recognize that more time needs to be devoted to training periodically, but they see the gains they get — higher productivity, less interruptions on your time, better service to customers, to name a few.

They also know opportunities for employees to learn impacts employee commitment. Here is a look at how the pillars for building employee commitment (as explained in detail in Chapter 2) are influenced by your coaching efforts to teach.

> ✔ **Development:** Among the five pillars for building commitment, the pillar of development is impacted the most with your teaching efforts. Employees are getting opportunities to grow in their skills, knowledge, and abilities — this is development at its best.

> ✔ **Focus:** Your coaching efforts to train also help employees get a better understanding on how to do their jobs. This better understanding gives employees a clearer picture and more focus in carrying out their day-to-day job duties.

> ✔ **Accountability:** When your teaching efforts include reinforcement, they impact the pillar of accountability. Your teaching efforts send a clear message that your employees are expected to apply what they've learned. In addition, their sense of achievement serves as a great driver of accountability to do their jobs well.

✔ **Gratitude:** This pillar is influenced by the feedback you give to reinforce success in learning. The fact that you're willing to spend time (and often, money) to help employees develop also expresses gratitude for many staff members.

✔ **Involvement:** By working with your employees to gear teaching efforts to what they need in their jobs and having them be active participants in the instruction they receive, you impact the involvement pillar. Their efforts help shape the quality of their learning experiences.

Chapter 15

Building Career Self-Reliance

In This Chapter

▶ Exploring the ever-changing career marketplace

▶ Coaching to prepare employees to manage their own careers

▶ Teaching staff how to make opportunities happen

*Y*ou may have heard the saying, "They don't call it fun, they call it work!" If you won a multi-million-dollar lottery, would staying on the job for a number of years still be one of your top options? For many people, if fortune dropped in their laps, work would drop out, because work is what people do to make a living.

Yet, at the same time, work is so much a part of people's lives. Beyond just the economic support that jobs provide, many people seek fulfillment in their work and seek to have meaningful working careers. They want careers that give them satisfaction, challenge, and opportunities for growth. This is where coaching comes in.

Coaching managers help prepare employees to take advantage of opportunities for fulfillment and growth in their working careers. The coaching tools covered in Chapters 5 through 14 help to do this. They not only help drive performance but they also help employees develop their skills and abilities — factors that lead to career growth and satisfaction. This chapter shows you even more ways.

Coaching for Career Growth

Changes in the workplace have created a volatile job market, but one with many diverse opportunities. The old employment relationship of giving loyalty and getting security has become a scarce commodity (see the "You can't stay — you've been rightsized" sidebar). Employers still need commitment even if they can't offer long-term job security — which for some employees has less appeal anyway in today's work environment (see the "Other trends a-happening" sidebar later in this chapter). At the same time, employees aren't necessarily going to give commitment without something in return — usually something more than just a good salary and stock options. For many employees, career growth opportunity is a big part of that something in return.

You can't stay — you've been rightsized

The working world is one of change — sometimes rapid change. In particular, the concept of *a womb-to-tomb career* — going to work for one company and spending the rest of your working career there — is something of past generations. Layoffs have became a common practice and aren't due just to economic slumps. Creative terms from *downsizing* to *rightsizing* have come to mean the same thing: Like or not, you don't have a job here anymore and this is not the place from which you will retire one day. This so-called *rightsizing movement* (although many companies still have not figured out the right size to be) is due to several key factors, including the following:

✔ **Mergers and acquisitions:** The practice of buying and selling companies or linking them together has caused job cuts due to redundancy in job functions created from the merger. You don't need two accounting or human resource departments.

✔ **Organizational restructuring:** *Restructuring* is the reorganizing of work functions and people in those functions, due to mergers or competitive pressures. Sometimes, this leads to departments being combined, grouped differently, or redesigned in work flow — with fewer people needed to do the work.

✔ **Outsourcing:** *Outsourcing* is sending internal functions to outside companies. Sometimes a product of restructuring efforts, companies outsource many kinds of functions that are usually in support of the core business or that they view can be done more cost-effectively by the outsource service.

✔ **Investor pressures:** As the American economy of the 1990s boomed, more and more companies sought to *go public,* allowing investors to purchase stock in their companies. However, companies that are public often face pressure to keep the stock price high to please investors. This pressure sometimes leads companies to make changes, including job cuts, to keep costs down and profits up.

✔ **Business shifts:** Many companies change their business strategies, emphasizing new products or services and de-emphasizing the old ones. These shifts in strategy, usually in the attempt for growth, sometimes are accompanied by a loss of jobs in the less-emphasized areas of the business.

✔ **Technology:** Technology, in the form of automation, may cause job cuts because fewer people are needed to do the same work. Technology can also create jobs because new skills are needed to design or work new machines and gadgets. Technology also drives some of the shifts in business strategies, for example, capturing the online market and forgoing direct mail sales.

Explaining the message

Your coaching role with your employees' career development is one of support. This means you care about what happens with their careers and are interested in assisting where you can in their development, but you're not their benevolent leader or savior who will take care of their careers. At the same time, you don't want to play a totally hands-off role that says "You deal with your own career growth and don't look to me for support."

To best help coach and prepare your employees for today's work environment, help them understand the message of *career self-reliance.* The heart of this message is take responsibility for your own careers; don't expect others to take care of them.

Here are the key points of career self-reliance that you can share with your employees:

- ✔ **You are the greatest determiner of your own career development.** Recognize the world you work in and the fact that it is ever-changing and less likely to provide one place for your whole working career. Recognize that no one is just going to give you opportunities for growth and advancement. You can get support, but you must be the driver of what you want to achieve.

- ✔ **Build a positive track record.** Make positive contributions in every job opportunity you have, regardless of what kind of situation. You're building skills and meaningful experience, along with a track record of quality performance so that managers in the future — whether within the organization or outside of it — will see you as a valuable performer to have on their teams.

- ✔ **View yourself as a skills vendor.** This means you have skills and knowledge to meet the needs of employers. Managers and other key constituents are, therefore, your clients, and you are a service provider to them. You want to deliver quality service that satisfies their needs so that they view you as a valuable contributor.

- ✔ **Look to grow broadly not just vertically.** Measure career growth by more than advancement up a hierarchy or career ladder (see the "Career webs, not ladders" sidebar). Expand yourself in terms of breadth and depth: Lateral moves, taking on new roles, being involved in special projects are but a few of the ways that you gain valuable experience.

- ✔ **Know thyself.** What are your talents and interests? Pursue opportunities that best meet your desires and tap into your talents. At the same time, recognize your strengths as well as your weaknesses. Be willing to work on improving your package — yourself — while maximizing your strengths.

Career webs, not ladders

How people progress in their careers has changed to some degree. The metaphor used to be the ladder. If you were ambitious, you would rise up the corporate ladder or hierarchy into significant positions of management. Today, you see people progress in their careers like they're traversing a spider web. The following figure gives you a contrasting look at how career paths traditionally flowed, up the career ladder, and how they now often progress in a web-like fashion, going in different directions: lateral movement, moving out, moving out and then up, changing career paths, and growing in job scope while still in the same role. The idea of traveling up the corporate ladder in one organization for most of a career occurs less and less these days, and often, a career-web progression is done through changing companies.

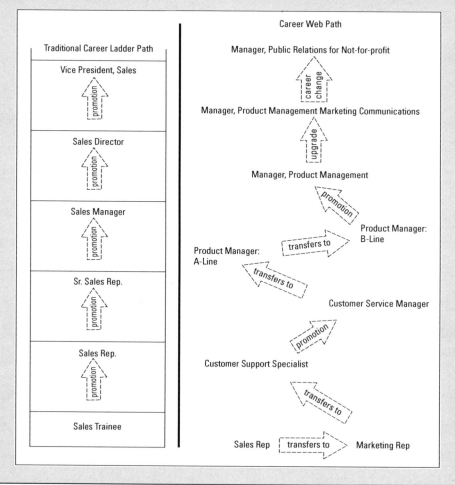

Remember that careers are as much webs as they are ladders in their development. Be open to new experiences and opportunities for learning and training so that each opportunity is a building block for your future.

✔ **Build relationships along the way.** Combine what you know with who you know, giving respect and dignity to others so that you have a solid foundation of constructive working relationships. It is not about kissing anyone's anatomy or playing politics. It is about getting to know the people you work with and, regardless of who you like or don't like, about establishing working relationships in which others view you as a quality person, not just a quality performer.

Other trends a-happening

As a result of layoffs and job insecurity, other trends have emerged that affect the world of work and careers. Here are a few:

✔ **Job hopping is hopping.** Pick up any article about careers and you will see comments such as, "The average person will have seven to ten jobs and three or more careers in his or her working life." That's a lot of job changing and career changing — not just working at different places but working in completely different occupational fields. It's not uncommon now to see some people with an average tenure in their jobs of two to three years. If people used to have such an employment history, they were considered _job hoppers_ and were a great liability to hire. Not so today. Now if someone has been in a job for 15 years or more, employers may wonder what's wrong with that individual — does that person lack energy and creativity?

This also means that more and more people want to enjoy their work situations and are often less tolerant of less-than-satisfactory conditions, such as working for a lousy manager. Many employees also want opportunities to learn and grow, so if conditions aren't right or opportunities are seen elsewhere, employees voluntarily move on.

✔ **Work is more team-based and multi-functional.** A generation ago, when people worked in their jobs, they did one or perhaps a few main functions. They served as one piece in the overall puzzle, acting as narrow-based specialists. While some jobs still function this way today, you often see people working in teams within work units — and sometimes across departments. The idea of a cross-functional task team is commonly used in many organizations. Work is often project-oriented, instead of being a set of tasks that an individual does, and employees often have multiple functions that they work at.

✔ **Emphasis on technology, information, and service.** The growth industries of the American economy revolve around technology, information, and service — often all three together. High-tech is where it's at as e-commerce and dot-coms are springing up like weeds in a vacant lot. Technology is providing innovation to enhance health, to access information, and to shop at home. Think of anything you would like to have or experience and some business is probably offering a service to meet that desire or need.

Counteracting resistance

As you communicate the important message of self-reliance discussed in the previous section, you may find that some employees don't initially understand the message of working to be career self-reliant, and others may not like it.

✔ **Don't-get-it types:** For employees who initially may not understand the message well, you may see them take a wait-and-see approach to everything. Asserting themselves and taking initiative aren't behaviors they usually exhibit in their own careers, let alone in how they work in their jobs. You can coach them to develop by helping them define behaviors that help them succeed and by creating work opportunities that provide challenge to use those behaviors.

✔ **Don't-like-it types:** For employees who don't initially like this message of taking charge of your own careers, you often may hear comments like, "I work hard, how come I haven't been promoted?". These employees have *entitlement syndrome,* thinking that they are owed a career with good progression and salary increases because they come to work every day. Don't debate them. Give them time to let the message sink in. In future conversations with such employees, tutor with questions, asking them questions such as the following:

   • What are you doing to prepare yourself to be promotable?

   • What skills are you working to develop?

   • What needs do I, your manager, have in running this group and what are you doing to meet them?

These questions are the beginning of getting don't-like-it-types to take action that moves their careers in positive directions.

In spite of resistance, don't stop educating your employees with the self-reliance message — continue to have discussions about it. Share articles that help educate your employees about the world in which they work. And above all, avoid these pitfalls in your coaching efforts:

✔ **Don't reward noise.** Just because one of your employees wants a certain opportunity or bigger role and complains loudly, you don't have to give the person the opportunity or role. Let the merit of a person's performance determine who is ready to take on bigger or better opportunities.

✔ **Don't feel obligated to do something.** As you explore career interests with your staff members, you will hear about their ambitions. Sometimes these are career desires that you currently can't do anything to help the person achieve.

Your role is to support their efforts — you're not obligated to do for your employees. Where opportunities to gain work experience or receive training can be provided, do so. Avoid feeling guilty and thinking that you have to give your employees promotions or fulfill every career desire they have. This action on the part of a manager breeds dependence, not self-reliance. Let business needs, along with employee performance and initiative, be the keys to determine what career opportunities people get to experience.

✔ **Don't give employees what you think they want.** Sometimes, managers have very good intentions, but those intentions don't translate into actions that their employees appreciate, especially when you insist that employees take on certain assignments or roles that they don't really want — even though you know such opportunities will be good for their careers. Sometimes the actions from managers involve telling employees what they should do and what steps they should take for their careers — even though the advice isn't asked for and doesn't meet with employees' career interests. Avoid making assumptions or thinking you know what's best for someone else.

Let employees manage their own careers. Pass on your knowledge and experience and mentor with messages that promote career self-reliance, instead of imposing your will on what employees should do with their careers. Give assignments based on the needs of the business and the interests of the employee. To find out about an employees' interests, start by listening and tuning into what you see and hear from them. (See the "Being in touch" sidebar for more information.)

✔ **Don't set goals and then not follow through on them**. Sometimes, when managers attempt to support employee career development, they set goals around such issues as part of the performance-review process. These goals often have something to do with getting training in certain areas or getting opportunities for certain work experiences. If the employees don't follow through and meet these goals, some managers think that the staff members have been negligent in their responsibilities, and that's just too bad.

Often, though, opportunities for learning and growth don't happen because managers don't follow through on what they said they would do. When employees are told that the company won't give the financial investment to go to the seminars agreed upon or that the manager really doesn't want the employee taking on other responsibilities, employees often wonder why the goals were set in the first place. If actions don't follow commitments you make, the message of career self-reliance rings hollow.

Being in touch

George is a manager who makes the effort to get to know his staff. In coaching them to deliver quality performance, he occasionally has discussions about what motivates them and what their career interests are. He supports efforts to upgrade their skills and gives recognition when they produce outstanding performance. As a result, his staff members feel that George cares about their work situations and that he is someone they can talk to about their careers or other issues.

George encountered two problems, however, affecting his staff. In one instance, the company decided to soon close one of its field offices — an office that contained one of George's field engineers. The employee, of course, was worried about his job situation. Because of past conversations, George was aware of the employee's willingness to relocate, should the right opportunity to come up, and his desire to get into other engineering work that George's group did at the home-office. Because George had an opening in his home-office area, he worked with the employee and the move was made. The employee is now on a path for learning and a new career experience.

In the second instance, George had an employee who enjoyed his work as a field engineer and had been a good performer. The employee came to George one day and informed him about a family problem. His wife and children needed to move to another part of the country due to family reasons. The employee was in a quandary because he truly wanted to stay with the company. George had an opening in another region, one state over from where the employee's family was going to move. Because field engineers are out in the field much of the time anyway, George was able to shift the home base for this position to where this employee needed to live. The company gained by retaining a top employee and the employee gained by getting an opportunity that met his personal and career interests.

Because George was in touch with his employees and they with him, he knew their needs and interests. His support was in the form of being creative and providing opportunity that also served the needs of the business. The employees had managed their careers well. They had performed reliably and let their interests and needs be known to their manager. Good matches were made as a result — that's coaching for career development and self-reliance.

Certainly opportunities aren't always available to help out in situations like the one George encountered. The key here is to be in touch with your staff and aware of their interests and to work with them first on what is possible. Awareness, good communication, and creativity often lead to good career solutions.

✔ **Don't hold reliable people back.** Don't punish good performers by keeping them in the roles in which they reliably deliver quality performance and subtly blocking opportunities for learning, taking on new responsibilities, or pursuing other internal positions of interest and growth. When employees are no longer challenged and are working for managers whose actions seem to communicate "stay as you are" (any words of encouragement don't matter), they feel held back or stuck. Such management behavior often spurs the opposite of what's desired.

The truly self-reliant and top performing individuals won't stay put and will move on to get the growth opportunities you tried to block — often leaving the organization to do so.

✔ **Don't appear disinterested.** Giving the message of career self-reliance to your staff doesn't mean that you step away and don't play a role in assisting your employees' career development. Some managers make this mistake: They don't engage in conversations to explore career interests and don't care about opportunities for staff to get training or broaden their experiences. The focus is on having employees do their work — period.

Such disinterest doesn't stimulate employee retention and sometimes serves as an obstacle to employee growth. Good performers look to move to where better opportunities for learning and growth are supported.

Focusing on Preparation

Your role isn't to manage your employees' careers (you have your own to work on), but you do need to focus on preparing people to manage their own careers and build success with them. This emphasis is twofold: helping employees develop the work behaviors and habits to be productive and positive workers, and helping employees develop the skills and competencies to be valuable contributors. After an initial discussion on getting started, these two areas of emphasis are discussed in the following sections.

Starting the discussion

The quarterly checkup review, as discussed in Chapter 7, lends itself nicely to having discussions with your employees about their career interests — not necessarily every quarter but at least twice a year. These meeings also give you a chance to reinforce the importance and meaning of becoming career self-reliant.

As you explore their interests, ask questions, such as the following:

✔ As you look to your future, possibly three to five years from now, what role or occupation would you like to have and why?

✔ What are the competencies — the skills, knowledge, and abilities — that you need to do that job?

✔ What experiences would be beneficial to gain for your proposed job role?

✔ What are you planning to do to prepare yourself for that job?

✔ As your manager, how can I support your efforts?

These questions ask your staff members to look to the future. Too often, people are caught in the present. To prepare your employees to be self-managing in their careers, the effort starts by looking ahead to have a sense of direction. In addition, these questions get the employees understanding your and their roles in this process: Yours is to support, theirs is to work on their own development.

These questions not only stimulate a good discussion and provide you insight, they also allow you an opportunity to mentor and tutor to help prepare your staff to build solid track records in their performance.

Performance isn't just the work someone does; it also includes behavior. The mentoring and tutoring aspects of coaching (covered in Part III) happen informally as you work with your employees.

Professing to have professionals

If you have an opening in your group and are faced with two candidates who were equally qualified in terms of their technical competence, who would you select? Tough question, right? Suppose, however, that one of the two candidates sounds bitter, complaining about her past employer, and gives you a list of the duties she doesn't like, while the other applicant consistently expressed herself in a positive and upbeat manner. Now who would you hire? Easy question, isn't it?

Just because people have technical skills, knowledge, and education doesn't mean they have the work habits and work ethic that makes for an effective employee. You want to hire people who are both technically competent and professional. In coaching to prepare your staff to manage and achieve success in their own careers, you want to mentor with messages that help them work as professionals, which is about behavior, not occupation. Being *a professional,* as defined here, is about how you work and conduct yourself in getting the job done. It's about your interactions with others and the work ethic you display in your actions.

To help prepare your employees for building and maintaining success in their careers, mentor them to work as professionals. In your coaching discussion, do the following:

1. **Define what working as a professional means.**

2. **Ask your employees to give you examples of behaviors that fit this definition.**

   Feel free to offer some examples, too.

3. **Ask your employees, of the professional behaviors identified, which do they need to demonstrate in order to be successful in their jobs today and in the future?**

4. **Follow-up periodically to assess their progress at adopting these behaviors.**

The likelihood is that, together, you can easily come up with ten or more behaviors that fit the definition of working as a professional — and find that all of them are needed to be effective. Here are the ten behaviors of professionalism that I stress:

✔ **Exhibiting a can-do manner:** This is the behavior that gives you the impression that a positive attitude is behind it. When people show a can-do manner, their body language comes across as alert and receptive — no slouches, grimaces, or rolling of the eyes. The tone comes across as sincere and interested as opposed to monotone or sarcastic. They carry themselves in an upbeat fashion.

The can-do manner shows itself in people's moods. Moodiness, good days and bad days, and chronic complaining aren't evident. Even-keel and a positive attitude are the norms. The can-do manner also shows itself in people's willingness to do the little things to get the job done. Such professionals, as the old commercial goes, are willing to do windows — no task is beneath them.

✔ **Showing a willingness to learn:** People are, of course, capable of learning, but not all are open to it. The ever-changing world of business and the career marketplace requires people to be open and willing to learn. Professionals desire opportunities to receive training and to learn from new experiences. Know-it-all disease is pushed aside. Regardless of the quality of the learning opportunity, professionals walk away getting something of value out of it. They are teachable.

✔ **Having flexibility:** The expressions of "rolling with the punches" and "going with the flow" are what the behavior of flexibility is all about in the workplace. Flexibility is the ability to adapt to change from small to big, and to then move forward and continue to perform well.

Flexible behavior is much in demand in today's rapidly changing work environment. Professionals can deal with the discomfort and ambiguity that often are a part of change by staying positive and in control and by focusing on the projects that need to be done.

✔ **Being a team player:** Nearly every manager wants a team player, but they are often hard to find. This behavior is about taking individual talents and blending them with others to get work done. It is about being able to help when asked and offer assistance without being asked. It is not only lending a hand but also sharing information and welcoming others into the group.

Professionals who are team players are able to work cooperatively versus competitively in collective situations. They are able to fit in with the group and focus on the goals that the group needs to accomplish.

Career coaching exercise

As you have career coaching discussions with staff members about what it means to work as a professional, use this fun exercise. Using the list of ten professional behaviors in the "Professing to have professionals" section of this chapter, do an assessment comparison. Your employees assess themselves on how well they make these behaviors common practice and you assess them, as well. (You can also turn this around and have them assess you while you assess yourself.)

Here is a simple scale to use in completing the assessments:

✔ **High:** Consistent practice; makes the behavior work well.

✔ **Medium:** Does the behavior some of the time; room for improvement on being consistent.

✔ **Low:** The behavior is not shown very often; see the need to do much better.

Compare notes through one-on-one discussions. Talk not only about what the ratings are but why your staff members see themselves as they do and how you see them. Have both you and the employee give the explanations based on observations, not on interpretations or perceptions (see Chapter 5). This makes for an open and interesting discussion and helps you with your employee identify areas to work on as well as work on ways to reinforce positive efforts.

✔ **Taking initiative:** Professionals who take initiative function as self-starters. They don't waste time in waiting to be told what to do — when they see something needs to be done, they act. Taking initiative also entails the willingness to seek out information and answers, to reach out and connect with others: making that phone call, setting up that meeting, or taking some other action to help make things happen.

✔ **Being creative:** When I mention this professional behavior, some people react with a sorry-don't-have-the-talent response. Being creative isn't about being brilliantly innovative or having the ability to make great inventions. Instead being creative as a behavior of professionals is about offering ideas and about thinking of ways that help get the job done the best way possible. Ideas are often like batting in the game of baseball. The best hitters in baseball aim to bat .300, and not many hit this mark (but they make millions if they do). That means they are only successful 30 percent of the time. With ideas, not every one will be accepted or a hit. But you have to keep swinging.

Professionals who are creative do just that. They speak up and offer thoughts and ideas aimed at helping get the job done better. They bring their minds as well as their bodies to work.

✔ **Producing reliably:** This behavior is about taking responsibility and being productive; delivering results, not about being busy; getting work done with quality, thoroughness, and timeliness — on a consistent basis.

Professionals who function as reliable producers are the employees you can count on — when they take on a job, you have the confidence it will get done well. Excuses aren't part of their vocabulary and repeated mistakes aren't part of their work habits.

✔ **Communicating constructively:** This behavior is about showing good judgment and awareness in interacting with others. It is about not suffering from foot-in-mouth disease: No one gets offended, turned off, or agitated when you speak.

This behavior is about expressing messages the best way possible: Not shying away from the point or looking to be nice, but being direct, sincere, and respectful. It is about recognizing each person as an individual and not expecting that everyone will respond to how you say things the way you would. Concern for individuals is taken under consideration. This professional behavior is also about being able to listen and understand messages that others express without being judgmental — giving others the opportunity to be heard. In sum, the constructive communicator allows for two-way conversation during which important points are expressed and heard, and respect for the other person is maintained.

✔ **Solving problems:** This behavior is about focusing on solutions rather than finding fault, blaming others, getting defensive, or complaining about the problem and doing nothing about it. Having a solutions-focus is about engaging in ways to fix the problem. A problem solver uses other professional behaviors in dealing with problem situations — can-do manner, constructive communication, creativity, and initiative. The behavior is about taking action and focusing attention in positive directions to make something come out better.

✔ **Being service-oriented:** Ronald Nykiel, in his book, *You Can't Lose If The Customer Wins,* refers to an expression that you can't teach pigs to dance. His point is that no matter how much training in customer service you provide, it will do little good if you have employees who aren't service-oriented to begin with.

Being service-oriented is about seeing that your job involves providing quality service to others — external as well as internal customers. It is giving people the help they need in a courteous and responsive fashion. Having the orientation to serve customers well is the best tool for having any kind of job security.

The talks I give about working as a professional are commonly part of presentations about making yourself resilient in your career. One time, after a presentation at a public forum, a gentleman came up afterwards and thanked me and asked, "Where were you 30 years ago?" The talk caused him to reflect back on his work career and see the difficulties he'd had in trying to be viewed as a good employee. He could see some of his own inconsistencies in his behaviors and work habits. This list of ten behaviors provided him a focus to use going forward. Now that's someone open to learning — a true professional.

A major part of coaching and preparing your staff to manage their own careers is developing recognition of the behaviors and work habits that build positive track records. Discussions about this list of professional behaviors, or about what you see as professional behaviors to exhibit, help build recognition. It gives people a focus in their performance to go beyond just the job at hand, tuning in to getting the job done well and making a positive difference in doing so.

Sharpening skills

Coaching your staff to prepare them to manage their own careers also involves developing the competencies to be effective performers. Look at competencies as the skills, knowledge, and abilities to have to perform a job well. Work with your staff to look at what they need in their current roles and what they need for their future interests. (Refer to the "Starting the discussion" section earlier in this chapter for questions that get to the heart of this.)

What are the skills or knowledge areas people should look to develop to enhance their career growth? One answer doesn't exist for this question — the answers vary based on individual needs and interests. But if you read about what is happening in the career marketplace, see ads in newspapers or online services, or talk with outplacement or career transition professionals, you get a sense of what's important. So taking all that into consideration, here is a baker's dozen, many of which may be applicable to you and your employees:

- **Product and systems development:** This is a fairly wide range of skills and knowledge that involve having the ability, regardless of what field you work in, to build the products your company sells or build the systems and applications that your company's employees need to do their jobs.

- **Job-technical skills and industry-related knowledge:** These are two sets of competencies that are effective when seen and developed together. Job-technical skills, discussed in Chapter 14, are the skills that go into the day-to-day workings of your job. The job title often defines what this skill set is. Accountants do accounting, engineers do engineering, and so on. Industry-related knowledge is understanding the business context in which you work. Knowing how to do police work is the skill set of a police officer's job, but understanding the field of law enforcement and municipal government is the industry-related knowledge that's important to have.

- **Process development:** This is the operations-oriented skill set — the ability to create, organize, or redesign processes to have a more efficient work flow. It is about impacting how work gets done so that it gets done in a simpler, more timely fashion. This often involves being able to create structure out of chaos.

✔ **Computer applications:** This is the ability to utilize, in your work, the various tools of technology that computers offer — from word processing to graphics. It includes being able to access the online world of the Internet, too.

✔ **Technical support:** This set of competencies is about keeping the systems running (such as computer systems and telephone systems) that employees use to do their jobs, as well as supporting customers in the use of the products a company sells to them. Tech support involves responding to the end user and keeping their tools or products working, perhaps even doing the repair necessary for these products to work.

✔ **Sales and marketing:** These are two sets of skills that often go hand-in-hand. Who does sales in their jobs? Nearly everyone. The ability to persuade someone else to support an idea is, in effect, "selling." The ability to promote an idea, program, or service that creates interest is "marketing." Both skills are sometimes overlooked but they are critical to success in many people's jobs.

✔ **Teamwork:** More and more work today is organized into some type of collective arrangement: project teams, cross-functional task teams, or in-unit work teams. The ability to work well with others is, therefore, increasing in demand. Skills for building good teamwork involve communication and problem solving, as well as thinking of others and organizing efforts to coordinate with them.

✔ **Facilitation:** This is the ability to pull people together and help them move forward to resolve issues or get work done. It is exercising personal influence along with organizational skills. Facilitation is one of the foundations of effective leadership.

✔ **Customer service:** Everyone you deal with is a customer of one sort or another. Providing some form of assistance, information, or support to others goes on in every job, whether the recipients are internal or external customers. The behaviors and skills involved in carrying out these functions are not only important to learn but are often one of the keys to success in your job.

✔ **Compliance and control:** This set of skills and knowledge takes in the regulatory and security issues that affect many businesses today. It involves understanding legal affairs and government workings that can help a company gain approval for getting its products out in the marketplace or that can keep a company from getting into hot water from an action it takes. In addition, it may involve knowing how to keep a workplace safe from any kind of harm or knowing how to secure vital information and other business secrets.

✔ **Training:** Training is the ability to teach others. In so many jobs, people need to be able to teach others how to do certain things, and a lot more goes into training than people often realize. Share Chapter 14 with your staff as a good start.

✔ **Communications:** This skill set involves the ability to express thoughts clearly and convincingly in writing. It sometimes involves the ability to deliver formal presentations that captures people's attention. (You have, on the other hand, probably been to presentations that helped cure insomnia!) Most importantly, this skill set involves interpersonal communications that are critical in everyone's job — the ability to listen to and truly understand others, along with the ability to express yourself constructively and clearly.

✔ **Leadership and coaching:** This is the ability to take charge, to influence, and to make results happen with others and to do so in ways that inspire commitment. See Chapters 1 through 14 and 17 through 20 for further details!

Many of these competencies are major functions of certain occupations. But they are also the abilities, knowledge, and skill sets needed to perform many jobs. When your employees put attention to developing these competencies, they are focused on preparing and growing themselves, which translates into career self-reliance.

Onward Ho

Coaching to build career self-reliance with your employees is an active, ongoing effort for both you and your employees. You're not managing their careers for them — your efforts are of support:

✔ Providing information and having mentoring discussions to help your staff members understand the importance of managing their own careers; of working as professionals; and of developing the skills, knowledge, and abilities that help them perform well today and in the future.

✔ Working with them to identify areas to work on and to set plans that help prepare and develop them for career success.

✔ Helping provide learning and work opportunities that allow for career growth and contribute to business success.

✔ Making introductions to help employees expand their contacts and exposure in the organization.

✔ Communicating the needs of your department and of the business overall.

✔ Providing ongoing performance feedback.

Your coaching efforts can also teach them how to learn of opportunities within the organization, including those in your own group, and how to pursue them. Doing so requires them to listen and learn, to take initiative, and to reach out. Here are some additional tips to heed that you can show your employees who want to grow in their careers:

✔ **Get to know each area of the organization.** Encourage your staff to find out who the executives of the organization are, what functions they manage, and what messages they hear about where the company is going and what the important issues are to the business. Understanding these issues helps employees know what is going on in the organization and develop a broader understanding of how things work.

✔ **Get to know department managers' needs and challenges.** This strategy applies within employees' own groups but also to other areas in the organization where they may have interest. Encourage staff to talk to other managers and ask questions to find out their needs and challenges, starting with you. As your staff understands where needs and challenges exist, they know what they can offer to help satisfy those needs and meet the challenges.

✔ **Increase visibility and exposure.** This step involves efforts to build relationships and give good performance, not playing politics or kissing up. Encourage your staff to introduce themselves to other staff and managers in areas in which they have interest, to informally talk and keep in touch, and to occasionally have lunch to visit with others in these areas. It also involves volunteering to be on special assignments or cross-functional teams to gain exposure and meet others in the organization.

Don was a technical contributor and had hopes one day of moving up to become a technical manager. When a cross-functional task team was created to develop some key personnel policies for the organization, he volunteered to be the representative from his department.

Don went forward and made a good contribution to the task team, which took place over the course of the year. He attended all the meetings, followed through on all the assignments, and offered ideas that helped the team do its work. What Don gained most of all from his participation was exposure to different people in the organization and especially the management of the company. His contributions were seen as valuable on the team. Toward the end of the year, an opening for a supervisor's position came up in Don's area. He applied and was selected to take on the role. What he realized was that two actions made a difference in getting this promotion — his reliable performance and his visibility from the task team. All the other internal candidates hadn't taken steps to show leadership or contribute in other areas to help the company. Don had.

✔ **Build your career portfolio.** Your portfolio is a record of your accomplishments and skills. Performance reviews often reflect what assets you have shown and developed. The idea is to continue to develop skills and to make contributions that build a positive track record. Document this track record: Save products of work and other evidence of the performance contributions made.

✔ **Identify opportunities and offer proposals to add value.** When employees understand the business, understand managers' needs, and have the tools ready to contribute to meet those needs, they shouldn't wait. They should take the initiative and offer ideas and solutions, starting with putting the proposal in writing. In it, ask them to outline the opportunities or needs they see, the services or solutions they have to offer to meet them, and the benefits that the group gains. Then have them sit down with you to discuss the proposal and see what happens. Nothing ventured, nothing gained.

Sometimes these efforts lead to employees taking on new projects or roles within your group and sometimes they lead to handling new opportunities that have them move on into other groups. In either case, you have coached employees to take charge of their careers and to make the most of opportunities (empowering them) and have helped influence employees to grow within the organization (retaining their services).

The fear that some managers face is that if they support employees learning and growth and teach them how to seek opportunities, they will lose those valuable employees to other places. Such fear sometimes becomes the reason that little support is provided.

Certainly, sometimes people leave and go elsewhere to work. But if you work for a manager who pushes you to be responsible for your own career yet at the same time takes an active interest in your growth, including your being able to take on opportunities elsewhere in the organization, is this an organization that you want to leave? Not likely.

Influencing the Pillars of Committment

Efforts of coaching for career self-reliance help employees move forward and take charge of their own careers. They also help stimulate employee commitment. Here is how the pillars of commitment (as outlined in Chapter 2) are influenced from your career-coaching efforts:

✔ **Focus:** Mentoring with the message of career self-management and with efforts that help prepare employees to manage their own career development gives them a sense of direction and, therefore, focus.

✔ **Involvement:** Coaching for career self-reliance encourages employees to take initiative and to seek opportunities that shape their own futures. Success is dependent on their getting involved to help make things happen in their own careers.

✔ **Accountability:** Your coaching efforts encourage your staff to take responsibility for their own actions and progress with their careers — this is accountability at its best.

- ✔ **Development:** Your coaching efforts, as described in this chapter, encourage employees to work on growing their skills and behaviors for quality performance.

- ✔ **Gratitude:** This pillar is less directly influenced than the others. However, employees' quality performance, gained from focusing on building a positive track record, is sure to be appreciated by others that work with you.

Chapter 16

Making the Plan: Coaching For Development

. . . .

In This Chapter

▶ Learning the process and strategies for employee development

▶ Creating development plans to guide the efforts

▶ Coaching to gain improvement in employee performance

▶ Dealing with behavior and personal issues that get in the way

. . . .

A major part of the emphasis in managing as a coach is on development of your employees. Doer managers (defined in Chapter 1) tend not to put much emphasis in this area — you do your job; I'll do mine.

Under the coach approach, developing employees is an important part of how time is spent at work. It is about strengthening and growing employees' skills, knowledge, and abilities so they can perform self-sufficiently and at high levels. This is all done in the context of maximizing the resources being paid for to get high productivity in return.

The primary emphasis when you coach for development, therefore, is on increasing levels of employee performance. Yet, at the same time, it is about stimulating career development — helping people progress in their careers. The two aims often fit together. If the employee is developed to perform at greater levels of skill and capacity, he is likely to move ahead in his career to take on bigger and better roles.

Coaching to help make employee development happen is focused and organized in nature. Development plans are put together to guide the efforts. You and the employee then manage by plan and watch the development occur. (Kind of like watering a little bud and watching it grow into a flower.)

Defining Development

Development, as discussed in this chapter, has two areas of emphasis:

- ✔ **Increase competency and capacity levels.** You want to take employees who are at an acceptable level of performance and grow them to perform at stronger and more self-sufficient levels.

  For example, you want to take a steady sales associate and develop her to perform as a seasoned veteran who sells to executive-level clients. Or you want to take an accountant and grow him to do financial planning and analysis work, as well.

- ✔ **Improve performance.** In this case, the emphasis is on taking someone performing at a less-than-satisfactory level and getting that individual up to an acceptable or competent level of performance. Work on improvement before you consider working on development.

  For example, when a sales associate often falls below quota, you work with that employee so that performance gets up to the competent level it needs to be, that of meeting the quota each period. Or, you want that accountant to improve accuracy to consistently maintain the general ledger.

Following the Yellow Brick Road when Developing for Growth

Unfortunately, what generally happens in discussions about development issues between managers and their staff members is, well, not much.

- ✔ Development issues are discussed every now and then, but often little results.
- ✔ Behaviors or other areas of performance that the employee should pay attention to aren't talked about.
- ✔ Attention is given to areas that aren't relevant to the employee's performance.

These are all misguided and unfocused efforts. The following two sections help you stay on a clear path toward employee development.

A process to follow down the road

To attend to and guide employee development, look at the coaching effort as a process. In a process, key elements or steps occur, and the process is ongoing and evolving. Coaching for performance and career development involves a five-step process.

1. **Assess employee competencies and explore needs and interests.**

   The following questions represent the issues you want to explore with your employees.

   - What job-related skills, knowledge, and abilities does the employee have — from the ones of strength to the areas of weakness?

   - What does the employee need for future growth?

   - What are the employee's interests for performance and in career development?

   Chapters 12 and 15 can also provide you with helpful questions to use as you attempt to gain further insight into these issues.

   Often, the checkup review (recommended to be done quarterly — see Chapter 7) and the formal annual performance evaluation conference serve as useful forums for these discussions. They require that you give your employees honest and clear feedback —both positive and negative — about how they are performing. Without sincere and constructive feedback, development efforts don't have the proper focus.

2. **Clarify the organizational needs and competencies required.**

   Arm yourself with two sets of data:

   - What are the challenges and needs of your department, currently and in the future?

   - What are the needs of the business overall, currently and in the future?

   Provide this information to your staff members so they see two main points:

   - What is important in running the business from a group level and organizational level.

   - What direction are the group and company headed?

   If you're coaching for career self-reliance with the people on your team (see Chapter 15), ask them their views on the needs of the department and the business overall. Compare notes together. And if they don't have a clue, give them this big picture information but also encourage them to tune in to what is happening in the organization.

3. **Analyze and prioritize career issues and development needs.**

   Determine what to work on for employee development to meet business needs — create a match between employee and company needs that makes the development effort relevant. If employees have other interests unrelated to their current job situations or future growth in the organization, redirect the focus to what is relevant and needed.

   Here's an example: "So you say you want to become a rock music star and working here is your day job. Sounds neat. Because you plan on staying employed here for awhile, let's talk about developing those computer skills you're going to need to tackle some upcoming challenges we have in the department."

   If improvement is needed in an area of performance, start there before worrying about working on growth. (See the "Oh No, A Personnel Problem: Coaching to Improve" section later in this chapter.) In essence, get the foundation of the house in order before you work on adding new floors to it.

4. **Mutually construct a development plan to target the selected needs.**

   This involves building a road map together to formalize and focus the development efforts. The plan allows both you and the employee to manage the development effort. You're building involvement and accountability from the get-go. What to write into the plan is detailed in the "Crafting the plan" section later in this chapter.

   Don't be overly ambitious and target a bundle of areas for development. Usually one or two is enough and is all that you support with each staff member. You want to take a long-term view with your development efforts. It's not about what assignments or tasks you need to learn to do for next week. It is about growing employee skills and capacity levels for bigger and better performance.

5. **Follow up to review progress and support ongoing development.**

   This step makes the process continuous and focuses on getting results that benefit both the employee and the business. It ties development to a regular part of employee performance — not an extracurricular activity that everyone forgets about when they go back to work.

   Set the frequencies for checkpoints at a reasonable level. Weekly check-ins for a long-term effort usually aren't relevant. Tying into the checkup review you have each quarter (see Chapter 7) may work just as well. Tailor to what best fits the development plan.

This five-step process provides you a focused approach for coaching for career and performance development with your employees. It takes threads of discussions about performance needs and career interests from scattered conversations into a guided tour so you know how to move down the yellow brick road. (This is what Dorothy needed in *The Wizard of Oz.*) It also defines how both parties play a role in helping to make employee growth happen — the employee is the driver, and you are the supporter.

Don't promote promotions in your development efforts

Don't fall into this trap. "Hi, employee. I know you want to get promoted. Tell you what. If you jump through these three hoops I have here for you and do so successfully in the next three months, you will get promoted."

If you send a message like this, you will feed into a frenzy some employees have about promotions. The eager ones, the ones big on seniority, or those with a distorted view of their own self-worth and talent may bombard you with questions like, "What does it take to get promoted to the next level? When can I get promoted?"

Promotions aren't employer- or God-given rights that are bestowed on people for being loyal or worthy subjects. The frenzy that some employees exhibit is part of an assumption that a schedule and plan exist for when they will get promoted. They just think that you haven't given them the information about how to make it happen.

Promotions also aren't prizes that people get for winning a contest or enduring a period of time. They aren't like some class in school in which the teacher spelled out what efforts and assignments to do to earn an A. If you respond to questions about what one has to do to get promoted as if you have a simple formula to follow, you set yourself up for making promises you often can't or don't want to keep.

As part of your ongoing efforts of coaching for career self-management and development, help your employees understand promotions. Here are a few tips to help build this understanding:

✔ **Ask them to take the perspective of a manager.** In your coaching discussions with staff, ask them this question: "If you were a department manager who had the opportunity to promote someone in your group, what would be the reasons for granting the promotion?" This question usually sparks an interesting discussion. Answers certainly can vary, but staff members most likely will say that those who deliver quality results are reliable, work well with others on the team, and show the capability to take on greater responsibility are the ones who should be promoted.

The sum of these thoughts answers the question, "Who gets promoted?" The biggest factors on who gets selected to move up in an organization involve merit, not time on the job; performance, not who talks a good game. Promotions are earned. (Of course, some promotions make you wonder how some people worked their way up into the positions they have. Did they have some revealing pictures about the CEO?) This kind of a discussion often helps employees put their attention on delivering top performance versus waiting and wondering how to get anointed.

✔ **Tell them what creates promotions.** Promotions most often come about because a business need exists and, therefore, an opportunity is given to meet that need. The same goes for why managers get the approval to recruit and hire someone when new or open positions exist. Sometimes, opportunities that could be promotions are filled by hiring people from outside the organization because no one internally has shown the quality performance and readiness to take on the role.

Let your employees know that promotions don't usually operate by a schedule. The opportunities for them happen as business needs present themselves to be filled, which happens any time and all the time.

✔ **Advise them to do the job they want to have.** With a few exceptions, the loudest whiner isn't at the top of managers' list as the person to promote. Tell the individuals on your team that letting their desires for career advancement be known is fine, but they should go out and let their performance do the talking for them.

Following this advice also means the following:

- Tuning in to the needs of the group or other areas of the organization

- Taking initiative

- Taking on responsibility to help

- Offering and acting on good ideas that help meet needs

- Building positive working relationships

For example, why should you be promoted to team leader when the team members don't see you working hard and often see you getting in conflicts with them? On the other hand, if you consistently produce results, go above what is asked for to help the group do even better, and are well respected by the team, sooner or later, promoting you to team leader is an easy decision to make.

What occurs today in the fluid nature of business organizations is that opportunities for advancement occur because people take initiative and carry out responsibilities that fill voids. This sometimes leads to upgrades in current positions and sometimes to the creation of new positions.

✔ **Create development plans that help prepare your employees.** While there's no telling when opportunity for advancement is going to knock, nor are there any guarantees that when it does that the employee will be given it, you can work with employees to prepare themselves for opportunities, should they come knocking. The worst thing is to have it pass the employee by because he or she wasn't ready to handle it.

Remind your staff members of this message and then, as you work with them to construct their development plans, focus on areas that will help prepare them for the future opportunities that they desire within the organization. As part of this planning effort, keep in mind that career advancement sometimes involves taking steps in sideways directions (instead of upwards) that eventually lead to people moving upwards. Therefore, work with your staff to help them to grow in depth and breadth.

Coaching for career development focuses on performance and on stimulating career self-management, not on promotions. Promotions aren't guarantees, so don't fall into the trap of promising them to any of your staff, and don't make them goals of development plans. Let them be the rewards — ones that may even come unexpectedly — for people growing in their capabilities and delivering quality performance.

Some construction work: Building the plan

Creating a development plan is done as a collaborative effort with you and your employees. You don't write the plan for your employees. If you do, even if it is the greatest plan since the invention of the light bulb, it becomes your plan, not theirs. This point becomes even more critical when the target of your development effort is on improvement in performance that is deficient rather than being on an area for growth (see the "Oh No, A Personnel Problem: Coaching to Improve" section, later in this chapter, for further details).

People support most what they help create. For development plans to be effective, they must belong to the individuals for whom they are created. Thus, employees need to be part of the collaborative effort to create development plans if they are to own and drive them. As covered in the "A process to follow down the road" section earlier in this chapter, you help by assessing performance, giving direction about the business, and providing input to assist in shaping the development plan. Your role in the overall development process is to support, which includes helping to reinforce accountability along the way.

Targets to shoot for in the plan

I've seen managers who think they are creating development plans when writing annual performance reviews. In such attempts, what usually happens is the manager writes something — usually a suggestion or two for areas to get training in the coming year — in the development section of the appraisal form so that nothing on the form is left blank. This is often done without any discussion with the employee.

While the performance-review meeting is a good opportunity to work on development because performance is being evaluated, making a few suggestions on an appraisal form is not a development plan. In addition, a list of a few areas in which to get training is not development. Training is one of many strategies for helping to make development efforts happen, but learning for learning's sake is not career or performance development.

The key, then, is to create development plans *with* your staff members (not *for* them) and to include the ingredients that a good plan has (as described in the "Crafting the plan" section coming up later in the chapter). You also want to know what areas to target. When the development emphasis is on growth, the focus of the development plan should be on the outcomes or level of performance you are helping the employee to reach. You want to target the levels of expectation for competent performance. Here are some areas to target for growth in a development plan:

✔ **Strengthening or building skills to deliver greater levels of performance.**

Example: Helping a junior engineer grow in skills to play a more independent role in projects.

Example: Helping a product manager develop formal presentation skills for delivering effective presentations to customers at marketing seminars and trade shows.

✔ **Developing certain behaviors to increase performance effectiveness.**

Example: Targeting efforts to help a customer-service representative understand how to greet and service customers in a way that makes them want to come back for more business.

Example: Developing a fairly inexperienced sales representative to listen and present himself with polish so that customers' key decision makers see this individual as their main contact for business.

✔ **Developing certain skills and behaviors to handle new or changing situations.**

Example: Helping everyone in the warehouse, which needs to have more coverage, become able to handle all shipping, receiving, and traffic functions.

Example: Ensuring that one of the technical support specialists, who has transferred into your inside sales group, masters the skills and duties to handle a sales role.

✔ **Building competencies to handle greater level of responsibilities.**

Example: Delegating to one of your staff the responsibility to handle all technical support and maintenance activities for the department's new inventory management system.

Example: Delegating to one of the junior recruiters in the human resources department the responsibility to coordinate all hiring of temporary and contract staff for the company.

✔ **Grooming someone to handle a new role now or in the near future.**

Example: Developing your successor to handle management of your group so that you're able to move on in the near future to a bigger and better role in the organization.

Example: Creating the role of project manager to coordinate the growing volume and demands of the customer accounts you oversee in your group, and developing one of your staff members to handle the new role

✔ **Grooming someone to take on a new role sometime in the distant future.**

Example: Developing a recruiter in your contract staffing branch, who desires to one day move into a sales role, to understand and support sales operations while still maintaining his current job, because you expect an opening will occur sometime in the future.

Example: Grooming one of your staff, based on her interests and the anticipated growth of the business, to handle a first level management role should the opportunity come to pass, as you think it may.

The target you and the employee want to achieve is what's most important. Coaching for development means putting focused attention on increasing employees' levels of performance and capability, which often includes career growth. It is outcomes-based (as opposed to signing an employee up for a training class and thinking that will cover the development effort).

Crafting the plan

Creating the development plan with your staff members is akin to setting performance plans, as covered in Chapter 6. In fact, including the development plan as one of the goals for your employees to accomplish (as part of their performance plans) is a great way to marry the development effort with performance management.

Figure 16-1 shows you a format for a development plan with the key ingredients in it. Here is a look at each of these ingredients.

Development Plan

Employee _____ Date _____

Development goal:

Action plans:
(What steps the employee will take and what the manager will do to support to make the development goal happen. Include applicable target dates.)

Checkpoints:

How to measure (as applicable):

Figure 16-1:
A work-
sheet for
development
planning.

✔ **Development goal:** This is the area being targeted for the employee's growth. Stay away from having a goal that's just learning for learning's sake: for example, learning computer skills or management skills. Instead, consider the impact: Develop computer skills for what use? Develop management skills for what purpose? The answers to these questions are what development goals are all about.

Development goals are outcomes-based. They are often broad in nature, but should be written in specific, action-oriented terms with a meaningful purpose to them. They define a level of performance to be achieved.

Instead of "Learn computer skills," a development goal could read as follows: Develop and apply upgraded computer skills that enable you to produce the department's operations reports each month in a timely and accurate fashion.

✔ **Action plans:** Action plans are the meat and potatoes (or the ripe vegetables to it if you're a vegetarian) of the overall development plan; in other words, the concrete substance. They define the activities and steps that the employee will take to achieve the development goal, as well as what you will do to support the effort. Define them in specific and action-oriented terms, identifying who is responsible for what effort with target dates, as appropriate, to when steps should happen.

Putting your name in the action plans at least one time increases the likelihood for success in the development effort. While the plan is the employee's, your support shows that you care and tells the employee that he isn't on his own — a very positive and motivating effect.

✔ **Checkpoints:** Checkpoints map out the efforts of follow-up. They are the dates and frequency that you and your staff person are to meet to review progress with the development plan and update it accordingly. Tailor the frequency to the needs of the development effort. In many cases, because development plans are more long-term in nature, progress reviews once per quarter work well.

✔ **How to measure:** This component of the plan defines the means for measuring progress and outcomes. This can be done by gathering feedback from others, reviewing the products of work, checking off steps in the plan completed, and using a combination of measurement sources. Certainly, your observations and feedback, as well as those of the employee, are good to use in the mix of ways to measure what has happened.

Strategies for the action plans

Action plans are the substance that drive the entire development plan. They are the activities and efforts to be carried out that move the employee towards reaching the development goal.

What are some strategies that are helpful to have in development plans? Here is a list to consider that covers training and educational efforts, work activities and experiences, and working with mentor-types who can help — including you.

- **Formal training classes:** This strategy can be fulfilled through many channels, including college courses, outside seminars with training companies or professional associations, in-house offerings, or training sessions for your group that you organize with an outside professional or internal staff to teach.

- **Cross training:** Sometimes, the employee is taught by others how to do their job functions — referred to as *cross training.* Sometimes, an employee's development plan may include *being* the cross trainer, allowing that person to train someone else, thereby freeing up time to get into other areas of work.

- **Readings:** Reading articles, books, or information from the Internet helps with employee learning and development.

Reading alone without any connection to a task is a passive development activity. To make the most out of this strategy, have the employee share with you or others what he or she is learning from these sources.

- **Spending time outside the group:** Another helpful development activity is to allow an employee to pick up skills by spending time away from the work group. This may mean visiting another company or working with another department or office location within the organization. The idea is to see and grow from what others do. Outside exposure often broadens horizons of thinking.

- **Special projects or work assignments:** This strategy is about learning by building experience. It is being given responsibility to handle a project or important assignment that helps grow skills and knowledge. You have to provide the right level of guidance that the employee needs, but let the person run with the job and gain success from it.

- **Special committees or project teams:** These activities usually involve participating in inter-departmental or organizational-wide teams to work on special events or tackle important business issues. These teams are helpful in giving a person exposure to other people and functions in the organization and in gaining a broader-level understanding of the business.

- **Activities for higher-level exposure:** This strategy involves giving the employee more management-level exposure and visibility. It may mean including the individual in management meetings you attend, having the employee make presentations to management groups, or having the person represent the group at outside functions.

- **Manager-employee mentoring discussions:** This activity works best when scheduled. It is carried out through periodic meetings during which you teach or informally tutor skills or knowledge areas that are important for that person's development. Quite often, such efforts help in your own development, too.

✔ **Providing a coach:** Sometimes the best way for a staff person to develop new skills or meet new challenges is to get one-on-one coaching with an outside expert or consultant. You support the effort budget-wise and stay tuned in to see how the employee is progressing. Sanctioning the investment to work with a special resource often serves as a great boost and motivator for that person's development.

A sample to taste

In this section, I give you a look at a sample plan.

First the scenario: Work gets done in your group through project teams. You have served the role of project leader because usually no more than three teams were functioning at one time with a total of ten employees involved. Due to the pending growth in the business, you know that in the near future you'll be asked to oversee more projects. You see the need put someone in the role of project leader, as larger groups have done elsewhere in the company. The role is not supervisory but one that carries project management and leadership-by-influence responsibilities.

Paul, a member of your group, has shown some initiative and leadership abilities in working with fellow team members on projects and has expressed an interest in growing in this direction in his career with the company. You both agree to target this area for growth and to put together a development plan to help the effort. For the purposes of this example, you are a woman named Sue who is Paul's manager.

Employee: Paul Groth   **Date:** February 1, 2001

Development goal: Develop Paul to proficiently handle project leader responsibilities so that the project teams he manages meet their schedules, deliver the work products that their customers need, and work together in a positive and productive manner.

Action plans:

1. Paul will take up to two classes or seminars in project management and team leadership over the next three months. Sue will assist in finding the right courses and in allowing Paul the time to attend.

   When: Complete by May 1.

2. Paul will spend time with Sarah, the project leader in the engineering group, to pick up skills in project scheduling, resource allocation, and team facilitation. An average of three hours per week will be allotted for this effort over the next month or so.

   When: Start immediately and complete by March 15 at the latest.

3. Paul will assist Sue with the three current projects that the group is handling by taking on all status-review tracking and overseeing all product-documentation functions.

   When: Start immediately.

4. Paul will serve as co-project leader with Sue for the upcoming ABC Account project, slated to begin in mid March. Sue will ask the group to work through Paul for day-to-day management with the project. Paul's manager will oversee his efforts.

   When: Start approximately March 15.

5. Paul and Sue will hold one-on-one meetings every two weeks to discuss what Paul is learning through his classes, his time with Sarah, and the new responsibilities he is to handle. Paul is to be the driver of these meetings in terms of their scheduling and their agenda.

   When: Start the week of February 8.

Checkpoints: Meetings to review the overall progress with this development plan will be held on a monthly basis, starting at the end of February, for the first three months of this plan. Further checkpoints will be determined from there based on Paul's progress and the needs of the business.

How to measure:

1. Completion of Steps 1 through 3 of the action plans by Paul.

2. Sue's observations and feedback to Paul on his performance with Steps 3 and 4 of the action plan.

3. Sue will gather feedback from team members on the ABC Account Project about Paul's leadership by May 1.

This sample development plan represents what you want to do when creating development plans.

- ✔ The goal defines an objective that the employee is working towards achieving.
- ✔ The action plans map out strategies in clear and specific terms — who is to do what and by when.
- ✔ The action plans spell out key steps, not a slew of detailed tasks.
- ✔ The manager's name is in the action plans at least once, with some effort to support the cause.
- ✔ Follow-up review on the whole plan and ways to measure progress are defined.
- ✔ The plan is written with the employee, not the manager, as its focal point and its driver.
- ✔ The plan ties individual interests with business needs. It is development- and performance-based.

You can tell that this sample plan will be evolving. If Paul progresses as hoped and the business needs grow as anticipated, Paul will take on the project-leader role. It is likely then, after its first quarter, that the plan will be updated to focus on Paul's development in his new role. Coaching for development is an ongoing and evolving process.

The development plan, created collaboratively, provides a road map to help make growth happen. This is much better than having scattered and occasional conversations with little focus or clear steps for action. It is also meant to be a living document, not something cast in stone that you can't change. You're making best estimates on strategies and time frames when you start and are adjusting along the way. Make your follow-up efforts so that the plan stays relevant and so that both you and the employee stay accountable for its success.

Oh No, A Personnel Problem: Coaching to Improve

Coaching for development can be fun and rewarding. Through your support, your employee has mapped out a plan, and now you get to see employees grow and achieve success. They gain satisfaction and you get stronger levels of performance.

However, when you're developing for improvement, you aren't working on growth and building someone to be a bigger and better performer. Instead, you're dealing with issues in which performance is unacceptable and is having a negative effect of various magnitudes. Some of the common performance issues are examples such as the following:

- Sporadic attendance with increased absences
- Punctuality problems; difficulty in consistently being to work when scheduled
- Thoroughness and accuracy of work are lacking or inconsistent
- Output produced is of lower quantity than needed
- Timeliness in getting work done is inconsistent or behind schedule
- Lack of follow through or initiative slows accomplishment
- Periodic clashes or outbursts make working with others difficult
- Abrasive or challenging behavior rubs people the wrong way

It's in the approach

To solve a problem, you have to first recognize that one exists. Seldom in these performance-problem situations is the employee in question totally incompetent or all bad. In fact, in many cases, while less-than-satisfactory performance occurs in one area, the person does very well in other parts of the job. Here are a few examples:

- ✔ Sandy has the strongest computer skills of anyone in the group and she produces top quality work. However, she seldom meets deadlines with her reports.

- ✔ Lyle is the most capable performer in the group and helps everyone on the team learn to do their jobs better. He shows up to work late half the time, however, and that holds up the production process from starting on time.

- ✔ Carol does a great job. Ask her to do anything and she willingly takes on the assignment, getting it done on-time and with high quality — when she's there. Unfortunately, she calls in sick at least once every week or two.

- ✔ Bill is a brilliant engineer. He can solve any technical problem thrown his way. But when he needs to work in team-like situations, he clashes with other team members who no longer want to work with him.

- ✔ Tammy knows the business so well and has done a good job at growing her group and the volume of business it produces. At the same time, her verbal attacks on staff have alienated them to the point that turnover is high and many employees want transfers.

These examples represent situations you often see. You have an employee who has a lot of strengths and is a valuable contributor in your group, but that person's weaknesses are causing a problem. Unfortunately, many managers suffer from what I refer to as *avoidance disease:* Performance issues appear and the following efforts are what get displayed:

- ✔ Do work-arounds. Structure assignments or other situations so that you or others cover for what should be the responsibility of the individual to handle.

- ✔ Complain about the person to peers but say nothing directly to the employee.

- ✔ Make excuses for the employee. "Oh, that's just Bob," or "Yes, but Bob really knows his stuff."

- ✔ Give occasional, vague, unclear criticism.

- ✔ Act as if the performance problem doesn't exist at all.

- ✔ Put off raising the issue to the employee with the idea of addressing it at a better time sometime in the near future.

These actions, or I should say inactions, are means of avoidance. Managers who take this approach aren't dealing directly with the problem. What happens to the performance issues you avoid dealing with? They continue, and often grow into worse problems. Behavior that is rewarded is repeated.

Other times, after avoidance has been tried or when the performance issues are more troublesome, managers take the *hammer approach:* Yelling at the employee, threatening the individual's job, or putting the person on warning, usually as the first real attempt to address a performance problem. Most employees respond to this harsh approach with bitterness, covert to overt resistance, fearfulness to perform, and boisterous confrontation.

Neither the hammer nor avoidance-disease approaches effect much positive change in employee performance. Coaching, with the emphasis on working to achieve improvement, is the approach that works best. This approach is characterized by such actions as the following:

✔ **Focus on solutions:** When you throw technical managers a technical problem that needs to be solved, what do you see happen? Quite often, they go into problem-solving mode. They analyze the problem to get a firm understanding and then get creative in proposing alternatives for a solution, generating a lot of positive energy and some good solutions.

Throw the same group a performance-related personnel problem, and they want to either run away or kill it. Instead of running, use the same solutions-focused approach described with technical problems when the issue is people-related.

✔ **Remain in control:** When an employee isn't performing well, a lot of emotions come into play. You're disappointed, angry, or frustrated. Be aware of the emotions you feel and focus your attention where it needs to go — on defining a course for correction with the employee. Like driving on the roads, you need to have this frame of mind to be able to stay out of accidents and reach the intended destination.

✔ **Be helpful:** Work with an employee to map out a course of action for improvement in performance. To make it work, the employee must hear sincerity in your tone of voice and use of language. Employees generally work better when they see that a manager cares and is trying to help them resolve a problem rather than blaming, dictating, or ignoring the situation.

✔ **Stay firm:** Staying firm is letting people know the importance of an issue. It means not shying away from working out a solution. Be positive and respectful but insistent on seeing positive changes made.

✔ **Take action immediately:** You can get the best improvement if you take action when the issues start to surface. The longer you wait, the harder the problems become to deal with and resolve successfully.

✔ **Accept discomfort:** Many managers are susceptible to avoidance disease because dealing with personnel problem-related situations aren't comfortable. You don't deal with these situations, no matter the magnitude of the issue, for your comfort or the employee's comfort. You deal with them to create better performance that benefits you and the employee. Accept as a given that you may feel discomfort in the coaching effort, and you can then focus on what you need to accomplish.

✔ **Collaborate:** Make employees aware that you aren't trying to impose solutions. You're firm about wanting a solution worked out, but you're involving the employee. In fact, managers I have taught to coach for improvement often report that by working collaboratively in their approach, the employees come up with better ideas than the managers would have. This isn't surprising, because those closest to a problem can work often out solutions if given opportunity and support to do so.

Following these characteristics puts you in a coaching frame of mind and makes you ready to tackle performance issues with your staff members.

Set, hike, tackling the problem

Coaching for improvement in performance, which some people refer to as *counseling,* is a problem-solving effort. Tackling the concerns or weaknesses showing in an employee's performance is first about taking an informal, prevention-minded action — through using the tool of constructive feedback.

As discussed in Chapter 5, when given in a timely fashion and on an ongoing basis, constructive feedback — that is, positive and negative feedback, not praise and criticism — helps employees know where they stand in their performance. Using this coaching tool correctly means that when someone slips a bit in performance or gives you less than the standards you need, you have a situation that calls for negative feedback. And after the negative feedback is given, you have a discussion with the individual and work out steps for correction or better performance going forward.

In most cases, this simple, straightforward coaching with constructive feedback corrects problems on the spot and prevents performance problems from forming into patterns — continuous signs of similar, less-than desirable performance. When you find yourself giving negative feedback over and over again on the same types of issues, however, a pattern exists with your employee. When you see these patterns, you need to coach for improvement just like you coach for development.

Here are the steps to follow in your coaching for improvement effort with your employee:

1. **Define the performance problem.**

   Summarize the pattern of performance that needs improvement. Follow the guidelines in Chapter 5 for giving constructive feedback: be specific, direct, sincere, and offer observations, not interpretations. Stay away from stating why you think the problem is occurring; instead, avoid the assumptions and tell what you see happening in concrete, observable terms.

2. **Invite the employee into the discussion.**

   Listen closely so that you can understand the employee's perspective on the situation. As needed, explore possible causes for the problem. Discovering root causes helps you pinpoint solutions that help improvement happen.

   Don't debate, listen. Neither of you have to see exactly eye-to-eye on the problem. What you need instead is for both of you to understand what each other has to say. Quite often, by avoiding the blaming or other problem-dwelling focuses, the dynamic of the interaction has opportunity for openness, and you can both gain insight. Remember, you're here to be helpful; otherwise, why should anyone want to work with you for improvement?

3. **Collaboratively create the plan for improvement.**

   Follow the same format for creating development plans — refer to Figure 16-1. List the target as the "Goal"versus the "Development goal." The goal here is the expected level of performance you want to see from the staff person — come ready to spell that out and let the employee help define it with you for clarity. Work on the action plans, the substance of where the solution comes from, which should define which steps the employee will take to reach the goal, and what steps you will take to support the effort. Ask the individual for ideas — brainstorm together, if needed, so that this planning and solution-building is a two-way effort.

4. **Manage by plan and do your follow-ups.**

   The checkpoints to review progress are best if relatively short-term initially — say, two to four weeks out. As you complete each progress review with the employee, exchange feedback on what has occurred relative to what the plan defined and update the plan accordingly. Set your next checkpoint from there.

Plan on doing at least three follow-ups over a period of time with your staff person when you create a plan for improvement. Quite often, because focused attention has helped set a course for correction, you see immediate improvement. Holding follow-up meetings ensures sustained improvement (as opposed to short-term improvement), and keeps old habits from returning after the initial try.

Continuous follow-ups over time help keep positive momentum going and lay a groundwork for accountability to make the plan work. As progress is made, set the next checkpoint out farther; for example, 30 days the first time, 60 days the next time, and then 90 days. Make your goal to get this person's issue improved upon, sustained, and then maintained through the quarterly checkup meetings that you do with each of your staff (see Chapter 7).

Here is a sample development plan targeting improvement for an employee who has had difficulty in working with team members positively and productively. This is created by the employee and manager — it isn't created for the employee.

Employee: Joe McGee   **Date:** May 8, 2001

Goal: Consistently maintain working relationships with team members that demonstrate constructive assistance and respect, especially in situations when differences or conflict arise.

Action Plans:

1. Joe will maintain a sincere tone of voice and constructive use of words in interactions with team members. If angered by someone else, he will walk away and gather thoughts first so he can return, if needed, and express himself constructively.

   When: Start immediately.

2. Issues of concern that Joe has with any team member will be addressed one-on-one, with the emphasis on developing solutions together.

   When: Start immediately.

3. Sheila (Joe's manager) will serve as a resource Joe can go to when he needs to plan how he will handle challenging situations constructively.

   When: Start immediately.

4. Sheila will organize a conflict-resolution seminar for the whole team to participate in, and Joe will set learning goals from it and discuss them with Sheila.

   When: Seminar to happen by August 2001.

5. In project team meetings, Joe will speak up if he has a need to clarify his role and will offer ideas or help that aid team members in getting the project done.

   When: Starting at the June team meeting.

Checkpoints: Sheila and Joe will meet every two weeks for the first month, starting May 22, to do progress review on the plan, and will set further follow-up meetings from there.

How to measure: Sheila will solicit feedback from team members periodically as well as share feedback from her own observations. Joe will share feedback on his own efforts, especially in making his learning goals from the conflict-resolution seminar happen.

Dealing with difficult obstacles in getting improvement

Most often, when managers collaborate with their staff members to set plans and then do the follow-ups with them, they get improvement. Two circumstances that managers often find difficult to deal with, however, occur when performance issues are behavior-related and when personal problems are impacting the performance. Coaching for any kind of development is certainly not easy under these circumstances.

Hold onto the wheel — time to change behavior

Sometimes people can be quite capable in their work performance but the behaviors they display spur clashes, turn off customers, intimidate others, or just greatly annoy you. Whatever the case, this *toxic behavior* detracts from their performance and is a hindrance for future development or success.

Follow these steps to coach and develop the right behaviors for good performance. Refer to the development plan in Figure 16-1.

✔ **State observations, not interpretations:** You want to give specific, observations-based feedback about the person's behavior. Tell what you see, not your characterizations of how that person is. Demonstrate the behaviors of concern so that the employee can truly see what you're talking about.

Instead of saying, "You're nasty with your team members," give constructive feedback such as, "What I have noticed and heard from some of your team members is when disagreements occur, your tendency is to raise your voice loudly, talk over when others are trying to speak, make comments about how stupid people are, and not address the issues being raised."

✔ **Set the goal to define the behavior you want to see:** The level of performance you expect related to the behavior desired is the basis for the goal written in the plan. State the behavior in positive terms — what to do versus what not to do — and in specific and observable terms that define the picture of the behavior expected for good performance. Don't yet talk about desired behaviors; save that for the action plans.

For example, a goal can be as follows: "Maintain interactions — writing, speaking, and listening — with fellow team members that show respect and are constructive." The target has now been defined for what the employee is to aim for in his behavior.

✔ **Survey others:** To help measure progress, state up front when you set the plan that you will gather feedback from the sources involved with this person as a way to measure progress in meeting the goal. Sometimes, you may also want to survey these people, or even have the employee do it, to help give a specific picture of the difficult behaviors as a way to help understand the problem.

When you gather feedback for these purposes, try to obtain information through conversation instead of in a written survey, so you get more depth and clarity of information. Ask specific questions so you get specific feedback.

✔ **Define the new behaviors in the action plans:** With the employee, develop the solution of how the goal is to be met. Together, make sure the action plans clearly spell out what the employee is to do differently and better to make the goal happen. Stick with it until you have defined clear behaviors. The action plans serve as a reference guide for the employee on how to handle situations differently going forward. By developing them together, you both know whether training of any kind is needed or desired.

✔ **Grow from successes:** As you review progress with the plan going forward, and good behavior towards the goal is exhibited, analyze with the person what was done. Help the employee see his own lessons and stories of success.

✔ **Maintain accountability:** Follow through with checkpoints and ongoing constructive feedback on the behavior issue. People can change behavior and make it more positive, especially when attention and a sense of importance are attached to it.

The problem outside of work is affecting performance at work

Sometimes the cause for subpar employee performance stems from personal problems. Personal problems can be a number of different things: marital problems, problems with children, financial woes, drug and alcohol abuse, depression, or other emotional difficulties. Whatever the case, the employee's attention is on outside distractions, and performance at work is suffering.

Here are some tips to help deal with this sometimes sticky situation:

✔ **Manage performance:** Your role is to be a manager, not a doctor who diagnoses physical or mental health problems. What a relief! Therefore, keep your focus on the person's job performance and not on what you think may be happening in the personal life.

Follow through and work with the employee to put the plan for improvement together. Monitor progress and maintain accountability for good performance to happen.

✔ **Direct to resources that can help:** Many organizations have EAPs, *employee assistance programs.* These programs allow employees to work with a professional who can provide counseling or other assistance to deal with personal problems or give referrals to resources that can. These types of situations are usually handled confidentially so what the employee does can be kept private. If you aren't aware of what your organization has to offer or of resources in your community, contact your human resources department for assistance.

Don't start playing therapist, engaging in trying to help employees work through personal problems. The best way you can show concern is to let them know you want them to get the help needed and that you want to see them performing well on the job again. Unless you have suddenly become a licensed counseling professional, trying to counsel is like walking through a minefield. Listen enough to be aware, but don't play pop psychologist through which you may emotionally (if not legally) get yourself tangled in employees' personal affairs. When you keep your focus on demanding good performance, you prevent what is called *enabling* — excusing and allowing the problem to continue.

✔ **Accommodate as appropriate:** Sometimes, to sort through the personal problems, employees need time off or adjustments in their work schedules. Be willing to accommodate, under these two conditions:

- The person is getting professional help or taking some other action to resolve the personal problems. Have this step written into the performance plan.

- While on the job, the employee is committed to giving full effort to perform well. Steps to make the good performance happen should be the crux of what's contained in the plan for improvement.

When the exit door is needed

No matter what the performance issue is, if the improvement needed isn't happening despite your best coaching efforts, terminating or coming to a mutually agreeable exit for someone is a good thing to do. Coaching doesn't involve employing people who don't take full responsibility for nor demonstrate the capability to deliver the level of performance needed.

The plan you set with the employee is the key to managing and influencing the change you need in performance. Following through on your checkpoints helps you and the employee measure progress. In your follow-up efforts, if you aren't seeing signs of improvement and the performance is having a negative impact that can't be tolerated, set disciplinary consequences so the employee won't be surprised if you have to enforce those consequences. Carry out the consequences when you do your follow-ups if improvement isn't shown, but still develop a plan outlining a solution for better performance. Stay corrective in your approach. Other than severe incidents, use termination or an agreed-upon exit as a last resort.

The turnaround coach

Jack had a dilemma on his hands. He wanted Sam to step up to a senior level role in his engineering group, which Sam wanted as well. As part of the transition, Sam was to shift his project and customer support work to a less experienced engineer in the group, Joan, to handle. The transition effort was not progressing. Joan was struggling in trying to take on the new responsibilities and Sam was getting frustrated by it. Sam voiced to Jack and a few others that maybe Joan was not the right person for the job.

Jack had not been too involved in the issue up to this point, but upon learning how to coach and create development plans, he decided the time was right to act. He had a two-pronged coaching effort. First he met with Joan to provide feedback and work with her to create a plan to help her gain improvement in performance. They collaborated effectively and created a specific plan to help Joan turn her performance around. At the same time, as he suspected, part of the struggles Joan had been encountering were due to the infrequent and short training efforts by Sam.

Jack then met with Sam and worked with him to create a development plan to help him move to the next level as needed. The major theme in Sam's plan was that his success was to be measured by Joan's success, as targeted by the action plans.

Through Jack's coordination of the two plans, Sam and Joan started to work more closely together. Outward complaining about Joan stopped, as predicted in Sam's plan. Jack kept in touch with both to monitor progress. Joan's performance soon blossomed and, within two months (as had been the estimate), Sam stepped up into his new role. Through his efforts of coaching for development, Jack had taken a dilemma and turned it into a success for two employees.

Building on the Pillars of Commitment

In coaching for development in which you create plans to target either growth or improvement in performance, the five pillars for building employee commitment, discussed in detail in Chapter 2, are positively influenced. Here's how:

- ✔ **Focus:** The plans provide a clear target, direction, and road map to help make development happen. The effort replaces scattered and occasional conversation with concrete plans that are designed to help make good things happen. Clarity replaces ambiguity in the process.

- ✔ **Involvement:** This pillar is at the heart of the development effort. No plan of action or adjustment is done without the employee. That person first shapes what goes into the development plan and then becomes the driver to help make it happen.

- ✔ **Development:** Of course, the crux of the coaching tool discussed in this chapter is on helping make growth happen. The guided path of a development plan helps people see and measure their own improvement or development.

- ✔ **Gratitude:** As long as you continue to review progress, the pillar of gratitude is affected positively. The checkpoint reviews become your opportunity to give positive feedback, reinforcing success that the employee is making. In addition, as the development effort is being achieved, the rewards associated with the plan occur: new and better assignments, recognition for a job done well, and promotions, all of which are actions that stimulate feelings of gratitude.

- ✔ **Accountability:** This pillar for building commitment gets a good wallop from coaching for development. The coaching process for development has the employees owning the plan: Their success or failure comes as a consequence of their actions. When they are successful, the sense of accomplishment they experience from their own development is a great stimulator for people to push their own performance. And as long as you maintain your follow-up meetings, employees know that you want to see progress happen — that accountability matters.

Part VI
The Part of Tens

The 5th Wave   By Rich Tennant

"Your supervisor tells me you're the guy I talk to for fast tracking a project."

In this part . . .

The short chapters in this part are packed with tips and ideas that help you become a better coach.

Chapter 17

Ten Coaching Myths

In This Chapter

▶ Debunking myths surrounding coaching

▶ Getting a fresh perspective on the realities of coaching

A big factor that holds some managers back from learning to function as a coach is they are stuck on certain misconceptions or myths about coaching. These myths tend to fuel insecurities and reluctance to gain new skills, let alone put them into practice. This chapter contains ten such misconceptions.

You Can't Afford the Time to Coach

Of course coaching takes time. Everything you do as a manager involves the use of your time. The question to ask is: Who *can't* afford to put time into coaching?

When you function as a doer (see Chapter 1), and then attempt to shift to managing as a coach, the way you use time needs to change as well. Time becomes something you budget and balance. You use it more to help others be more effective instead of spending it primarily on your own activities. Coaching thrives on the use of quality time; that is, spending time with your employees that helps them go back to their jobs to perform effectively and self-sufficiently. Now that's time well spent.

Coaching Is Only about Being Nice to Employees

Although coaching certainly isn't about being mean to your staff, coaching is also not about being nice. Coaching doesn't focus on your personality; it focuses on your personal influence. What behaviors do you display that can have a positive influence on employee performance? Those behaviors go far beyond whether you are nice or mean.

Some managers are too nice and, as a result, aren't able to be direct and firm with their employees when they need to be. Other managers don't do the nicest thing you can do as a manager, which is to honestly communicate with your employees and give them constructive feedback that lets them know the pluses and minuses of their performance. Be assertive rather than nice and you'll make coaching work.

Without Any Good Role Models, Coaching Won't Work

Coaching isn't dependent on what your boss or other managers do. It is dependent on your own behavior and the tools you apply with it to stimulate employee performance.

While having your own mentors and role models certainly helps, not working to develop yourself to function as a coach because you don't have one can be an excuse to hide behind. You want your employees to take responsibility for their own actions, so do the same and take responsibility to give them the best coaching and leadership efforts you can.

Coaching Means Seeking Consensus on Every Decision You Make

This myth often comes out of the collaborative nature that coaching requires. Collaboration means working with your employees — it doesn't mean making all decisions by consensus.

You and your employees have different levels of responsibility. In some cases, you make decisions for which no input or discussion is needed from your staff, and that's the best way to handle the situation. In fact, they want you to make decisions; that's why you're in charge of the group. In other cases, because the responsibility for action rests with the employee, you have that employee make the decision. That's building accountability, and now you're coaching.

If You Hire Good People, Coaching Isn't Really Necessary

Hiring good people certainly helps and is a good practice. But it's after you bring someone on board that your real work as a manager begins!

Even good employees need direction, goals, feedback, training, and challenging work — all efforts that involve coaching. Management by this sort of osmosis approach — hiring good people and letting them be — is a hands-off approach that doesn't provide the guidance and support employees need to maximize their capabilities. And maximizing capabilities is the emphasis of coaching.

Employees Have to Ask for Coaching in Order to Be Receptive to It

At the core of this myth is the thinking that people have to want to be coached for you to coach them. Managing as a coach and applying coaching tools to your management practices are not based on who you think is coachable or who is asking for coaching. It's based on providing leadership and getting the best out of people's performance — efforts that make a business succeed.

Coaching doesn't require invitations from your employees. Your role as a manager requires you to work with your staff to deliver quality performance to meet the needs of the business. Coaching is an effective way to make that happen.

Coaching Collaboratively Doesn't Work When You Have a Disagreement

Sure it does. In fact, when you have a difference of opinion, working through it collaboratively is the best way to handle the situation. This means you recognize that you and the employee aren't going to see eye-to-eye on every issue, but that you're willing to listen to the other person's viewpoint and expect the same in return. It means you maintain respect for the other person.

Collaboration doesn't mean that you agree to something you find unacceptable or that you push your authority and browbeat the employee because of a disagreement. It means you are firm as necessary, but positive and willing to explore ideas with the employee. This dynamic is the key to resolving conflicts, and the involvement of others in developing mutually beneficial solutions is one of the reasons that coaching is successful.

You Can Be An Effective Coach Even If You Lack Technical Competence in the Area You Manage

This way of thinking assumes that a good manager can manage any function effectively. Not usually. When you don't have the technical competence for the area you manage, you often lack the understanding of what people do, so your credibility comes into question. When these obstacles exist for a manager, coaching employees becomes difficult to do.

As you move to higher levels in an organization and manage multiple functions, you certainly won't have the technical competence for all the areas under your responsibility. More often, your emphasis is on setting direction for the business and coaching managers to be effective managers — two areas in which you can have competence and credibility.

Coaching Involves Being Direct — People Don't Like That

Some managers have a hard time being direct with their employees. They worry they'll hurt their staff members' feelings, especially with sensitive issues. As a result, they give indirect or mixed messages or say nothing — all of which complicate the situations further.

Direct and blunt aren't the same thing. Blunt means being harsh and slamming the point so the other person takes it personally. Direct is getting to the point and doing so with tact. It is being sincere and honest with all the messages you express, from the positive to the negative. If you think your employees don't like this, consider this: Who doesn't like when someone is honest, clear, constructive, and to the point in communications?

In general, you'll find that people want you to be straight with them. Coaching employees is about working with adults, and most adults want to be treated like adults.

You Have to Be a Psychologist to Coach Employees

If this were the case, organizations would only hire psychologists to be managers — and businesses would likely fail because no one would have the expertise in the various functions of the business to help run it effectively.

Besides having technical expertise in the area you manage, no other background or education makes someone more or less suitable to coach employees. The aptitude to work with your employees and to want to understand them as people is what is needed first. From there, you can learn the tools that help you get the best out of their performance and stimulate their commitment.

Chapter 18

Ten Skills That Strengthen Your Foundation for Coaching

In This Chapter

▶ Recognizing skills that great coaches possess

▶ Brushing up on your coaching skills

*Y*our own development as a manager is a continuous work in progress. Work on developing the coaching skills throughout this book — there are over ten of them! (See Chapter 1 for a listing of these coaching skills.) In addition, develop other skills that build the foundation for effective coaching by taking college courses, attending seminars, and reading books.

The toughest person to manage in your group is yourself. When you work on yourself, you're in a better position to positively influence others and coach effectively with the tools provided in this book. For that reason, in this chapter, I list ten skills to help in the development of your coaching foundation.

Active Listening

People listen in a variety of ways, but active listening is the most effective way. It involves showing an understanding — verbally — of what someone else says to you, without passing judgment. It is a powerful skill that helps you manage stress, see where people are coming from, and spark people to speak up and get involved.

Assertive Speaking

This is an important interpersonal communication channel that goes hand-in-hand with active listening. Speaking assertively is about expressing yourself in a direct, positive, and confident way, both nonverbally and verbally, that maintains respect for the other person. It is speaking up to make your point but allowing others to be heard as well. It is being straight with people but doing so constructively. Because so much of what goes into coaching involves person-to-person communication, this is a vital skill to develop.

Time Management

Time management is about having organizational skills: knowing how to manage your schedule and your work flow, staying focused on priorities, and getting things done. Being organized is critical for management effectiveness. You may have difficulty rallying and organizing others together if you can't do it for yourself.

Meeting Management and Facilitation

The higher you rise in an organization, the more your time gets spent with others — usually in meetings. Coaching involves plenty of one-on-one interactions but also group-level efforts. Facilitating meetings so they run productively is quite a skill. Being able to facilitate them is part of this skill set that involves guiding the flow of the meeting so that it accomplishes results and has participation that is active, yet focused.

Change Management

Welcome to today's business world. No matter what industry or organization you work in, the one constant you can count on is that, sooner or later, something is going to change. Being able to use tools to manage the process of change and lead people through it is so important in today's business environment. Letting change just happen is good for chaos but not for progress and good performance.

Team Development

More and more work these days is getting organized around teams, and being able to coach groups that need to function as teams is critical to your success as a manager. Coaching on this collective basis is part of the skill set of developing units that work in teams to perform not only productively but also cohesively.

Problem Solving

Problems are part of every job situation; solving them is what people get paid to do. But how you solve problems effectively is something many people struggle with. Knowing how to approach problem situations and to apply tools to tackle them in a thorough and organized fashion are very useful skills to learn. These skills help you coach employees as you help them address and resolve the problems they face.

Conflict Resolution

Simply defined, a *conflict* is a difference. It can be a difference of views, work methods, or styles that lead to a clash. Conflicts are inevitable in any work environment; knowing how to manage them on a constructive (not destructive) track is an important skill for positively impacting productivity and working relationships.

Project Management

In many organizations today, much of the work gets done through projects, usually project-team situations, in which projects are done within work units as well as through crossfunctional groups. The managing of projects requires a wide range of skills, from planning tasks to keeping people on schedule. The ability to manage projects effectively dovetails nicely into coaching. In fact, coaching skills are so often what is needed when managing a staff that manages projects.

Leadership

Managing as a coach involves leadership, and coaching tends to be less effective when managers aren't effective leaders. Leadership involves setting a direction and sustaining a course of action to get there while influencing and inspiring commitment from others to help reach that desired direction. Leadership involves far more than position; it's about how you conduct yourself to get others to want to follow you.

Chapter 19

Ten Management Behaviors to Avoid

In This Chapter

▶ Reviewing ten bad habits to avoid

▶ Recognizing your own behaviors and working to improve on them

Applying the tools of coaching is an ongoing learning process. It requires hard work, a desire to grow, and self-awareness of your own behaviors. Occasionally, managers exhibit certain habits or behaviors that detract from their ability to effectively coach their employees. Here are ten such habits or behaviors to avoid.

You can use these ten habits as a checklist of behaviors to avoid as you look to develop your coaching skills. You can also use them as a tool for self-assessment, recognizing what habits you need to change.

Talking too Much, Listening too Little

Coaching works best through two-way conversation. The more you talk, the less you get this vital two-way communication. The more you talk, the less involved your employees become — and often the less they desire to interact with you.

When you listen, you find out what your employees need. Listening helps you gain insights and understand where people are coming from. It also serves to motivate people because it shows that you care.

Being Hands-Off In Your Style

A hands-off approach is often referred to as a *laissez-faire* style of management. While being hands-off means that you're not a micromanager — and this is good — this style also means that you're uninvolved with your employees. Your guidance, direction, and support are lacking. When you take a hands-off approach as your regular management style, everyone functions on their own.

As a result, people aren't developed or challenged. Goals aren't set nor are issues addressed. This style sets an atmosphere in which chaos can reign or status quo can live comfortably. Progress, increased productivity, and employee motivation — all of which are positively impacted by coaching — are also left alone.

Hovering Around too Much

This habit is the opposite of being hands-off. When hovering, you don't leave your staff alone; instead, you nag the heck out of them. You check up on every little thing they are doing. You keep an eye on every move they make.

Coaching is about spending quality time with your staff so they can perform for themselves. Then it's about letting them perform and meeting back later to review results. Hovering over people's shoulders decreases the likelihood that your coaching will be received with any credibility. You may need to lighten up and get out of the way.

Not Following Through and Following Up

Following through is doing what you said you would do. It is taking action to carry out the commitments you make. *Following up* is the checking back later to see what has happened or to review progress that has been made. When coaching, these two behaviors go hand-in-hand.

As a coach, you often set follow-up meetings in order to monitor progress with your staff members, and then you need to follow through and actually have such meetings. You also need to follow through on your end of the deal, taking the steps you said you would take to help support the employee's performance. Not doing so on both counts often frustrates employees, leaves issues lingering, and affects your credibility as an effective manager.

Focusing on Methods Rather Than Results

When managers focus on methods, they tend to get into a lot of discussions (if not heated debates) with their employees about how tasks and assignments should be done. The debates go back and forth over which is the right way to do the job.

The focus is not on the outcomes or results needed. Managers with this habit overlook that jobs can be done in different ways. Pushing people to do work in certain ways often stifles creativity and demotivates performance. Focusing on results gives people a target to shoot for and a standard by which to measure performance.

Managing Everyone the Same Way

Many managers suffer from this habit. They work with everyone in their group the same way. It works for some but not for others. Such a habit renders managers inflexible: They aren't able to tailor their efforts of guidance and support to fit individual needs. This takes away from their ability to manage highly experienced employees to inexperienced ones and of dealing with the variety of strengths and weaknesses people bring to their job. People aren't all the same. Coaching tunes into individuals.

Failing to Get to Know Your Employees Or Becoming Their Friends

These are the two extremes of manager behavior that deal with the relationship side of the coaching role. One of the aims of coaching is to build good working relationships with your staff. This involves getting to know something about your employees as people.

Some managers show little skill and/or great discomfort in talking with the people in their groups. They tend to focus strictly on business and then keep their distance. As a result, their staff often has little connection with them, and this greatly limits managers' abilities to motivate and exert personal influence.

The other side of the coin are the managers who know their people too well. They build friendships with their employees and share gossip and tidbits about personal matters. They become, as the expression goes, "one of the guys." Work becomes secondary and their leadership seldom is taken seriously.

Attending to Tasks Rather Than Goals

Some managers have the habit of getting stuck in the day-to-day affairs and tasks at hand. They aren't able to look ahead at what truly needs to get accomplished — the goals. If they have goals, they are written as a requirement but then tossed aside, and their attention goes back to the tasks of the moment. Or the goals are set as if they're an extra-credit project — nice to do if you can find the time, but they don't tie into real performance.

As a result of this habit, managers aren't able to set any direction or effect much significant change. They look to today and aren't able to chart a path to the future with their employees.

Failing to Bring Issues to Closure

Managers display this habit in a few different ways:

- ✔ They discuss and discuss issues but take no action to move anything forward.
- ✔ They have a hard time making decisions and showing any sign of decisiveness.
- ✔ They seek employee input on problems but don't do anything with it.

As issues linger on and the lack of progress becomes the norm, employees lose faith that anything positive is going to happen. They get tired of "all talk, no action." Manager credibility goes down because of this passive behavior.

Coaching requires assertiveness to be effective — you have to take action and conduct yourself in a positive and direct way, not shying away from taking action when it's needed.

Desiring to Do It All

Some managers have a hard time letting go. They want to be hands-on with every project and activity in the group. They love the work and want to handle all the issues that come up with it. Delegating is difficult for them to do and they are often quite burdened. Often, activities don't happen unless they are there to get everyone started. This behavior breeds dependency among employees. It also keeps people from developing and taking on meaningful responsibility — keys for increasing productivity and a big emphasis in coaching.

Chapter 20

Ten (er, 50) Ways to Build Commitment through Coaching

In This Chapter

▶ Understanding the five pillars of commitment

▶ Investigating ways to build employee commitment

*W*hen you have high levels of commitment from your employees, you see high levels of performance. Commitment also gives you a greater likelihood of retaining employees because people with a strong sense of commitment in their jobs aren't usually the ones looking to leave an organization for other opportunities. Getting this commitment is a critical part of a manager's job and is vital for an organization's productivity and growth.

Coaching is one of the best ways to inspire employee commitment. The five pillars of commitment, discussed in more detail in Chapter 2, serve as a useful framework for this effort. This chapter pulls this theme together as it provides you ten coaching efforts that impact each of the five pillars of commitment.

Impacting the Focus Pillar of Commitment

For the focus pillar, employees know what's important, what's expected, and what to accomplish. Here are ten ways to impact this pillar:

- ✔ Set goals and performance plans.
- ✔ Define results expected when you delegate an assignment.
- ✔ Create plans to spur employee development.
- ✔ Create plans to improve performance when it is at a level less than what's needed.

✔ Mentor with important messages that provide guidance to employees, and have them tune in to the behaviors that lead to good performance.

✔ Set parameters that the employee is to work within when delegating an assignment.

✔ Define action items to accomplish for the next status review meeting.

✔ Discuss and set priorities.

✔ Teach the message of career self-reliance to your employees.

✔ Clarify employee needs along with business needs, and use the matches between the two as the guideposts for developing and executing motivation strategies.

Impacting the Involvement Pillar of Commitment

For the involvement pillar, employees have a say into the planning, problem-solving, and decisions that affect their jobs. You can impact this pillar in the ten following ways:

✔ Mutually set performance goals and plans.

✔ Solicit employee input for solving problems and making operational decisions.

✔ Use instructional methods that allow employees be active participants in the training you provide them.

✔ Collaboratively set development and motivation plans.

✔ Tutor with questions so that employees play an active role in thinking and doing for themselves.

✔ Allow employees to determine how to best get assignments done.

✔ Use experienced employees to help train new employees.

✔ Allow employees to take the lead in discussions to shape improvements or solutions after you have given them negative feedback.

✔ Motivate a staff person by seeking the individual's involvement in meaningful project work.

✔ Ask employees to shape their priorities and action items for status reviews with you.

Impacting the Development Pillar of Commitment

The development pillar is about encouraging and supporting learning and growth opportunities that strengthen employees' skills and knowledge. Use the ten following tips to positively impact this pillar:

✔ Teach an employee how to carry out important job duties.

✔ Arrange for an employee to attend a relevant offsite seminar or conference.

✔ Set plans with employees for reinforcing professional development training they have received.

✔ Tutor with questions so that your staff solves problems themselves.

✔ Mentor by sharing your experiences that are relevant to a challenge the employee is facing.

✔ Delegate a challenging project through which the employee gains valuable experience.

✔ Take someone under your wing to help the person grow in leadership capabilities, in professional behavior, or in handling challenging job responsibilities.

✔ Work with the employee to set development plans, and support efforts to help make them happen.

✔ Organize efforts for some of your staff to share knowledge and conduct training for other staff members.

✔ Let employees take good ideas and bring them to fruition.

Impacting the Gratitude Pillar of Commitment

In the gratitude pillar, good performance efforts and outcomes are recognized and acknowledged. Here are some examples:

✔ Give positive feedback when a new skill has been mastered.

✔ Nominate the employee for the organization's recognition program.

✔ Write a note of appreciation to acknowledge special efforts.

✔ Reward the person with a favorable assignment for handling a tougher, less desirable assignment well.

✔ Provide positive feedback for meeting goals, helping other team members, serving customers well, and other situations of good performance.

✔ Take the employee out to lunch as appreciation for a superb job done on a project.

✔ Send a letter to your boss and copy the employee for a job he or she did well.

✔ Allow a day off, not counting against vacation, after an extended period of long work hours.

✔ Write a performance review that details an employee's contributions over the past year.

✔ Say thanks to employees as a regular practice for all the little things they do to keep your organization running well.

Impacting the Pillar of Accountability

Through the accountability pillar, responsibility is given and high standards are upheld. Here are ten ways to impact this pillar:

✔ Conduct status-review meetings when employees work on important projects.

✔ Facilitate postmortems at the conclusion of key events or significant projects.

✔ Give positive feedback for outstanding performances as they occur.

✔ Give timely negative feedback when performance slips.

✔ Allow employees to be the drivers of their own development and motivation plans.

✔ Set checkpoint meetings on assignments that you delegate and follow through to hold them.

✔ Conduct checkup-review meetings at least once every quarter.

✔ Let employees implement solutions that they develop to problems and follow up to review progress with them.

✔ Have employees set plans to reinforce and apply skills on which they receive training.

✔ Let employees make their own decisions that affect work at their level.

Index

• T •